# LIFE AND DEATH IN THE BRONZE AGE

# LIFE AND DEATH
# IN THE
# BRONZE AGE

*An Archaeologist's Field-Work*

*by*

SIR CYRIL FOX

*Routledge and Kegan Paul*
LONDON

*First published* 1959
*by Routledge & Kegan Paul Limited*
*Broadway House, Carter Lane, E.C.4*
*Made and printed in Great Britain*
*by William Clowes and Sons, Limited*
*London and Beccles*

© *by Sir Cyril Fox* 1959

# CONTENTS

v

CONTENTS

# ILLUSTRATIONS

## FIGURES

# PREFACE

Most people who will take up a book like this, about the Bronze Age in Britain—which came to an end between two and three thousand years ago—will have seen in their local Museum rows of hand-made pottery, some finely shaped and well-fired, others rather clumsy-looking and ill-baked, labelled 'Bronze Age', and coming from 'round barrows' in one or more parishes in the neighbouring countryside. These will have been described as 'beakers' or 'food-vessels' if found with skeletons, 'cinerary urns' if containing burnt human bones. Nowadays there is likely to be a plan showing whereabouts in the burial mound—barrow or cairn—the particular vessel was found: but with rare exceptions nothing further about its source to illuminate the enquiring mind.

It is the purpose of this book to show what a range of interest—ceremonial, cultural, structural, technical, economic, or geographic—Bronze Age barrow excavation can yield to patient and prolonged field-work, and the help, in the build-up of such knowledge, provided by chance discoveries of burial urns in ploughed-down barrows.

In the title, then, 'Death' represents persons important enough in the life of a tribe or group, in the Bronze Age of British prehistory, for the distinction of burial in barrow or cairn: 'Life' the evident pleasure the leaders and commonalty concerned took in elaborate funeral ceremonies.

The writer has been in Museum Service in England and Wales (Cambridge and Cardiff) for a quarter of a century (1923–48)—service which has involved him, as a professional archaeologist, in a good deal of work in Cambridgeshire, Suffolk, and the Welsh counties, including the digging of barrows; all but one of these, as it happened, proved to be of the Bronze Age, here dating from about 1700 to 450 B.C.

In this field-work I took great pleasure. I like measuring and plotting complex structures as their pattern gradually develops: I like the isolation of a thinly populated countryside to which such work usually takes the archaeologist, and the friendly contact with a couple of countrymen such as one employs for the heavy work. The tool of the responsible researcher in the exploration of earth-mounds is a trowel, but most field-workers of

xiii

my sex and my generation trained themselves to pick-and-shovel work also, and—within limits—liked it. Proficiency emboldened me, sometimes, to instruct my workmen on ticklish jobs: the pick is a necessary primary instrument for such research as I engage in, and can be handled with delicacy and precision when required.

My first barrow was dug in 1922, in collaboration with the Earl Cawdor, then a student at Cambridge, on Beacon Hill, Barton Mills, Suffolk: we removed the whole mound and afterwards replaced it—for it was a land-mark cherished by a rural countryside. It yielded fourteen secondary burials, some by cremation, others by inhumation; the grave-goods were not of great interest, but these small deposits gave me valuable training in 'discovery without damage' and in methods of recovery of delicate objects from damp soil.

Complete removal of the mound then seemed to me necessary: unless this were done one could not be sure that all the information on the early history of man in the region that it could yield had, in fact, been obtained. Such complete study of a barrow was a largely neglected, mostly forgotten, technique at this date, though it had been initiated and fully described by General Pitt-Rivers, the famous Victorian field-archaeologist, as far back as 1898. I now consider it unnecessary, for a fully-trained investigator.

On taking up a new appointment in 1925, that of Keeper of Archaeology in the National Museum of Wales at Cardiff, I was quickly and unexpectedly involved in a barrow dig, at Ysceifiog in Flintshire. Unexpectedly, because my field research in that region was officially concerned with Offa's Dyke, the well-known Mercian earthwork of the 8th century A.D.

Immediately thereafter invitations came to me from farmers who had found pots by chance, or persons barrow-digging in Wales who wanted me to come and see their work: this resulted in my writing-up their dis-coveries, urns or bronzes, which found a home in the National Museum. The sites were at or near Whitford, Flintshire; Holt, Denbighshire; Penllwyn, Cardiganshire; Whitland, Carmarthenshire; Castlemartin, Corston, and Rhoscrowther in Pembrokeshire. These last were specially interesting, as the following pages will show.

The barrow- or cairn-digging with which this book is mostly concerned, however, was my own work, wholly in South Wales, carried out during my tenure of the Directorship of the Museum: firstly, two barrows on land purchased by the War Department under a 1937 Defence Scheme—

Simondston and Pond Cairns at Coity, near Bridgend, Glamorgan—and thereafter six on airfields under construction during the Second World War, from the autumn of 1939 onwards—Six Wells 271' and 267', and Sheeplays 293' and 279' in Llantwit Major parish, and Sutton 268' in Llandow parish, all in Glamorgan; and South Hill in Talbenny parish, Pembrokeshire. The names are those given by the 'locals', the figures the heights above sea-level.

In this work, sponsored by the Ancient Monuments branch of the Ministry of Works, carried on, since it was war-time, in winter and summer alike, and under considerable difficulty, the competent help in the field given by my wife, Aileen Fox, M.A., F.S.A., was invaluable: my colleagues at the Museum, Dr. F. J. North (Geology), Mr. H. A. Hyde (Botany), and Mr. Colin Matheson (Zoology) in particular, moreover, gave me technical assistance. The difficulties referred to made some modification of the methods mentioned unavoidable, but without loss of anything essential, as I believe.

All these barrows (earth-mounds) and cairns (stone heaps) were described and illustrated in various archaeological journals, in the years 1926, 1936, and 1941 to 1943, shortly after the field-work on each of them was completed— a list will be found in the appendix. The pottery and other artifacts are preserved in the National Museum of Wales. A summary of the results attained in the later group was included in *The Early Cultures of North-West Europe* (C.U.P., 1950).

A famous Bronze Age pottery type, the Yorkshire 'Food-vessel', is not overlooked: a brief record, illustrated, of a barrow in the North Riding excavated by my friend Mr. D. M. Waterman, being included, as also is a summary record of Breach Farm Barrow, Glamorgan, an important link in the South Wales series, dug by my colleague Mr. (now Professor) W. F. Grimes.

The keen interest taken today by an educated public in the methods of, and results attained by, trained field-workers in all phases of British pre-history has encouraged me to reproduce in a shortened form the original records of these researches, without loss of any detail or omission of any illustrations essential to an understanding of the significance of the structures or finds discussed; I deal, it will be seen, to some extent with the technology of preliterate societies. I am greatly indebted to the owners of the copyrights—the proprietors of *Antiquity*, the Society of Antiquaries of

London, the Royal Archaeological Institute, the Prehistoric Society, and the Cambrian Archaeological Association—for permission to re-use this material, and for lending original blocks, or allowing copies to be made, of the illustrations. A map of England and Wales, below, shows the position of all the sites referred to.

Map A. Distribution of sites referred to in the text

PLATE I. YSCEIFIOG, FLINTSHIRE: Half the barrow excavated

(a) The grave pit

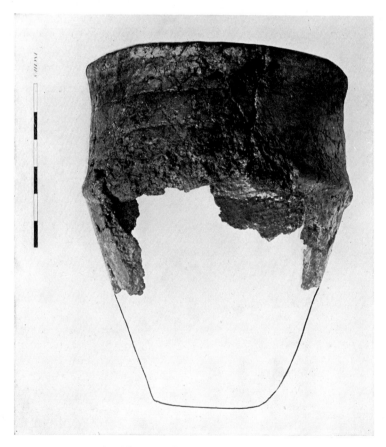

(b) The urn, from secondary burial

PLATE 2. YSCEIFIOG, FLINTSHIRE

# INTRODUCTION

## THE BRONZE AGE IN SOUTHERN BRITAIN

THE complexity of the cultural background of my Bronze Age barrows must briefly be set out, if we are to understand the wide range of human behaviour in the presence of death which they reveal and the stone structures in some of them. For a full account of this background the reader should refer to *The Prehistory of Wales* by W. F. Grimes, second edition, published by the National Museum of Wales in 1951. I would ask readers to pay more attention to the sequence than to the dating, which is by no means secure at present.

### *The Bronze Age in Southern Britain: Summary of the Cultural Sequence*[1]

*Neolithic Age*
  Begins about 2300 B.C.
  (Inhumation usual)

Chambered tombs and 'Long Barrows': tools and weapons of flint and stone: inhumation general: cremation late and rare. Pottery: round-based bowls, necked and ornamented. 'Beaker'-using people—the 'B' group—who inhumed their dead arrive, from Rhinelands (?).

*Bronze Age: Early*
  Begins about 1700 B.C.
  (Inhumation usual)

The 'A' Beaker people arrive from Brittany, the latter having a few small metal tools and gold ornaments. Avebury: Blue-stones transported to Stonehenge: Food-vessels develop from Neolithic wares. Beginnings of 'OHR' pottery. Intrusion of a ruling group (from Brittany (?)) into Wiltshire.

*Bronze Age: Middle*
  Begins about 1400 B.C.
  (Cremation usual)

'Wessex round-barrow Culture', rich in gold, under continental influence, develops in south Britain. Stonehenge reconstructed. Metal trade with Ireland active—via North

---

[1] For further information consult Glyn Daniel, *A Hundred Years of Archaeology* (1950); Stuart Piggott, 'Early Bronze Age in Wessex', *Proceedings of the Prehistoric Society*, 1938, pp. 52 ff.; Abercromby, *Bronze Age Pottery* (1912). A revised, low, dating for South Wales, suggested by Dr. H. N. Savory, will be found in *Archaeologia Cambrensis*, 1948, p. 79.

Wales. In Wales, as in Britain generally, cremation in similar barrows with elaborate ritual (enlarged food-vessels, or over-hanging-rim urns and pigmy cups) is usual.[1] Numerous finds of bronze weapons and tools. A vigorous community life ruled by chieftains, and kingship, is indicated.

*Bronze Age: Late*
   Begins about 800 B.C.
      (Cremation universal)

Tripartite (cordoned) and bipartite urns and debased pigmy cups in barrows. Late Bronze Age cultures of native origin are recognized in south Britain: 'flat' urn-fields with distinctive pottery, and 'ritual barrows', are two local manifestations.

The Early Iron Age begins about 450 B.C.

No early culture seems ever to have been uniform over the whole of Britain south of the Tyne–Solway line; one reason is that there are notable physiographic differences between east and west, geographically distinguished as the Lowland and Highland Zones respectively (discussed in detail in my *Personality of Britain*, also published by the Museum). These impose different habits of life. The Lowland is east of a line extending diagonally from south Yorkshire to Dorset inclusive, Wales of course being wholly in the Highland Zone. This latter zone has cultural contacts at times with Ireland.

The beginnings, the development, and the decay of the Bronze Age—or any other prehistoric period—in Britain, are, moreover, influenced by our geographical situation in relation to Europe. The most advanced cultures here, derived from early civilizations, develop in the south: we receive them attenuated by distance, and limited by the sea barrier. Some intruders may come from western Gaul or northern Spain; if so, they land on our southern coasts, or, rarely, by following the sea route up the Irish Channel, may land in Wales. They bring in, anyway, a culture higher than we possess at their advent.

1 As for the origin of cremation, which is not known prior to the Bronze Age, 'we need to explain how men became indifferent to preservation [of the body] which they had once been so anxious to secure. . . . We have not at present an historical knowledge sufficient to do this. . . . Fire is supposed to convey the immaterial essence, which was life, whither the particular beliefs of the group concerned require.' A. M. Hocart, *The Progress of Man*, p. 200; see also his *Kings and Councillors*, p. 21.

Invaders, however, are also likely to come from further north in Europe —the Rhinelands—entering east-coast harbours. They may be dwellers in that area under pressure from warlike neighbours, or a tribe moving west from central Europe, seeking a new home. The culture of these may be less advanced than our own at the time, but it will be different, and in a thinly occupied country the interaction of native and foreigner is likely to be ultimately beneficial to both.

Near to the time at which our survey begins, early in the second millennium B.C., the geographically imposed cultural trends referred to above were, as far as Wales—an important part of the Highland Zone—is concerned, modified by the exploitation of gold and copper deposits in east-central Ireland, the Wicklow Mountains.[1] The sea route for the valuable traffic thus initiated seems to have been from a harbour in Wexford (or perhaps from the Liffey at the present site of Dublin) to river mouths in North Wales: the distribution of early gold finds, on the map by Miss L. F. Chitty, F.S.A., in my *Personality of Britain* (Fig. 23, p. 50), does not suggest that, then, either Fishguard Bay or Milford Haven was used, as might have been expected. The gold route to the south in England may have been from the Flintshire coast down the Severn valley.

The Bronze Age trade generally is another matter. The distribution of finds in Pembrokeshire on Map C of this publication shows a belt between the estuary of the Taf, and Fishguard harbour, surely representing a cross-peninsular route for sea-traders unwilling to face the dangers of the all-sea route to Ireland round St. Ann's Head and St. David's Head with their scattered rocky islets.

Significant as these developments may be, it is most likely that knowledge of metal reached the centres of culture in south England from the opposite shores of the Continent (western France, Brittany in particular), before the Irish trade developed. This momentous event is held to date about 1700 B.C., shortly after neolithic settlements in the eastern and southern parts of our country had been overrun by a people called the Beaker folk,[2] chiefly a clever, tough, round-headed breed from northern France and the lower Rhinelands. The name covers our ignorance, being

[1] Probably by prospectors from north-west Spain bringing 'Passage-Grave culture' to Ireland: they will have had Mediterranean interests and connections.

[2] The culture replaced in Britain was that entitled 'Western Neolithic A'. See Gordon Childe, *Social Evolution*, Watts & Co., 1951, p. 167.

that of their characteristic pottery, two types of which, the B and A beakers (Figure 20), will have represented different, and successive, cultural groups.

The knowledge of metallurgy acquired by the leaders of these Beaker folk will have been that of the correct admixture of copper and tin to produce a compound—bronze—which provided a hard cutting edge for weapons—spears and daggers—or tools—axe, knife, and awl. They also appreciated, like every other vigorous race in the world, the untarnishable quality, colour, and weight of gold.

A group of chieftains, or more likely a 'Royal' dynasty claiming descent from a god—a type such as had for millennia risen (and fallen) in southern Europe and the Near East—seem to have gained a measure of control over the Irish copper trade: they were, at any rate, familiar with what must be regarded as the south British ends of some of the cross-channel traffic, the estuary of the River Taf, and Milford Haven. This is shown by the fact that they treated as a sacred site the remarkable local outcrop of a dense metamorphic rock (ophitic dolerite), the highest point of which, Preseli 'Top', is 1,760 ft. high. This range of upland dominates north Pembroke-shire, commanding uncounted square miles of the Irish Sea, and lies on a transpeninsular route from Fishguard Harbour to the Taf estuary, marked by a string of finds on the Bronze Age map. Knowledge of a local cult gained by the use of this route may account for their action in undertaking and carrying to a successful issue the transport of sufficient 'blue-stones' from Preseli to Salisbury Plain, and there creating the first stone construction at 'Stonehenge'.[1]

This achievement of course precedes the beginning of what archaeologists call the 'Wessex Culture'; that of a trading community with wide continental as well as Irish connections, covering a period of greatness as we now judge, from about 1450 to 1100 B.C., and initiating our specific, insular, Middle Bronze Age. This culture was brilliantly analysed by Stuart Piggott twenty years ago.[2] Barrows, mainly in the Stonehenge, Wiltshire,

[1] Eighty stones, weighing up to 4 tons each. I regard the Neolithic transport of a Bluestone for incorporation in Boles Long Barrow, near Warminster, as likely to have initiated the tradition, in Wessex, of Preseli as a sacred hill. The standard work on the prehistory of Stonehenge is by R. J. C. Atkinson (Hamish Hamilton, 1956). A possible transport route from Pembrokeshire to Salisbury Plain is set out on my Map A (p. xvi), by 'barge' up the Bristol Channel, making use of the tidal flow, and then up the Avon to the head of its tidal flow.

[2] *Proc. Prehistoric Society*, 1938, esp. pp. 94–5. His dates are challenged by H. N. Savory, *Archaeologia Cambrensis*, 1948, pp. 80–2.

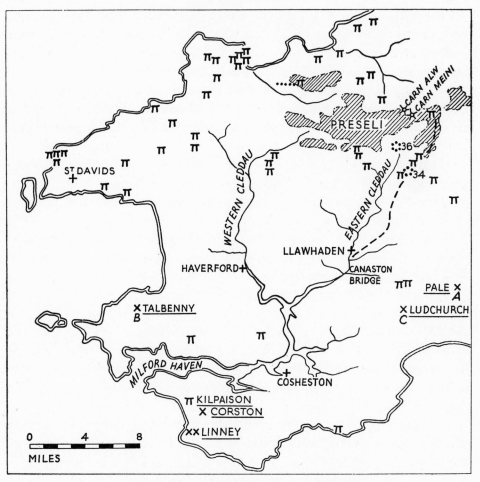

Map B. Sites in Pembrokeshire (underlined)

Π = Megalithic monuments                    X = Bronze Age burials

region, yield rich burial furniture: one elaborate symbol of authority is a mace-head of shale, studded with gold. Amber from Denmark is met with: blue faience beads, some manufactured in Egypt,[1] are frequently found, and were apparently being imported for a long time. Burials were at first by inhumation, but soon changed to cremation. The outstanding sign of technical and administrative capacity, visible to all, was the erection of the Sarsen Circle and trilithons in a new Stonehenge (Phase iii), which is the monument we see today.

[1] Beck and Stone, *Archaeologia*, 85, pp. 203 ff. See my Table, p. xxiv.

Such is the picture at the centre of power: at the periphery we shall find little of this wealth, but something which the inadequacy of much 19th-century archaeological technique failed to yield to the Wiltshire barrow-diggers, the elaboration of burial ritual.

To return to the pottery sequence: the chief wares in use during the Bronze Age are modifications of, and developments from, Neolithic ceramic: the beaker type seems to have died out. The first to appear was the 'food-vessel', associated with inhumation—and cremation—burials in Yorkshire barrows (Figure 47): in Wales varied—and somewhat debased—shapes are met with in cremations. Thereafter the familiar 'OHR' (over-hanging-rim) urn appears: the pigmy cup, so often found with it, is an element of the 'Wessex Culture'.

From about 1300 B.C. onwards, this practice of urn burial by cremation under round barrows seems to continue, in most parts of southern Britain, well into the first millennium B.C.: such primary burials are occasionally found without urns, and these may well be the latest examples of Bronze Age barrow-building, near the beginning of the Early Iron Age about 450 B.C. Now the 'OHR' urn is derived from the food-vessel. It is the most important ceramic in the Age: it comes to be, for several centuries, the almost universal receptacle for burnt bones in cremation burials in southern Britain. We should, then, know all about its 'history'—the changes in shape which it undergoes.

The hesitant character of the references in my text, however, to the date and sequence of 'OHR' urns found in my barrows reflects a fundamental difficulty. Urns of this type have long been classified in three phases according to the depth of the rim in relation to the shoulder and the body, and to the body alone, when the shoulder fades out—these having been regarded as a sequence in time: Phases i, ii, iii, as set out on this page from one of my barrow papers. A 'cordoned' type of urn is the ultimate derivative.[1] It is now practically certain that the development was too rapid for the variant forms to have dating value. In the Table (p. xxiv) all these are seen to be within the phase when the faience beads mentioned

[1] *OHR Urns in this Book:*

    Phase i     Narrow rim, shouldered, latish in the series: Fig. 53.

    Phase ii    Medium breadth of rim, shouldered: Fig. 35.

    Phase iii   Shoulder fades out or becomes a cordon: Fig. 5.

    Cordoned Urn, derived from OHR Urns: Fig. 69.

above were being imported from the Mediterranean region. No scholar would accept this phase as covering over seven hundred years (*c.* 1450–*c.* 700 B.C.) which is a likely range for the OHR urn as defined here, in our region.

Despite difficulties, an attempt is made in this book to present the barrow-burials studied in an orderly manner—that is, according to the dates provisionally assigned to each. The procedure fails, in part, because most barrows show secondary burials inserted here and there in the mound, which may be of any date in the Bronze Age later than the primary, and which have to be mentioned. It is moreover not possible to set out the data from all the barrows mentioned in a tidy form: there is a great deal of archaeological research on barrows, by no means uninteresting, which is essentially incomplete. Sufficient data cannot be obtained: the associations of an urn cannot be followed up: an S.O.S. from a local antiquary comes too late, evidence vital to a problem having been destroyed—and so on. Part of my second chapter will deal with such imperfect—but still significant—records.

Lastly, a late Bronze Age culture, localized in south Britain, which had no direct influence, so far as we know at present, on Highland Zone peoples, is represented by burials with 'Deverel-Rimbury urns'—as the culture is named from the first sites recorded. These urns are bucket-shaped, or biconical with 'lug' handles; applied decoration—cordons and ribs with finger-tip ornament—is usual. It is an 'urnfield' culture, with little or no visible sign above ground: but small earth-heaps long ago flattened out, no doubt originally marked most of the burials, and such urnfields occasionally show little barrows. Deverel-Rimbury urns, moreover, are found as secondaries in earlier barrows.

The contemplative mind, reflecting on the culture sequence in Middle Bronze Age Wessex and the influence this must have had on all Britain, will have little use for these late urnfields! It will dwell on the fact that the region is seen to present, for a space of time in the second millennium before Christ, in this remote and barbarous island, that heartening and inspiring phenomenon recurrent in the historical process, the rise to power, creatively employed, of a succession of able dynasts or of a dynamic priestly caste. Here, the achievement was based apparently on wealth obtained by trade with Ireland and Scandinavia, with Brittany and central Europe—also, as more than one student of the period has suggested, with

## A LIST OF 'OVERHANGING-RIM' VESSELS WITH DATABLE ASSOCIATIONS IN SOUTHERN BRITAIN[1]

| Site | OHR urn (Abercromby's classification) | Character of burial | Associations | | | | | Comments | Date |
|------|------|------|------|------|------|------|------|------|------|
| | | | Bronze | Gold | Faience | Other beads | Other objects | | |
| Hengistbury, Hants. | Type I, phase i | Cremation in barrow | — | Studs, gold cones | — | Amber | Pigmy cup. Amber and bronze halberd amulet | The associated objects were in the urn with the burnt bones of an adult | |
| Tynings East, Som. | Type I, phase i | Cremation (secondary) in barrow | Awl | — | Segmented beads | Jet | — | The associated objects were below the inverted urn with the burnt bones of an adult and child | |
| Upton Lovel, Wilts. | Type I, phase i | Cremation in barrow | Dagger, awl | Boxes, cones, plate, buttons | — | Amber | Grape-cup | The 'little urn' was inside a larger urn'. Both were 'near the ashes'. They were 'food vessels', not cineraries | |
| Normanton, Wilts. | Type I, phase ii | Inhumation in bell-barrow | — | Beads | — | Amber, encrinites | Pigmy (grape) cup. Double-axe amulet | | From about 1450 to 100 B.C. now seems probable for these urns |
| Stockbridge Down, Hants. | Type I, phase ii | Cremation (secondary) in barrow | Awl | — | Segmented beads | Calcite, jet, lignite | — | The associated objects were in the urn with the burnt bones of a child | |
| Bloxworth Down, Dorset | Type I, phase iii | Cremation in disc-barrow | — | — | Segmented beads | Amber | Bone tweezers | | |
| Oxsettle Bottom, Sussex | Type I, phase iii | Cremation beside inhumation in barrow | Extensible finger ring | — | Segmented beads, pendant | Jet, amber | Umbo of jet | The associated objects were in the urn with the burnt bones | |
| Easton Down, Wilts. | Type I, phase iii | Cremation: urnfield | — | — | Segmented bead | Amber, lignite | Bone pin | The associated objects were in the urn with the burnt bones of a child | |

xxiv

[1] This list is based on Professor Stuart Piggott's List in *Proceedings of the Prehistoric Society* (1938), pp. 102 ff., and Messrs. Beck and Stone's List in

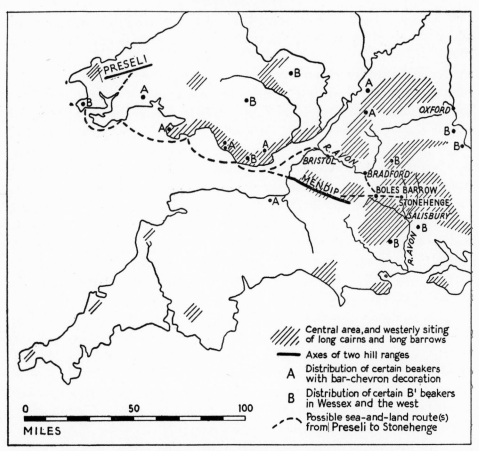

Map C. Preseli, Pembrokeshire, and Salisbury Plain: A water route

Mycenae.[1] For there is left to us not only the graves which reveal that, for any age, far-flung trade, but—Stonehenge: a rebuilt monument massive and unique, having a majestic dignity and architectural subtlety in the construction and placing of its elements, which in themselves suggest an Authority covering a great part of both Highland and Lowland Britain, on a basis, structural and political, laid down by the Beaker folk.

### RITUAL: ITS NATURE AND INFLUENCE

There are three important aspects of Bronze Age mound, or cairn, burial: the grave-goods, the structure, and the ceremonial: death and life.

[1] R. J. C. Atkinson, M.A., F.S.A., in a lecture: 1957. The incised daggers recently discovered on two of the Stonehenge sarsens are of Mediterranean form.

Few barrow-diggers in Britain have paid sufficient attention to the second and third elements: the writer in earlier days certainly did not. The possibility of ritual procedure before and during the burial of an important member of a savage community, and again at or after the raising of the mound or cairn, should always be in view during an excavation: a questioning mind, alert to any unusual or apparently inexplicable feature, or to the exact siting and character of a 'normal' feature, is essential. Such a mind will demand that I state what meaning I attach to 'ritual' in this connection: how is it revealed archaeologically? Ritual, says the *O.E.D.*, is a 'prescribed order of performing a religious or other solemn service'. It will be clear that only some actions in such a service leave traces: others cannot. In the former group is the lighting of sacred fires: the scattering of charcoal: the tread-marks of a procession of naked feet in a circle: and the dance.[1] With the latter are music and song. Again, some structures—the flimsy Hut under a barrow: the barrow which is built as a turf stack—demand explanations involving action and ceremonial.

If the archaeologist has in mind the possibility of these (and other features not apparently natural) surviving, he may find them here and there; if not, they will be dug away by his helpers before his unheeding eyes. He must be questioning every appearance, and alert to the unusual. Only when the work is completed, and all the features of the structure that survive reviewed in the order of their creation, can the appreciation of the ritual sequence begin. In our notebooks we get it all backwards!

Let us take an example: the evidence for ritual acts as exposed in the digging of a particular barrow. What is this deposit of wood-ash doing here? Why is it apparently trodden into the soil? Why was the mound flat-topped at this stage? Here is a row of small holes: what could they have been for? Was there a complete, or interrupted, circle of them? Is it a hut? if so, it was too flimsy to live in. Such are the questions: the answer to the last must be in terms of ritual necessity.

Ritual indeed seems to have become so elaborate and so sustained, that it moulded the final structure of some barrows—a flat-topped turf-stack being apparently evolved; while a dramatic finish to the series is provided by Six Wells 271' in Glamorgan, where the dead person is at the margin, not at the centre, of an obviously intense ritual activity. Myth and Ritual

[1] Gordon Childe, *Social Evolution*, 1951; J. G. Fraser, *The Belief in Immortality*, Macmillan, Vol. III.

have long been associated in studies of existing primitive tribes or early historical near-eastern peoples. The former has been defined as a narrative of what a significant person once did, or a god once ordained, and which validates the procedure for those who on suitable later occasions present it. The practice of Myth is the ritual. 'Ritual has been, at most times and for most people, the most important thing in the world.'[1]

Archaeology is incapable of dealing with myth, but ritual it can, as I hope to demonstrate, recover, and analyse, and appreciate. This mode of approach to barrow examination, this presentation of a ritual process, in so far as it is accurate and successful, is the best available. It is not merely the placing of the structures and objects in a time scale; our knowledge, indeed, of this aspect of the action is most unsatisfactory. It is, as the philosopher R. G. Collingwood affirmed of similar situations (field research on Romano-British sites) within his own experience, historical writing—the record of what men did in a long past time at a particular spot: and therefore since thought governs action, what they were thinking.[2]

[1] Lord Raglan, 'Myth, a Symposium' in *Journal of American Folklore*, 1956.
[2] R. G. Collingwood, *An Autobiography:* (Pelican Books) 1944, p. 75.

# 1

## A BARROW IN NORTH WALES

*Neolithic–Bronze Age Transition, c. 1700* B.C.,
*and Secondaries*

YSCEIFIOG, FLINTSHIRE

MY barrow digging in Wales began, as I have said, in 1925 in
Flintshire, when I was studying Offa's Dyke (a Dark Age, Mercian,
earthwork) in that county, being much puzzled by the gaps in its
course. At one point in Ysceifiog parish, however, it was intermitted for
what might have been, it seemed, a valid reason in the 8th century A.D.:
aligned on a small and slight ring-work (bank and outer ditch) with a
mound near the centre, it stopped at the ditch, and began again on the
other side. I sought and obtained permission to excavate the mound, in
search of that reason. It was not forthcoming, for the structure was not of
the Dark Age, but the work was otherwise rewarding.

Figure 1 shows the relationship described above, but suggests, perhaps,
a massiveness which neither the dyke (hereabouts), nor the ring-work,
showed; they were both heavily ploughed down, which accounts for the
'spread'.

When this round barrow, 67 ft. in diameter, was dug, no suitable technique for the type had been generally accepted in Britain, but the complete
removal of the mound had of course been practised by General Pitt-
Rivers nearly half a century previously. The method here adopted was to
turn the barrow over from end to end and to examine the whole floor for
a grave or graves. A vertical face was maintained, the section thus con-
tinuously presented being cut back a foot at a time (Plate 1). For determination of the position of any objects parallel rows of numbered pegs were
driven in, 1 ft. apart, on either side of the barrow, at right angles to the

I

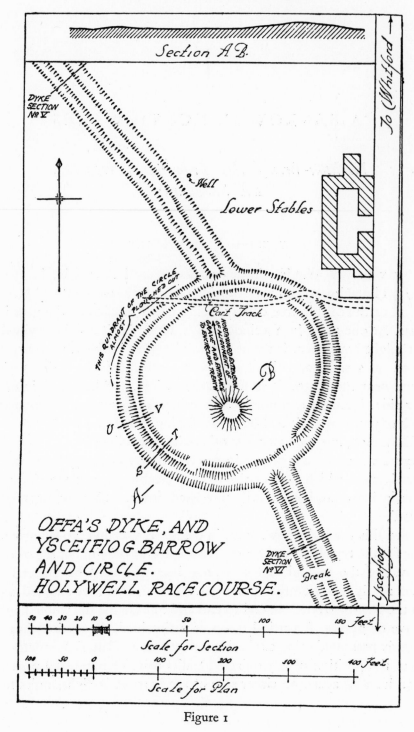

Section A B.

DYKE SECTION Nº V

To (Whitford

Well

Lower Stables

THIS QUADRANT OF THE CIRCLE ALMOST PLOUGHED OUT

Cart Track

NORTHWARD EXTENSION OF ALIGNMENT OF GRAVE AND ENTRANCE TO ENCIRCLING TRENCH

B

V

U

S

A

DYKE SECTION Nº VI

Break

Ysceifiog

OFFA'S DYKE, AND
YSCEIFIOG BARROW
AND CIRCLE.
HOLYWELL RACE COURSE.

50 40 30 20 10 0     50     100     150 Feet

Scale for Section

100     50     0     100     200     300     400 Feet

Scale for Plan

Figure 1

face. As the removal of the barrow advanced foot by foot the face was maintained in a straight line between pegs similarly numbered, and on the discovery of a deposit its position was fixed by measuring its distance from the appropriate right-hand peg along a line stretched to the equivalent left-hand peg, and secondly, by measuring its vertical position above or below ground level. The centre of the deposit marked C II on plan (Figure 2) 1 ft. 6 in. above the floor of the barrow, was thus quickly recorded as 25 ft: 18 ft. 6 in.: +1 ft. 6 in. The scale of feet on this plan indicates the position of one row of pegs. The sections (Figures 3 and 4) show the appearance of the barrow at significant stages of the work; the cross-section P–Q being afterwards built up from the data thus obtained and the daily record. The floor was tested at frequent intervals and holes dug when any indication of disturbance was met with.

When the barrow had been turned over from end to end, the existence of a circular trench 43 ft. in external diameter, concentric with the base-plan of the mound, was demonstrated (Figure 2).

The central space under the barrow thus defined was almost exactly 31 ft. in diameter. The trench was 3 ft. deep, the sides were as vertical as was possible in a gravelly subsoil. It contained no burials.

It was expected that a causeway, giving access to the central space, would be found: but a discovery made when the work was nearly completed accounted for its absence. This was a sloping passage-way leading *into* the trench from the north side (Section P–Q).

I now turn to the centre, where a cairn of stones (Sections 4 and 7) was found: oval, 10 ft. × 8 ft. in area and 2 ft. 6 in. high: about 1½ ft. below the barrow surface. A burial by cremation was found in the cairn; it was readily recognized as a secondary deposit (p. 8). When the cairn was removed its bottom stones were seen to be slightly below natural ground level—the position of which was by this time well known (Section G–H): this suggested that disturbed ground underlay the cairn. Excavation disclosed a large grave-pit (Plate 2), oval, 9 ft. × 7 ft. in area, which was unexpectedly deep; nothing was found until a point 5 ft. below the ground was reached. Here there was a natural layer of fine white sand, and on it a layer like porridge, with fibrous streaks, ⅛–½ in. in thickness. When the whole area was opened up, it was evident that a complete skeleton had originally been present: a curving line of gelatinous material and teeth represented the head, thick gelatinous lines the larger bones. A narrow

3

GROUND-PLAN OF YSCEIFIOG BARROW, SHOWING THE CIRCULAR TRENCH AND THE CENTRAL PIT-GRAVE WITH THEIR RESPECTIVE ENTRANCES. AN ATTEMPT HAS ALSO BEEN MADE TO SHOW THE AREAS OF THE FLOOR OF THE GRAVE, Q OF THE BURIAL DEPOSIT, AND OF THE CAIRN

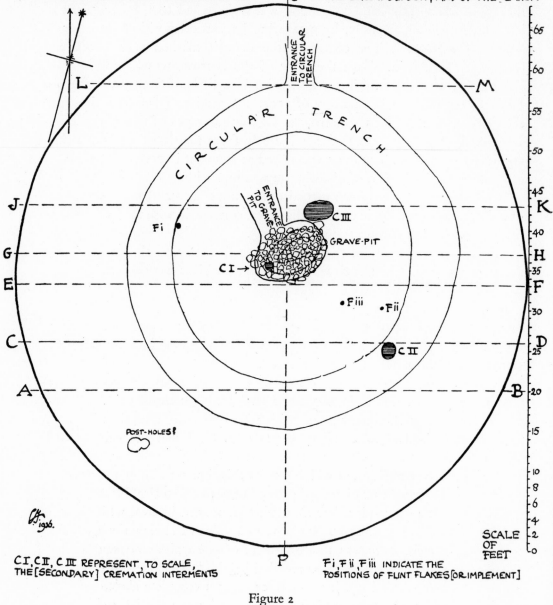

CI, CII, CIII REPRESENT, TO SCALE, THE [SECONDARY] CREMATION INTERMENTS

Fi, Fii, Fiii INDICATE THE POSITIONS OF FLINT FLAKES [OR IMPLEMENT]

Figure 2

4

(a) The ditch of the circle

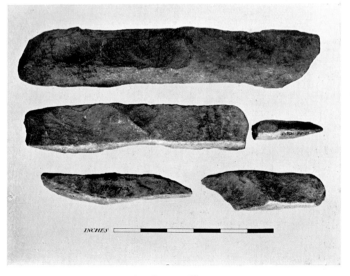

(b) Stone slivers

PLATE 3. YSCEIFIOG, FLINTSHIRE

PLATE 4A. KILPAISON, PEMBROKESHIRE: The hole containing primary burial; headstone and footstone

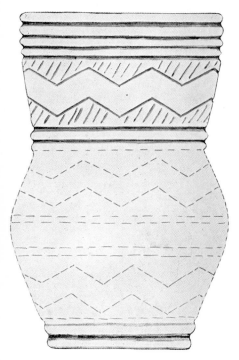

PLATE 4B. PALE BACH, CYFFIC, CARMARTHENSHIRE: Beaker

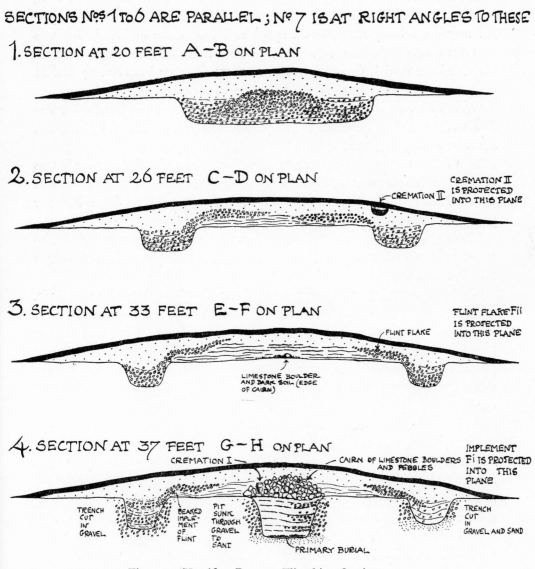

SECTIONS Nºs 1 to 6 ARE PARALLEL; Nº 7 IS AT RIGHT ANGLES TO THESE

1. SECTION AT 20 FEET  A—B ON PLAN

2. SECTION AT 26 FEET  C—D ON PLAN

CREMATION II

CREMATION II IS PROJECTED INTO THIS PLANE

3. SECTION AT 33 FEET  E—F ON PLAN

FLINT FLAKE

FLINT FLAKE Fii IS PROJECTED INTO THIS PLANE

LIMESTONE BOULDER AND DARK SOIL (EDGE OF CAIRN)

4. SECTION AT 37 FEET  G—H ON PLAN

CREMATION I

CAIRN OF LIMESTONE BOULDERS AND PEBBLES

IMPLEMENT Fi IS PROJECTED INTO THIS PLANE

TRENCH CUT IN GRAVEL

BEAKED IMPLEMENT OF FLINT

PIT SUNK THROUGH GRAVEL TO SAND

PRIMARY BURIAL

TRENCH CUT IN GRAVEL AND SAND

Figure 3. Ysceifiog Barrow, Flintshire. Sections 1–4

black layer bordered the deposit, thick at the head end: it was probably a rug and pillow of fur or hair.

The flat oval floor of the grave-pit measured over 7 ft. 9 in. × 4 ft. 2 in., and the body will have been laid out on its long axis, head to north-east. All round the body there was a space 12 in. or more in breadth: it was found to accommodate five persons conveniently. Sir Arthur Keith identified the burial, from the teeth, as that of a man between 35 and 45 years old. No implement and no pottery was found with him.

On one side of the pit disturbed ground was noted: this indication was followed up and an entrance to the pit revealed, 4 ft. wide and 5 ft. long, cut in two sloping steps.

This discovery prompted a re-examination of the circular trench: it was negative: there was no way up on to the inner area from it. The personages who walked into the trench stayed there: those who walked down into the grave-pit were posted there already!

These observations enabled us, perhaps for the first time in Britain, to reconstruct an elaborate procedure of burial in the early second millennium B.C. in Britain.

Since the entry into the grave-trench is north of that into the grave-pit, the approach of the mourners, and the bearers of the body, will have been from the north, as indicated on Figure 2. We can then account very simply for the eccentric position of the grave-circle within the ring-work: it provided the longest direct processional way which could be obtained, while keeping the line of that work a reasonable distance at all points from the barrow. The greater circle, then, will have been made prior to the burial: it kept, no doubt, the commonalty at a distance.

What, then, was the procedure adopted? What in particular was the function of the trench, 3 ft. deep, with a 'blank wall' opposite the sloping entrance to it (Figure 4, P–Q)? It was suggested, in 1926, that the inner area must have previously been consecrated by a suitable ritual process: only the elect of the tribe or community in whose hands lay the carrying out of the last rites on a dead chieftain might set foot there. (Some readers may recall the remarkable 'funeral enclosure', 90 ft. × 30 ft. in area, with primary interments, exposed by Pitt-Rivers under the great mound of Wor Barrow, on Handley Down, Dorset.[1])

The bearers of the dead man, then, entered the trench by the sloping

[1] *Excavations*, Vol. IV, Pl. 249.

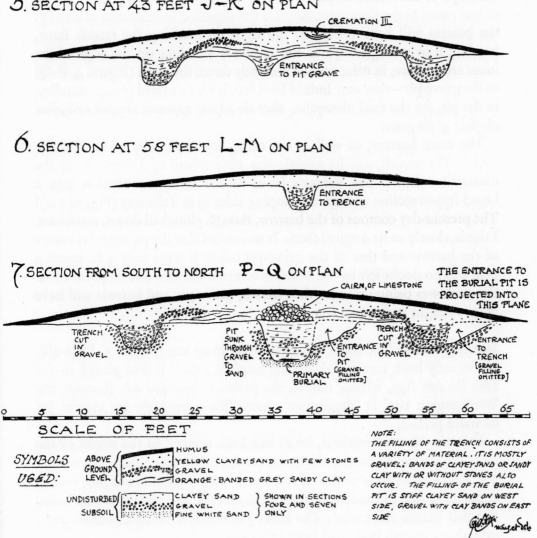

5. SECTION AT 43 FEET J–K ON PLAN

CREMATION III

ENTRANCE TO PIT GRAVE

6. SECTION AT 58 FEET L–M ON PLAN

ENTRANCE TO TRENCH

7. SECTION FROM SOUTH TO NORTH P–Q ON PLAN

CAIRN OF LIMESTONE

THE ENTRANCE TO THE BURIAL PIT IS PROJECTED INTO THIS PLANE

TRENCH CUT IN GRAVEL

PIT SUNK THROUGH GRAVEL TO SAND

PRIMARY BURIAL

ENTRANCE TO PIT [GRAVEL FILLING OMITTED]

TRENCH CUT IN GRAVEL

ENTRANCE TO TRENCH [GRAVEL FILLING OMITTED]

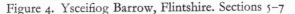

0  5  10  15  20  25  30  35  40  45  50  55  60  65

SCALE OF FEET

SYMBOLS USED:

ABOVE GROUND LEVEL
HUMUS
YELLOW CLAYEY SAND WITH FEW STONES
GRAVEL
ORANGE-BANDED GREY SANDY CLAY

UNDISTURBED SUBSOIL
CLAYEY SAND
GRAVEL
FINE WHITE SAND
} SHOWN IN SECTIONS FOUR AND SEVEN ONLY

NOTE:
THE FILLING OF THE TRENCH CONSISTS OF A VARIETY OF MATERIAL. IT IS MOSTLY GRAVEL; BANDS OF CLAYEY SAND OR SANDY CLAY WITH OR WITHOUT STONES ALSO OCCUR. THE FILLING OF THE BURIAL PIT IS STIFF CLAYEY SAND ON WEST SIDE, GRAVEL WITH CLAY BANDS ON EAST SIDE

Figure 4. Ysceifiog Barrow, Flintshire. Sections 5–7

way, and standing in it, *handed over the body* to those of 'the elect' awaiting it on the inner area. The 9 ft. of lateral space which separated the axis of the slope to the trench from the axis of the approach to the grave-pit is, as was noted at the time, necessary for the dignified transference of a body: the bearers will have turned to the right on reaching the trench floor, handing it over lengthways to the receivers standing on the edge of the inner area. These, in turn, carried the body down the slope (Figure 4, P–Q) to the grave-pit—they may indeed have handed it to a third group, standing in the pit, for the final obsequies, *since the sloping approach stopped well above the floor of the grave.*

The earth barrow, as well as the cairn, was built very soon after the burial. The trench, cut in gravel, was everywhere of U-section, as the illustration shows: one winter's frosts would have converted it into a broad-lipped section with gently sloping sides as at Talbenny (Figure 31a)! The present-day contour of the barrow, though ploughed down, conforms, I think, closely to its original form. It was noted that the present-day centre of the barrow and that of the grave-pit below it were only 4 ft. apart: a post was no doubt left by the builders to mark the true central point while the earth was being brought: thus trench, grave-pit, and barrow will have been wrought with equal care.

*Secondary Burials.* The more important one, in an urn (Figure 5, Plate 2b), has already been mentioned. In the original report it was placed in the Late Bronze Age, within, that is, the period *c.* 800–450 B.C. (because the 'overhanging rim' is 'degenerate', more like a cordon): we cannot yet be more precise.

For two other cremations, holes had been scraped in the slopes of the mound, one on the south, the other on the north-east sides. The former was identified as the remains of a woman 'with a small lower jaw, not an uncommon jaw in modern British womanhood, and usually a sure index of small stature and make'. The latter provided no definite indications— save that a human body had been cremated.

*Flint Artefacts.* At various points in the mass of the barrow three flint flakes with secondary working were found. One is a thin scraper broken in antiquity, patinated blue-grey; another a typical round scraper of cherty flint, likewise imperfect. The third, and largest, was struck from a nodule

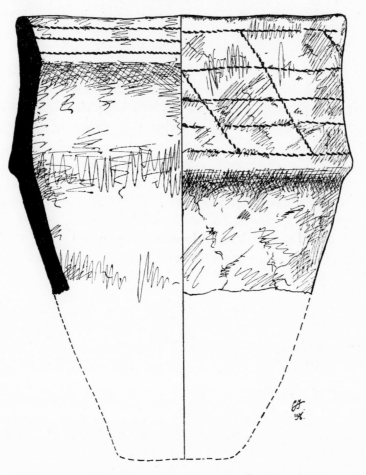

Figure 5. Ysceifiog, Flintshire. Urn: secondary burial. Scale ⅓.

of fine-quality dark flint, and shows no patination other than the glassy surface which may be characteristic of Early Bronze Age flint tools. The position of this specimen in the barrow is known, as it was found *in situ* under the gravel deposit close to the trench. It is therefore certainly as old as the primary burial—and probably contemporary. The flake surface shows no secondary working; the upper surface shows pressure-flaking at either end. This fine flaking was probably continuous from end to end along one side, but a large flake was subsequently struck off, giving the tool a V-shaped outline on this side—it was thus converted into a hollow scraper. There is little doubt that small tools of this class, in a flint-less

9

district, were shaped and re-shaped from time to time to suit the job in hand.

*The Circle.* Neither time nor money was available in 1925 to look for the entrance to the circle—if it has one—that is to say if the ring-ditch were not completely closed after the ceremony. There is no clear indication on the ground today. I did, however, examine this structure at ST on plan (Figure 1 and Plate 3a): it was 49 ft. overall, the ditch being 3 ft. 9 in. deep (Figure 6); 2 ft. 6 in. of silt had accumulated since it was dug. A group of five slivers of mud-stone (Plate 3b), stuck upright and in alignment, was found at the very bottom. These were certainly contemporary, and suggest a survival of megalithic—i.e. Neolithic—tradition as represented in North Wales, Bryn Celli Du (Anglesey).[1] In a second trench, U–V, close by, none was found, and I wished my circumstances had permitted extensive research on this point also.

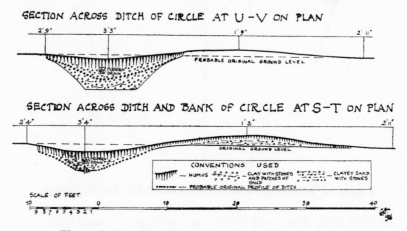

Figure 6. Ysceifiog, Flintshire. Ditch of circle: sections

Why the Offa's Dyke builders used the circle as part of the boundary instead of carrying their dyke across it is a proper but unanswerable question. The area may have had a sinister reputation, as an abode of spirits, and the peasantry have been unwilling to desecrate it. On the other hand, it has been observed that the dyke is hereabouts incomplete; control by the King's officers may have been lax.

[1] W. J. Hemp, 'Bryn Celli Du', *Archaeologia*, 80, Pl. LVI, and S. Piggott, *Neolithic Cultures of the British Isles*, p. 195. A ring of upright stones was set in the circular ditch.

Lastly, since out-door studies tend to be allied, some readers may be interested to know that from a study of the cremation material, the Botany School, Cambridge, identified seven tree species as being in the neighbourhood in the second millennium B.C.:

*Betula alba* (Common Birch)     *Crataegus* (Hawthorn)
*Salix cf. fragilis* (Crack Willow)     *Alnus glutinosa* (Common Alder)
*Sambucus nigra* (Common Elder)     *Quercus* (Oak)
*Corylus avellana* (Common Hazel)

Any convenient firewood was therefore used for these pyres, and perhaps this disposes of a suggestion that the sole use of oakwood for the purpose, which has been recorded, had a ritual significance.

*Summary.* Under the Ysceifiog Barrow was a central grave-pit, containing the primary burial, that of a man 35–45 years of age: the date suggested is the dawn of the Bronze Age, *c.* 1700 B.C. A trench encircling the grave was dug before the burial took place, and there were entrances to both trench and grave on the north side—facts which have formed a basis for the recovery of an elaborate ceremonial.

The grave-pit and trench were filled in: a cairn was raised over the grave-pit: a barrow was then constructed partly with the excavated material, partly with material obtained probably in the neighbourhood, but *not* at the base of the barrow. Secondary burials by cremation were inserted in the barrow, one being associated with an overhanging-rim urn of advanced —or rather debased—type held to date in the Late Bronze Age, *c.* 800–450 B.C.

The circle (bank-and-ditch) was a very slight work. Slivers of slaty rock stuck upright at the bottom of the ditch at one point must have been contemporary with its construction. The placing of the entrances to the trench and grave-pit provide an explanation of the eccentricity of the barrow within the circle.

# 2

## (a) FIELD ARCHAEOLOGY IN WEST
## WALES, 1925–6

A FORMALLY organized dig has been chosen to introduce my subject: in this section I deal with barrows dug by others which 'The Museum' was invited to 'write up', in the early years of my work in Wales. These illustrate the variety of casual experience which may fall to the lot of a professional archaeologist.

I also deal briefly with the pottery sequence of the Welsh Bronze Age Barrows, illustrated by examples acquired during the same period, much in the same way.

We have concluded that the cremation without grave-goods and the structures at Ysceifiog were survivals of a Neolithic tradition. One of the barrows we shall now discuss provides a remarkable example of such survival.

A BARROW ON KILPAISON BURROWS, RHOSCROWTHER, PEMBROKESHIRE

### Early Bronze Age

The peninsula whereon the town of Pembroke is situated, which presents at its most southerly point the well-known sea-mark of St. Gowan's Head, consists of a ridge of Old Red Sandstone rising to a height of over 200 ft., the main axis of which runs east-south-east and west-north-west.

South-west of Rhoscrowther village the peninsula is little more than one mile in breadth, and from the ridge hereabouts a fine view is obtained; on the one side the open sea, on the other the beautiful estuary of Milford Haven. From the wide sandy beach of Freshwater West, 200 ft. below, the south-westerly gales have driven masses of sand on to the very crest of the ridge; the area thus enveloped is known as Kilpaison Burrows (Figure 7). The plateau was probably free from these accumulations in prehistoric times. The Devil's Quoit, a well-known dolmen, is on the margin of the sand-covered area, and deep within it, 420 yds. south-east of the dolmen,

Figure 7. Kilpaison, Pembrokeshire. Map showing barrow site

is a barrow, exposed by a violent storm which shifted the sand, in 1925. In that summer it was excavated by local archaeologists, who invited me to come and see it and 'write it up'.

'The barrow was circular, and just over 4 ft. in height at the centre: it was composed of reddish clayey earth.' Similar soil was obtainable, we were told, a quarter of a mile away; but it is probable that when the plateau was clear of sand it could have been dug in the immediate neighbourhood.'

'In the centre of the mound (Figure 8, C I, and Plate 4a) was a megalith of the local conglomerate, its base sunk 1 ft. 3 in. below the original ground level. It was 4 ft. high (above ground), 2 ft. 4 in. in greatest breadth. Stones of moderate size were piled round it, but not to the top. South of this upright stone there was a smaller mass of the same stone (2 ft. 7 in. in greatest diameter) which lay on the original surface of the ground; the interval between the stones was 4 ft.'

Half-way between them (Figure 9) a circular basin-shaped hole had been

13

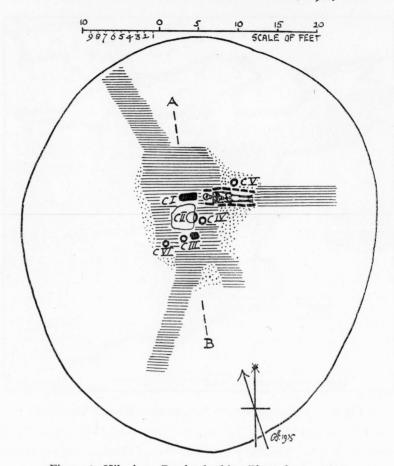

Figure 8. Kilpaison, Pembrokeshire. Plan of excavation

made, 1 ft. 5 in. deep and the same in diameter, very smoothly and carefully hollowed. Its walls were blackened with charcoal and it contained a deposit of burnt bones—the primary burial.

The deposit was sent to the late Sir Arthur Keith, who recognized 'nothing among the burnt bones except human remains—apparently of one individual. The skull bones are remarkably thin and the sutures unclosed; no fragment suggests a big bone: I infer the person cremated was a young woman—but the evidence is not at all decisive.'

The symmetrical disposition of the large stones in relation to the burial (Plate 4) left no doubt in the mind of an observer that they were intimately connected with it, and that the whole must have formed a dignified and

14

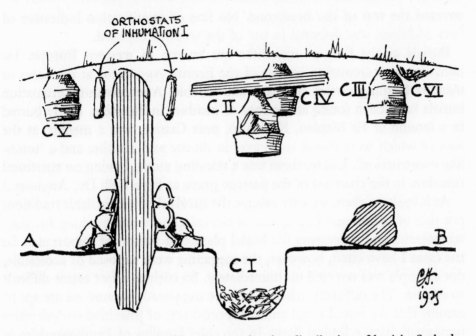

Figure 9. Kilpaison, Pembrokeshire. Section showing distribution of burials: Scale $\frac{1}{24}$

impressive setting to the ritual of interment. (One was reminded of the headstone and footstone employed in Christian burial in this country from the 7th century A.D. onwards; the setting of the broad face of the larger stone at right angles to the alignment of the monument intensified the resemblance.) It was thought desirable to examine the subsoil below the megalith to make sure that this did not cover a cist-burial: excavation was also undertaken to see whether the smaller stone was one of a circle round the megalith. In both cases negative results were obtained.

That these stones were not permanently visible memorials may be taken as certain. Charcoal (traces of the funeral pyre?) lay here and there close to the burial on the original surface of the ground—it would have been carried to a depth of 5 or 6 in. by the action of earthworms had the surface been exposed subsequent to deposit. Again, the smaller stone was merely laid on the ground, and could easily have been displaced: had the memorial been permanently visible, we may be sure that this stone would have been firmly set. See the lower zone, A–B, on Figure 9.

When the ceremonies connected with the burial were completed, the barrow as we now see it was erected. Its crest before excavation just

15

covered the top of the headstone. No line of stratification indicative of later additions was detected in any of the sections exposed.

Burials at the foot of megaliths are known in western Europe. Inhumation and cremation burials of the Bronze Age occur at the bases of menhirs forming circles at Tuack and Crichie, Aberdeenshire: cremation burials have been found at the foot of menhirs in Finistère. Partly buried in a mound at Er Manieu, Kermario, near Carnac, was a menhir, at the foot of which were found small axes in diorite and fibrolite and a 'tomb-like construction'. Lastly, there was a standing stone, having no structural function, in the chamber of the passage grave at Bryn Celli Du, Anglesey.[1]

At Kilpaison, then, we may assume the survival of a megalithic tradition; not that of communal burial, but of the standing stone marking for contemporaries and successors the burial place of a person of importance. In the cases I have cited, however, the megaliths were exposed or accessible; our example was covered up immediately. So curious a fact seems difficult to explain. The difficulty arises, it may be suggested, because we are apt to assume that the burial ritual and ceremonial acts of primitive communities necessarily have a logical basis. In the chief families of Pembrokeshire (a peninsula which lies in the path of that seaborne culture to which both the Irish and British megalithic monuments bear witness) memories of the Great Age of stone sepulchres might have survived for centuries, ending in a meaningless tradition which, at Kilpaison, resulted in a menhir being entirely covered up in a circular earthen mound of Bronze Age type. The disposition of the stones of this monument moreover reflects a burial rite which had been replaced by cremation when they were erected. The very terms one instinctively employs to describe its elements—headstone and footstone—suggest inhumation.

Thus the character of the monument, and the relative position of its elements, alike seem to reflect cultural disharmonies. We see old customs combined with new ideas and new rites: an interaction one would expect to be manifest at the dawn of the Bronze Age in a region wherein is situated an upland so venerated in the Megalithic period—and later—as Preseli Mountain, from which came, as we have noted, the 'blue-stones' of Stonehenge.

It is not a matter for surprise that the peculiar features of the Kilpaison

[1] W. J. Hemp, *Archaeologia*, 80, pp. 179 ff.

Barrow cannot be exactly paralleled elsewhere. In conditions such as we have envisaged, sometimes one, sometimes another element of antique usage may survive, more or less enfeebled and transformed; uniformity of devolution is not to be expected.

It has been assumed in the course of the analysis that the primary burial at Kilpaison is not later than the mid-second millennium B.C.; but only *a priori* reasons for this opinion have as yet been stated, and there was with the burnt bones no urn or associated object to confirm the attribution. Numerous secondary deposits now to be described were found at a high level in the barrow, numbered C II to C VI on the plan, Figure 8, and these provide a limiting date for the primary: but whether it is close enough to be of any value to us, is questionable.

In the centre of the barrow, then, quite close to the surface, almost vertically over the primary burial, was a thin slab of stone 3 ft. in greatest diameter. On levering this stone up, it was found to cover a large inverted urn, C II, not otherwise protected. On clearing away the surrounding clay it was found to be perfect; when lifted it 'fell to pieces' (as I was told) and out of it 'rolled a smaller urn', practically undamaged. Both vessels are sketched in Figure 9 in their original positions; the smaller contained a deposit of burnt human bones—those of a boy 11–12 years of age.

The larger pot, diagrammatically restored in Figure 10, has a deep over-hanging rim and well-marked shoulder; the foot is unusually small. The breaks in the sectional outline cannot be filled with the material available, but the original profile is fairly certain: it is a crudely modelled piece. The smaller vessel (Figure 11 and Plate 5a), on the other hand, is a beautiful example of the potter's art: the proportions are admirable, and the orna-ment—made by pressing a twisted thong into the wet clay—is carefully spaced and wrought. That many pots of the Middle Bronze Age should be well shaped is not a matter for surprise when the quality of the tools and weapons of the period is considered; the designs of dagger and rapier, of spear-head and palstave, show a sure instinct for form and balance of parts; but I do not think that the aesthetic quality of the best examples of the sepulchral pottery of the Age is sufficiently appreciated. On the little vessel under discussion the balance between horizontality and verticality in ornament is evenly held—the zigzags being broken at intervals by a group of five parallel vertical lines. Internally, the moulding of the lip—the bevel—forms an admirable and strictly limited field for ornament; its

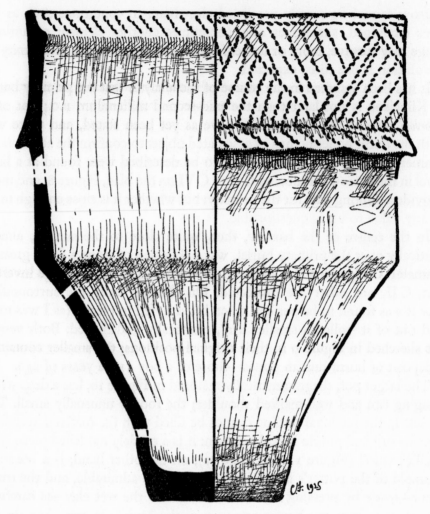

Figure 10. Kilpaison, Pembrokeshire. Secondary burial C II: OHR urn. Scale ⅓

well-defined lower angle casts a shadow within the pot, providing a needed balance to the external moulding and shoulder-cordon.

The three other secondary burials by cremation shown on Figures 8 and 9 are alike in that the (inverted) urns, which contained the ashes, were unprotected by covering slabs; they were so close to the surface of the mound that their bases had decayed away.

The ornament of two of these, like those hitherto described, has been produced by impressing a twisted cord in the wet clay. The urn which

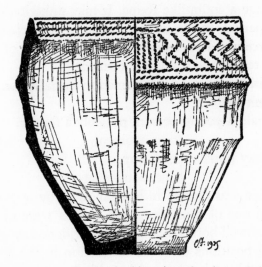

Figure 11. Kilpaison, Pembrokeshire. Associated vessel, burial C II

represents the cremation burial recorded as No. V, of which only the rim and a fragment of the body survive (see Figure 12), is decorated with diagonal herring-bone pattern incised with a sharp point. This decoration was present on the upper part of the body of the urn, as well as on the corrugated rim. Incised decoration is commoner in the beginning of the Middle Bronze Age than later on: the bevelled rim here is shallower than that of the other pots, and it may be half a century older than its neighbours.

The only other burial needing mention here is that by inhumation on the east side of the monolith. The skeleton was fully extended, on its back, nearly due east and west (head to west). A series of small orthostatic slabs

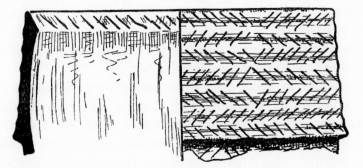

Figure 12. Kilpaison, Pembrokeshire. Rim of urn with incised ornament

19

on either side made a coffin-like frame. It may unhesitatingly be referred to the Christian period. In this appropriation of an ancient burial mound, then, we may perceive a late example of that continuity of tradition which gives special interest to the primary interment.

Sir Arthur Keith's report on the cremation burials found in the barrow may be briefly summarized:

Primary burial: A young person, possibly a female.

Four secondary burials: { two, women, one, boy, one, adult man

The barrow then was erected in honour of a young person, possibly a woman, and two out of four secondary burials were of women. Abercromby and Greenwell both remark on the evidence afforded by barrows that women held positions of social distinction in the Bronze Age. The burial of a child with such ceremonial as this barrow provides, moreover, may indicate that 'something like an hereditary headship' prevailed amongst the communities in Britain.

Our urns present characters which are widely distributed in Britain, but in my view the influences which went to their shaping and ornament derive from the north-east rather than from the south-east: this is suggestive. An early ceramic type, the handled beaker, reached the Brecon region *c.* 1500 B.C., from the Eastern Plain by a route which lay in all likelihood north of the Thames, and Yorkshire and East Anglia influenced North Wales in the food-vessel period, perhaps a hundred years later.

These secondary burials with urns, then, may be dated about 1100 B.C.

Since the same rite—which seems to have replaced inhumation, in Britain generally, at the close of the Early Bronze Age—was used for the primary burial, this may be dated about 1400 B.C. The monumental stones associated with the primary burial indicate the survival of a Megalithic tradition. Lastly, the inhumation burial points to the mound having sacred traditions still attaching to it in the early Christian period.

I am fortunate in being able, from personal experience, to follow up such a monument as Ysceifiog, with that on Kilpaison Burrows. Both illustrate, I suggest, a prolonged Neolithic–Bronze Age transition, to be expected in the Highland Zone. At Ysceifiog we have the great earthen circle (apparently with a decadent stone ring), but inhumation is still practised: at Kilpaison the burial rite is cremation, but the Megalithic idea

PLATE 5A. KILPAISON, PEMBROKESHIRE: Secondary urn

PLATE 5B. CORSTON BEACON, PEMBROKESHIRE: Cist exposed

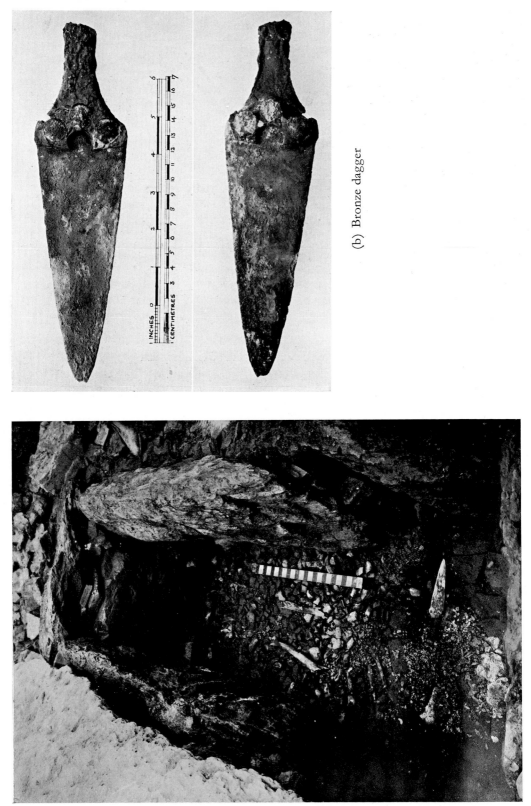

(b) Bronze dagger

(a) Cist with lid removed

INCHES.

PLATE 7A. CWM-DU, BRECKNOCKSHIRE: Handled
beaker

PLATE 7B. LINNEY BURROWS, PEMBROKESHIRE:
Food-vessel

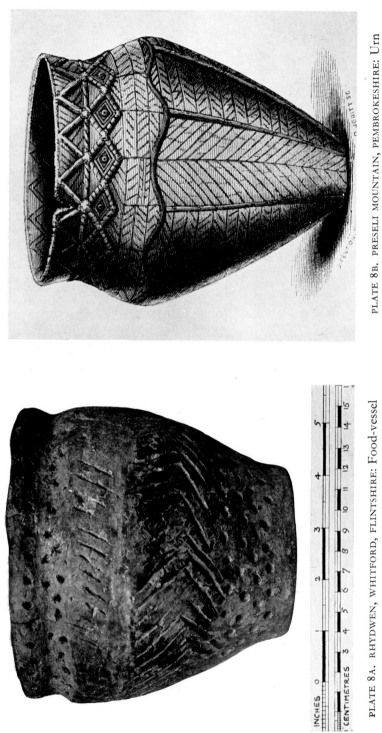

PLATE 8B. PRESELI MOUNTAIN, PEMBROKESHIRE: Urn

PLATE 8A. RHYDWEN, WHITFORD, FLINTSHIRE: Food-vessel

survived in the monolith. It is easy to realize how confused the leading family of any local community could be when its minds were fed by conflicting traditions in ritual—no doubt also in behaviour: the 'correct' ordering of the business of life and death.

Another point, of general interest, arises out of the study of the urn with elaborate ornament. The concentration of this feature on the upper half (the rim and shoulder), characteristic of the type, has never to my knowledge been discussed; but it seems to arise naturally from the physical ceremony of deposit of burnt bones in the vessel, from the pyre. *The mourners are looking down on it.* The classical urns, decorated all over, were designed for shelves in a tomb chamber.

### CORSTON BEACON, PEMBROKESHIRE: A ROUND CAIRN

## *Early Bronze Age*

On the same uplands as the Kilpaison monument, but in Hundleton parish, is an example of the use of great stones in another manner, in the early Bronze Age. Corston Beacon is a round cairn some 60 ft. in diameter and 5 ft. in height (Figure 13) on the highest point of the plateau, just within the 250-ft. contour, which commands extensive views of Milford Haven to the north and Freshwater Bay to the west. The writer was 'called in' in 1927 to supervise the lifting of the coverstone of a great cist which had been exposed below ground level in the centre of the cairn (Plate 5b): tackle was obtained and Mr. W. F. Grimes (then on the staff of the National Museum) and I got to work, cleared the domed coverstone (Figure 14) over 9 ft. long and estimated to weigh nearly two tons, and, with the aid of a local firm of builders, lifted it clear. On the floor of the cist (Plate 6a) was a male skeleton in an advanced state of dissolution, about 5 ft. 4 in. in height, probably, Sir Arthur Keith remarked, of 'Beaker type'. This floor was clean and without dust; the overhang of the coverstone prevented the washing-in of earthy matter, and this stone had itself been buried in clean small stones to a depth of 4 ft. Such care for the dead I had never before observed.

Corston, then, provided my first direct contact in the Highland Zone with the round-headed invaders who first attracted metal-workers into Britain, and then exploited native ores. On the right side of the skeleton (B on plan, Figure 13) lay a flat riveted knife-dagger, 7 in. long (Plate 6b)

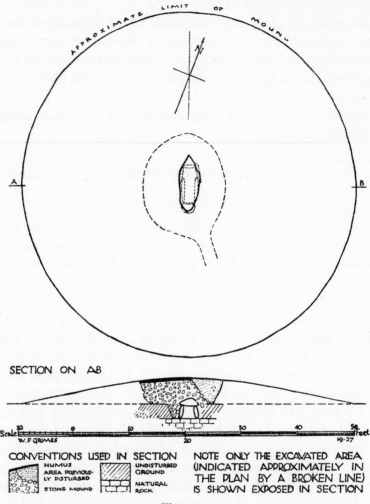

CORSTON BEACON A CAIRN IN HUNDLETON
PARISH PEMBROKESHIRE : GROUND-PLAN AND SECTION.
GROUND-PLAN

SECTION ON AB

CONVENTIONS USED IN SECTION

HUMUS
AREA PREVIOUS-
LY DISTURBED

UNDISTURBED
GROUND

STONE MOUND

NATURAL
ROCK

NOTE ONLY THE EXCAVATED AREA
(INDICATED APPROXIMATELY IN
THE PLAN BY A BROKEN LINE)
IS SHOWN EXPOSED IN SECTION

Figure 13

(with a handle probably of wood, not horn): it is drawn (by W. F. Grimes)
in Figure 15, and is a fine example of a famous early tool and weapon,
though the pommel has perished. A map (Figure 16) shows the distribution
of the type in Britain, and the probable directions from which came such
precious and expensive goods before bronze-smiths made them here.
Spain was no doubt the principal source of the copper, with Ireland

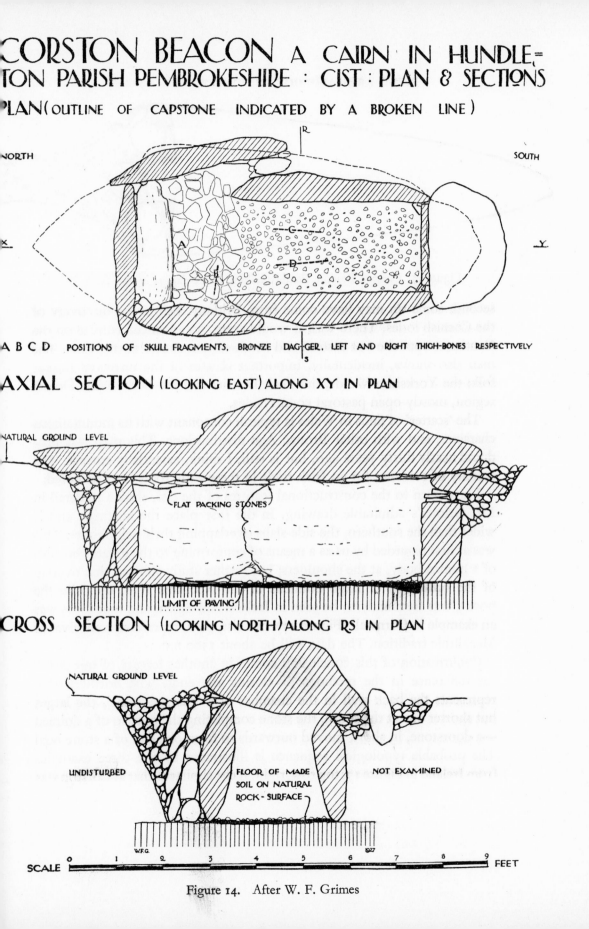

# CORSTON BEACON A CAIRN IN HUNDLE=TON PARISH PEMBROKESHIRE : CIST : PLAN & SECTIONS

**PLAN** (OUTLINE OF CAPSTONE INDICATED BY A BROKEN LINE)

NORTH

SOUTH

X

Y

A B C D   POSITIONS OF SKULL FRAGMENTS, BRONZE DAGGER, LEFT AND RIGHT THIGH-BONES RESPECTIVELY

**AXIAL SECTION** (LOOKING EAST) ALONG XY IN PLAN

NATURAL GROUND LEVEL

FLAT PACKING STONES

LIMIT OF PAVING

**CROSS SECTION** (LOOKING NORTH) ALONG RS IN PLAN

NATURAL GROUND LEVEL

UNDISTURBED

FLOOR OF MADE SOIL ON NATURAL ROCK - SURFACE

NOT EXAMINED

W.F.G.                                                1927

SCALE   0   1   2   3   4   5   6   7   8   9   FEET

Figure 14.   After W. F. Grimes

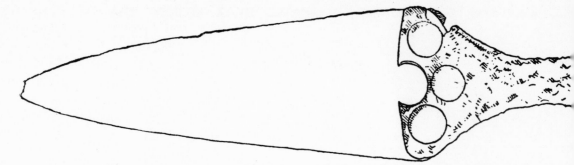

Figure 15. Corston Beacon, Pembrokeshire. Knife-dagger in cist. Scale $\frac{2}{3}$

second; some tin may have come from Brittany, before the discovery of the Cornish lodes. There was, it would seem, no advanced culture on the Continent opposite our eastern and south-eastern shores at that time. The map also shows, incidentally, important centres of the intrusive Beaker folk: the Yorkshire Wolds, the Peak District and the Berks-Wilts-Dorset region, mostly open pastoral countrysides.

The 'scatter' of finds in Wales is typical: consonant with its mountainous character, and with other Bronze Age distributions. This map was produced nearly thirty years ago, but is still, I think, essentially correct. The scarcity of evidence for an Irish trade in these early tools is to be noted.

I now turn to the constructional features of the cist, shown in detail in Mr. Grimes's admirable drawing. In the first place the northern end is wider than the southern, the side-slabs overlapping their neighbours. This was at first regarded by us as a means of conforming to the greater breadth of a human body, at the shoulders; but further study showed that overlap of the orthostats of large dolmens of the Neolithic Age, opposite the portal, was frequently to be seen in Ireland and Spain, and that there was an example in Cornwall (Figure 17): our cist, then, represents a survival of Megalithic tradition. The date will be about 1500 B.C.

Confirmation of this conclusion comes in another feature of our cist— the difference in the methods of closing the ends. The northern slab represents the back wall in the chamber of a 'passage-grave', the larger but shorter one at the south, the stone completing the portico of a dolmen —a doorstone, in short, moved outwards to form one end of a stone box! The probable typological sequence is illustrated by the three examples from Ireland in Figure 17, top row, right. A cist similar to that at Corston was

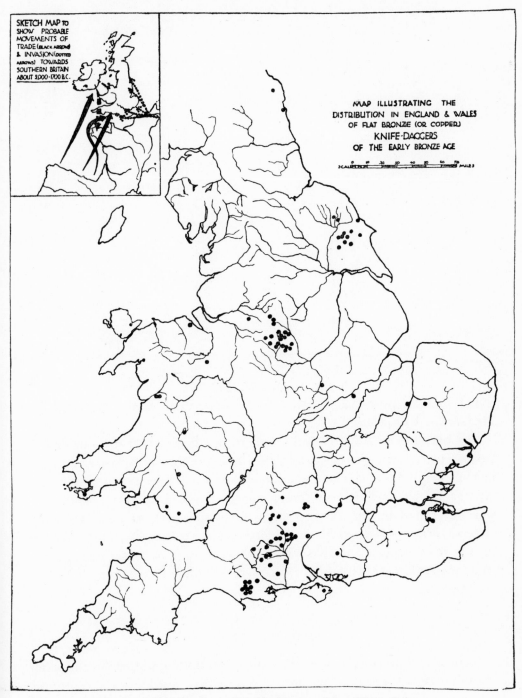

Figure 16. Distribution of Knife-daggers. After W. F. Grimes

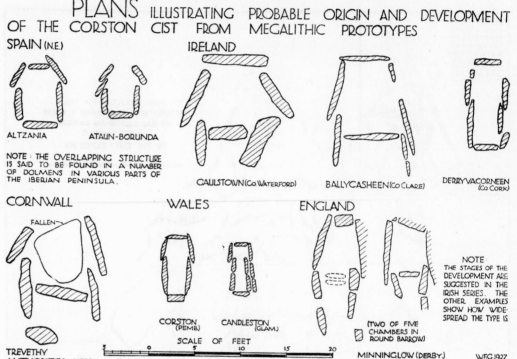

Figure 17. After W. F. Grimes

found in 1919 near Candleston Castle, Glamorgan, and is recorded in *Archaeologia Cambrensis* for that year.

The positions of Corston and Candleston, adjacent to a harbour and a landing place respectively, convenient for sea traffic between Ireland and Britain, may be relevant to the adoption of the design: this is a valuable pointer, for we much want to know *why* the Beaker folk knew about, and were interested in, Preseli Top (Introduction, p. xx), so far from their areas of primary settlement in Britain, and every scrap of evidence for such Irish contacts is valuable. The gold trade (see p. xix) is not very relevant; it seems to have taken, mainly, the Dublin Bay–Anglesey–North Wales route.

### A CIST AT CROSSHANDS, LLANBOIDY, CARMARTHENSHIRE

#### Middle Bronze Age

A further example of the persistence of Neolithic tradition (in this case the stone circle) well into the Bronze Age is the presence at the centre of a wrecked barrow (No. 2) at Crosshands, Llanboidy, in west Carmarthen-shire (Figures 18a and 18b) of a small cist, only 1 ft. in area, of slate, with burnt bones in an urn, inverted, of 'OHR' type. Around it was a ring of quartz stones—in other words, a 'stone circle'!—but it was only 4½ ft. in diameter, and the stones small. The site of this barrow, as the map and plan show, is relevant to the curious survival demonstrated in this struc-ture. It is on an isolated upland 650 ft. above sea-level commanding a view of the whole basin of the river, one of the sources of which is Preseli Mountain, 9 miles away to the north. Prolonged influence of early religious ideas is here and there to be expected, in this remote but significant region.

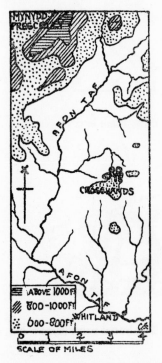

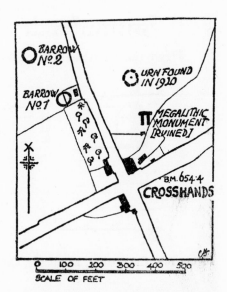

Figure 18a. Crosshands, Llanboidy, Carmarthenshire. The region

Figure 18b. Crosshands, Llanboidy, Carmarthenshire. The barrows

The urn, inverted, had been struck by a plough-share and only the upper part was recovered; it was of a type well illustrated in contemporary secondary cremations in another barrow at Crosshands, across the road, a hundred yards away. Figure 19a shows the excavated area, 19b the two cremations met with. These and the OHR urns are reproduced in measured drawings in *Archaeologia Cambrensis*[1]; the student will here find examples of early forms with thin rims and well-marked 'shoulders' as well as later ones with bevelled rims; one has incised, and two cord-impressed, ornament, while a fourth has a horizontally corrugated rim.

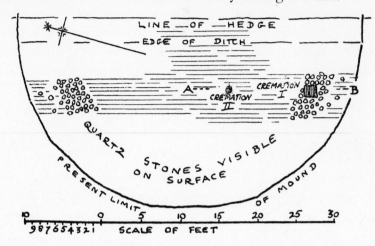

Figure 19a. Crosshands, Llanboidy, Carmarthenshire. Plan: barrow No. 1

Figure 19b. Crosshands, Llanboidy, Carmarthenshire. The burial urns: barrow No. 1

### BEAKER BURIAL: PALE BACH, CYFFIC, CARMARTHENSHIRE

#### *Early Bronze Age*

'Rescue work' of the type we are discussing, early in my Museum service, introduced me to the burial customs of those remarkable, able, round-headed invaders, the 'Beaker folk', mentioned in my Introduction:

[1] 1925, pp. 278 ff. and Figs. 5–8, 11–13.

the range of shape of their pots is illustrated in Figure 20. Such work can seldom be illustrated so vividly as in the little drawing, Figure 21, of a gateway on the farm of Pale Bach, Cyffic, Carmarthenshire. This gateway occupies the site of a burial mound or cairn, now completely levelled, in the centre of which was a stone cist! The covering stone had been swept away, but the well-made cist was not noticed until the wear-and-tear of iron cart-tyres on the approaches to the gate caused attention to be

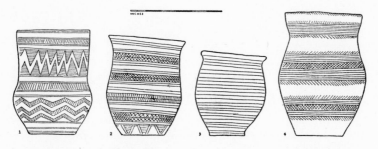

Figure 20. Beaker types in Britain. 1, 'A'; 2-3, 'B'; 4, 'C' After W. F. Grimes

Figure 21. Pale Bach, Cyffic, Carmarthenshire. Cist in gateway

drawn to it. I made a sketch on the site and collected the beaker sherds from the helpful owner; unfortunately, more than half the vessel was unrepresented in this group. The beaker had been placed in a natural hollow on the inner face of the slab which formed the east wall of the cist. When found it was in small fragments: the farmer notes that the stones marked 'E' and 'N' on the sketch were sunk by the weight of traffic through the gateway: the stresses thus set up are more than sufficient to shatter an ill-baked pot. Outside the cist a border of stones is seen: the space between these and the cist was packed with smaller pebbles.

The beaker is light pinkish-brown with 0·3-in. walls. The surface is smooth, as is usual; a chevron pattern and hatching are defined by grooves made with a blunt-ended tool. Rim, neck, and foot were horizontally moulded. The tentative reconstruction is illustrated on Plate 4b; the bar-chevron ornament is usual, being seen on several beakers from South Wales.

# (b) POTTERY FROM BURIALS IN WEST AND NORTH WALES, 1925–6

THOUGH in this section I continue my comments on Bronze Age pottery found by chance here and there in Wales, the attitude of mind is necessarily different: the actual sites of discovery could not for a variety of reasons be visited, and my interest is confined therefore to the urn or food-vessel itself.

## A HANDLED BEAKER FROM CWM-DU, BRECKNOCKSHIRE

### Early Bronze Age

Among the beaker class of pot none is more attractive than the small group of handled vessels, in which I became interested at the beginning of my work in Wales. The example from Cwm-du, Brecon (Plate 7a), comes from a cist in the cairn known as Pen Gloch-y-Pibwr, situated on a crest of the Black Mountains, 2,155 ft. above sea-level. It is clearly visible from the Crickhowell–Brecon road up the Usk valley, near the hamlet of Gaer: hereabouts no doubt was the dwelling of the chieftain so notably interred.

The elderly visitor who brought the beaker, whom I heartily welcomed in my room at the Museum, remarked that he was reminded, when nearing the cairn for the first time, of the 'Grammarian's Funeral'—'Well, here's the platform, here's the proper place'; and wondered if Browning had experienced the sort of effort required, before he wrote the poem. It has frequently been remarked that barrows and cairns are placed on the skyline of hills as seen from an accessible and fertile area of lowland; but the height of this cairn is certainly unusual.[1]

The scheme of ornament of our beaker is shown in Figure 22; it is wrought in notched technique. The limited range of motifs—zigzags, straight lines, and linked hexagons—is displayed in horizontal bands on the body of the vessel, and the handle is similarly decorated.

It will be noticed that the beaker has a bevelled rim: enquiry, in 1925, showed that ten out of the fifteen known beakers with the feature, unusual at this phase of our pottery sequence, come from eastern England. Again of sixteen known handled beakers twelve come from this same part of the country and four more were found in the Peak district of Derbyshire— an important early centre of occupation in prehistoric Britain, linked by a route not yet worked out to South and West Wales. Readers who have

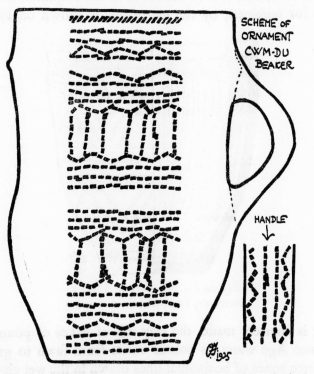

Figure 22. The Cwm-du Beaker, Brecknockshire. Scale ½

1 *Archaeologia Cambrensis*, 1925, pp. 12–16.

access to my *Personality of Britain* will find the Beaker distribution in Britain mapped in Figure 2.

## TWO 'FOOD-VESSELS' FROM WELSH BARROWS

### *Early Bronze Age*

The 'food-vessel' type of ceramic comes into use at the beginning of the Bronze Age, and is primarily associated with inhumation burial. It represents an important development, primarily in eastern England (p. 71, below) from Neolithic wares, and it ultimately replaced the invader's pottery, the beaker: characteristic examples from Yorkshire with loops above the shoulder are illustrated in most text-books. Thongs may have been inserted in the loops, for holding, as a ritual procedure. A derivative form from an inhumation burial in a barrow on Linney Burrows, Castlemartin, Pembroke, near and to the south of the Kilpaison barrow (p. 12), sent to me for comment by the excavator, is shown on Figure 23 and

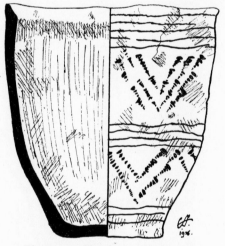

Figure 23. Food-vessel. Linney Burrows, Pembrokeshire. Scale ⅓

Plate 7b. It is coarsely made, the clay full of flakes of pounded stone— typical Bronze Age ware: its colour varies from fawn to greyish black. There are three zones of horizontal lines drawn in the wet clay with a tool having a narrow flat end, alternating with two zones of chevrons drawn with double or triple lines, made with a notched tool worked from below upwards. The potting is poor, but the potter was working in a good tradition: the zonal and repetitive features of the ornament are characteristic in Britain of the 1700–1500 B.C. period: beakers also illustrate them. This vessel shows, however, a hall-mark of *native* ceramic at this time, the internal bevel of the rim. Another food-vessel shape met with in the west is represented by an example from a barrow at Rhydwen, Whitford, Flintshire, also in the National Museum of Wales (Plate 8a and Figure 24). As in the case of the Linney pot, the section on the left shows the structural form; on the right the ornament is displayed.

When I was working in Cambridge I had occasion to study a beaker found in the neighbouring county of Huntingdon, decorated with rows of deep cylindrical holes, made by pressing a hollow reed into the soft clay, and withdrawing the little cylinder thus separated. Deep holes stabbed in the unbaked pottery are not infrequent in vessels of this period; but the bulge around the hole thus produced differentiates the technique from that produced by the reed which removes, instead of merely displacing, the clay. I had supposed the technique to be confined, in Britain, to the Eastern Plain, and it was therefore of great interest to observe that though

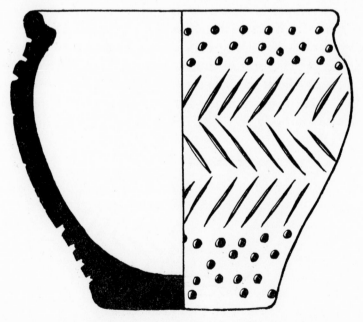

Figure 24. Food-vessel. Rhydwen, Whitford, Flintshire. Height 5.7 in.

stab technique was used on the middle zone of the Whitford vessel, the deep holes which form the other zones of ornament were cylindrical, and that each presents a small raised cone at its base—as shown in my drawing. The ornament on the Whitford vase is much rougher than that on the Huntingdon beaker, and the vessel itself is coarsely made; but the similarities detailed above can hardly be accidental, though a likely route for people of the Beaker culture to North Wales from central England has yet to be worked out.

### MIDDLE BRONZE AGE POTTERY: OVERHANGING-RIM URNS AND 'PIGMY' CUPS

The overhanging-rim urn, examples of which have already been illustrated (Figures 10 and 12), the standard type of burial pottery in the cremation period (*c.* 1400 B.C. onwards) in Britain is derived from the 'food-vessel' (itself occasionally used for the ashes of the dead, as we have seen). A good example of the transition is a pot in the National Museum of Wales from Holt, Denbighshire, covered with 'maggot ornament' of Neolithic derivation, which contained burnt bones. The rim is broader than is any true food-vessel, but cannot yet be described as overhanging.

A vessel sometimes associated with such urns in the full Bronze Age, not uncommon in Wales, will be known to everyone interested in our Bronze Age past—the pigmy cup, called 'incense-cup' in 19th-century archaeological papers, because some examples have pierced sides: we do not, in fact, know what purpose they served. I illustrate an example from Varlen, in the hill country near Llywel, Brecon, with impressed twisted cord ornament on body and base (Figure 25): we shall discuss the type later on (p. 54).

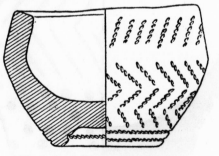

Figure 25. Pigmy cup. Varlen,
Llywel, Brecon

34

LATE BRONZE AGE POTTERY: 'ENCRUSTED' URNS: FROM
BURIALS IN WALES

A development from the food-vessel parallel to that of the 'OHR' urn,
of a pot large enough to hold a mass of burnt bones, is the encrusted urn,
represented by five examples in Wales. The type originated in north-
eastern Britain; two, having food-vessel features, from Jedburgh, Rox-
burghshire, and Branthwaite, Cumberland, are on record. Both show the
then novel pattern of zigzags in relief above the shoulder, and the survival,
on the shoulder, of the loops on some food-vessels, mentioned above.

The vase from Plas Penrhyn, Anglesey, Figure 26, at present unique,
and sadly fragmentary, contained burnt bones. It is of food-vessel shape,
and provides a manifestly early example of the raised-lozenge pattern, in

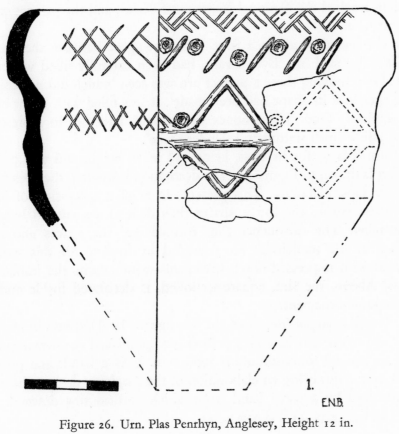

Figure 26. Urn. Plas Penrhyn, Anglesey, Height 12 in.

the form of opposed zigzags separated by a horizontal ridge. The incipient rosettes also are characteristic of a new style. Elaboration such as this attained its maximum when the type reached northern Ireland, and there are two encrusted urns found in Britain to match the overseas development—one from Penllwyn, close to the little port of Aberystwyth, Cardiganshire, and another from Preseli Mountain, Pembrokeshire. The ideas their style represents thus came back from Ireland, illustrating our western sealinks in the Late Bronze Age.

As a work of art the Cardiganshire pot is indeed superior to any Irish specimen. Its discovery is curiously appropriate, for a grave-digger in the chapel cemetery of that village hit with his spade the coverstone of a small cist 3 ft. below present ground level. The labourer, the minister of the congregation, and a well-known local archaeologist all, successively, rose to the unusual occasion, and the urn, with a detailed account of its situation, reached the National Museum of Wales, and the present writer, in due course.

The cist measured about 2 ft. × 1 ft. The space between the urn and the cist walls, said Mr. Eyre Evans, had been carefully filled with small stones. On removing these a perfect urn was seen 'which did not collapse until a sketch of its shape had been made'. It was filled with burnt bones, not completely fired. These bones were found, later on, to represent 'a man of rather small stature and slender make'.

The urn is large for its class, being $13\frac{1}{2}$ in. in height and well proportioned; it is drawn in Figure 27. The decoration is graded, the upper zone being the most elaborate. This presents in relief a succession of linked semi-circles: within the lower spaces thus defined are curved bands in similar relief. The cartouches thus formed and the spaces above the junctions of the semicircles are occupied by knobs. All this work is decorated with impressed-notch ornament—which turns the knobs into rosettes! Above, the rim, square-sectioned, is decorated inside and out with the same ornament.

The Preseli example (my Plate 8b) was figured by Thurnam in his well-known paper on 'Ancient British Barrows' published in *Archaeologia* in 1873[1]; its present whereabouts is unknown. It is a handsome pot, the pattern on the rim being an elaboration of the Anglesey design: the bulge is emphasized by a wavy band from which vertical ribs descend. The

[1] Vol. 43, Fig. 32, p. 353, and note p. 352.

(a) Stake-holes, and stone revetment of Beaker barrow, north-west side

(b) North side: Stone-holes between stake-holes and revetment

PLATE 9. TALBENNY, PEMBROKESHIRE

(a) The barrow on completion of digging: the primary grave in foreground

(b) Secondary burial, urn and pigmy cup *in situ*

PLATE 10. TALBENNY, PEMBROKESHIRE

(a) Kerb of enlarged Barrow (left); 'Beaker' revetment (right). North-west side

(b) Ditch and other constructions, from outside (North)

PLATE 11. TALBENNY, PEMBROKESHIRE

(a) Stones and stone-holes of enlarged barrow south-west side (see plan)

(b) Succession: Lip of ditch and rim of enlarged barrow, on east side (see plan)

PLATE 12. TALBENNY, PEMBROKESHIRE

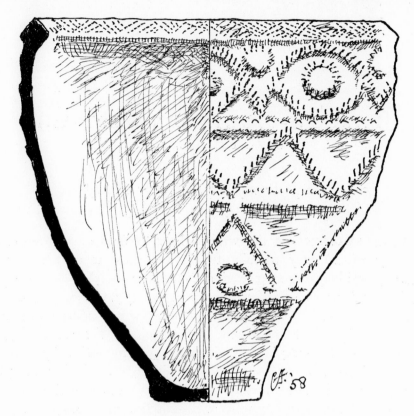

Figure 27. Urn. Penllwyn, Cardiganshire. Height 13½ in.

whole of the vessel has a close-set incised pattern. The importance of the mountain in our period heightens its significance. One of the closest parallels in the Irish series to our group is that from Gorey, Wexford— the county of gold-bearing gravels.

The date of this most interesting urn-type is about 800–600 B.C. The metal trade, in gold and copper, probably accounts for its presence on both sides of the Irish Sea, but there is a parallel, eastern, development, many urns from Late Bronze Age cemeteries showing similar vertical patterns having been found in southern England. Examples from Latch Farm, Christchurch, Hants, will be found in the *Proceedings of the Prehistoric Society*, 1938, and the problems which the western series presents are discussed in a paper by the author in the *Antiquaries Journal*, 1927.

# 3

## BARROW-DIGGING IN WEST AND SOUTH WALES

### *Early Bronze Age (Beaker Phase)*

OBSERVATIONS on the writer's later method of barrow-digging (1938–42) may usefully follow the account of the first one (Ysceifiog) dug after leaving Cambridge (1925) in the Cambridge technique and the records of early barrows (1925–7) the digging of which he did not control. In the 'quadrant method', as it was called, two trenches were dug at right angles across the highest point of the (often ploughed-down) barrow, working inwards from the margin—primarily at two of the four points—to learn about its composition, and whether it has been enlarged or no, and if so, how: enlargement may be symmetrical or lateral. All ritual or structural features met with—a stake circle for example, or an internal stone-ring showing that the barrow has been enlarged—are followed up laterally: the approach to the primary burial in or near the centre may thus be long delayed. To barrow-diggers, today, the characters of the structure, which give a clue to the procedures accompanying burial of important people, primary or secondary, are of great significance. A glance at the later plans in this volume will show better than any description the number and variety of such features: and since the exact extent of the excavation, when incomplete, is indicated, the reader can appreciate *why the dig took on the pattern thus shown*. Absence, as well as presence, of internal structures is intriguing: a row of empty stone-holes under a barrow, for example, reveals a phase of demolition and reconstruction. In one large barrow the writer found a secondary burial straight off by determining the axis of a *lateral enlargement* of the mound, and digging a narrow trench along it (the one aligned south-easterly, on Figure 29 below).

A variety of building techniques in 'composite' barrows (stone and earth or turf) have been studied: and vertical-walled turf mounds (for ritual control), rings for ritual dances, and other unusual, or hitherto unnoticed, features have been demonstrated.

The fundamental measurements are those that provide a plan, and sections: with the exact position of all burials and structural features. When these are completed, the finds studied and the whole 'written up', a new kind of problem emerges: what are the limits of inference from the observed facts which the writer should recognize and conform to? The limits in the case of Ysceifiog were those directly arising: but it will perhaps be seen by the reader that the growth of experience and the development of technique, in these later researches, beginning at Talbenny, Pembrokeshire, have extended the range of attainable knowledge.

One other point of importance arises at this stage. The sequence of my barrows, which will now be examined, covers the range of cultures in the Bronze Age of the Highland Zone, from Beaker to late Urn-type, *c.* 1700 to *c.* 450 B.C., fairly well; but there is one important gap—the adequate record of barrow burial associated with a 'food-vessel'—representing a weakening of the intrusive beaker activity, and a resurgence and development (primarily in north Britain) of the Neolithic tradition in pot-making. Now my friend Mr. D. M. Waterman, working in a technique similar to that which I employed in Pond Cairn (q.v.) and other barrows, found 'food-vessel' burials in Quernhow, a round barrow in the North Riding of Yorkshire 6 miles north-north-east of Ripon, beside the Great North Road $1\frac{1}{4}$ miles west of the River Swale: it was 3 ft. high and 77 ft. in diameter. With his kind permission, I have summarized his results and used his plan and other illustrations to fill the gap referred to (p. 71 below).

The series begins, then, with a 'Beaker barrow'.


## SOUTH HILL BARROW, TALBENNY, PEMBROKESHIRE, *c.* 1550 B.C.

*Argument.* Within a temporary circular wooden fence sited on a coastal plateau was a small stony heap containing an Early Bronze Age beaker.[1] A barrow (with a stone revetment) was raised thereover. In the Middle Bronze Age the revetment was in part dismantled when an enlargement of the barrow was undertaken; in the course of this enlargement the design was changed, involving demolition of new work. The completed structure

[1] *Arch. Journ.*, 1942, pp. 1 ff., and my Figure 32.

39

had a retaining wall and was ditched; the secondary burial (by cremation) was so placed as to suggest axial planning.

*Site.* Talbenny parish includes the seaward half of a patch of long-cultivated upland in Pembrokeshire 8 miles west-south-west of Haverfordwest, overlooking St. Bride's Bay. South Hill is the south-western portion of this plateau; a barrow is sited at its highest point, 236 ft. above sea-level (Figure 28). This is a mile from the Atlantic Ocean at the tiny rock-infested

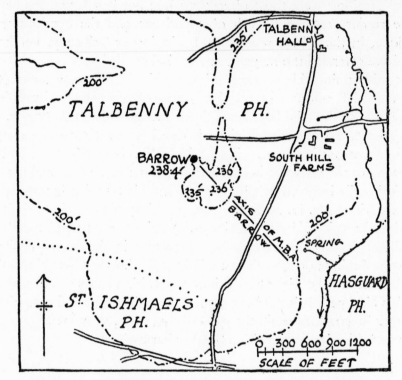

Figure 28. Talbenny, Pembrokeshire. Site of South Hill Barrow

landing-place known as Mill Haven; one of the two rills which combine to form the combe (and therefore the Haven), rises in full view, a short distance away from it. There is thus a physical link between plateau and landing-place, and the barrow is crest-sited from the north-west. Looking in this direction, then, a noble seascape and landscape is seen; on the skyline are St. David's Head, Ramsey Island and its rocky islets. On the east side of the barrow the plateau rises slightly, then slopes gently to a brook flowing south; there are springs on the plateau margin which prevent this brook running dry in summer.

South Hill Barrow is the only burial mound in this part of Talbenny parish; it is not marked on the Ordnance map. The underlying rock here is the Red Marl division of the Old Red Sandstone, a formation which occupies the greater part of the district north of Milford Haven and which provides a tenacious red clayey soil and subsoil. Locally there are patches of glacial drift, on one of which the barrow is situated. Glacial action has provided, in addition to such sandy or marly clays, boulders and pebbles of igneous rock. The district in general was undoubtedly heavily forested in antiquity, but the Atlantic gales, so frequent on this exposed coast, must have kept the higher ground, including the Talbenny upland, fairly open.

*Procedure.*The excavation of the barrow (Figure 29) was begun on the usual lines, trenches being dug to the apparent centre—the highest point of the mound—from the four cardinal points and the general character of the structure thereby discovered. Lateral clearances along the lines of a revet-ment and a stake-circle (Plate 9, A and B), outer kerbing (Plate 12b), ditch, etc., were carried out as required: a secondary burial—shown on the plan—was found (Plate 10b): and the exact centre of the structure having been ascertained (Figure 29), extensive clearance (400 sq. ft.) of the central area was made in a (vain) search for the primary deposit. It was war-time: all the necessary data relating to the construction and to the later history of the barrow, had been recorded; but the basic problem was unsolved— was there a primary deposit, and if so where? It was then decided to make use of a mechanical excavator, and to remove the remainder of the barrow mass (consisting mainly of tenacious clay) within the revetment. Moving forward in a circle around the opened centre, clearing down to ground-level and piling up the spoil on its outer flank, a caterpillar-wheeled 'Rapier' carried out work estimated to occupy four men for at least three weeks, in two and a half working days. Plate 10a shows part of the spoil heap referred to above, looking across the area formerly occupied by the barrow; the machine moved on the timber platforms which are seen lying about. Every scoop-load was watched by myself and my helpers; no exten-sive disturbance of the 'floor' (the original ground surface below the barrow) could have been present without being seen, though only momentarily,

41

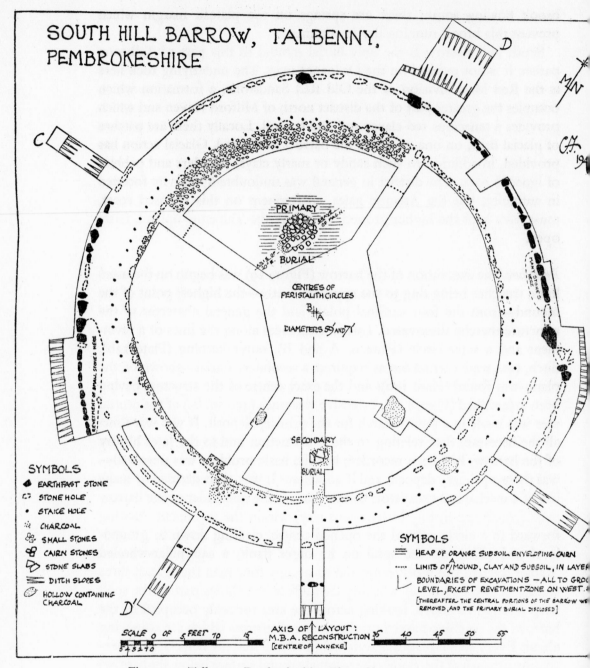

SOUTH HILL BARROW, TALBENNY, PEMBROKESHIRE

PRIMARY BURIAL

CENTRES OF PERISTALITH CIRCLES

B A

DIAMETERS 59 AND 71

SECONDARY BURIAL

SYMBOLS
- EARTHFAST STONE
- STONE HOLE
- STAKE HOLE
- CHARCOAL
- SMALL STONES
- CAIRN STONES
- STONE SLABS
- DITCH SLOPES
- HOLLOW CONTAINING CHARCOAL

SYMBOLS
≡ HEAP OF ORANGE SUBSOIL ENVELOPING CAIRN
⋯ LIMITS OF MOUND, CLAY AND SUBSOIL, IN LAYER
L BOUNDARIES OF EXCAVATIONS — ALL TO GROUND LEVEL, EXCEPT REVETMENT-ZONE ON WEST.
[THEREAFTER THE CENTRAL PORTIONS OF THE BARROW WE REMOVED, AND THE PRIMARY BURIAL DISCLOSED]

SCALE OF FEET

AXIS OF LAYOUT:
M.B.A. RECONSTRUCTION
[CENTRE OF ANNEXE]

Figure 29. Talbenny, Pembrokeshire. Plan of barrow excavations

as the shining teeth and keel of the scoop, starting at ground level, moved inwards and upwards into the overburden. And while a small secondary burial deposit could easily have been lost sight of, or not seen at all, in the mass of disintegrating soil which the method (however carefully employed, as in this case) creates on the working face, anything of the size and character of the secondary already found would certainly have been located and the machine stopped in time. My workmen and I (and the 'driver') of course got more expert as the work progressed; and, as it happened, the primary deposit was not reached until the machine had practically completed the circle mapped out for it.

The little cairn (seen on Figure 29) was struck, and a few marginal stones torn away; the machine was 'called off' and the deposit—the 'primary burial'—carefully examined (Plate 10a). With its examination the work on the barrow ended.

The experiment may then be regarded as successful. But I should not like to repeat it, even under the favourable conditions (i.e. machine and driver under my personal orders) which I enjoyed. It is a nerve-racking business, and a few seconds inattention with so powerful and rapid an agent of removal might render useless days of unremitting effort, and result in the complete loss of a vital deposit. The machine was, however, only employed when the barrow and the subsoil had been *studied for five weeks*, and everything material known about its structure and that of the soil and subsoil below it. As a method of investigating a barrow *de novo*, the use of a mechanical excavator is of course wholly inadmissible.

The complexity of the problems presented by the barrow and the partial character of the scientific excavation renders my published plan (Figure 29) of the areas uncovered, which usually provides a sufficient indication of the nature of the structure, perhaps too technical. This plan, then, is here supplemented by a reconstruction (Fig. 30), in which the barrow is shown as though wholly excavated, and in which ruined constructions are restored to their known original form and position.

*The First Phase: The Beaker Barrow.* This barrow occupies the area defined by the inner ring of stones on the reconstruction; its limits are also shown on the sections, Figure 31, as 'margin of Beaker barrow'.

*The Wooden Fence.* As the plan of the excavation, Figure 29, then shows, a complete ring of stake-holes approximating to a true circle, and varying in diameter from 60 ft. to 64 ft., was found under the mound. A characteristic series is seen in Plate 9a. The number of holes is 96, of which four overlap or duplicate others, possibly with intention. There are two interspaces, west-north-west of the centre, side by side, 3 ft. 7 in. and 4 ft. in breadth; the remaining interspaces range from 1 ft. 6 in. to 2 ft. 10 in.: an overwhelming percentage (93·3%) is concentrated within narrower limits, namely, 1 ft. 8 in. to 2 ft. 6 in. The stakes were driven in, and the holes range in diameter from $2\frac{1}{2}$ in. to $3\frac{1}{2}$ in., being up to 1 ft. in depth: they represent the earliest construction on the site. The evidence for this lies in the northern sector where, being encroached on by stone-holes of the revetment of the primary barrow, *they have been sought and found at the bottom of these shallow holes* (Plate 9b)! That the stake-holes, then, represent a wooden, almost certainly wattled fence (with a double gate of entry on the north-west side no doubt closed by hurdles), ringing the area within which the 'burial' was to take place, is a reasonable inference. That such an enclosure was constructed implies, furthermore, that the area where the burial rites took place was hallowed for the purpose. The great majority of stake-holes were filled with fine, dark earth; the stakes must either have rotted in position, or the ground occupied by the holes of the drawn stakes (which is outside the primary barrow) must have been untrodden long enough for them to become filled with humus. We shall have occasion to refer to this stake circle later on (p. 49).

*The Primary Deposit* (Plate 10a). A small mound of stones and clay, and wood carbonized by decay covered an area of about 6 ft. in diameter in the north-west quadrant of the barrow (see plan and section, Figure 31, B). The stones of the mound could have been collected in the immediate neighbourhood; they ranged from 4 in. to 12 in. in diameter. The base of the little mound was a foot below ground level; that is, an area approximating to 6 ft. × 6 ft. had been excavated to this depth before it was raised. At one place a flint implement was found; at another the base and part of the body of a pottery vessel—a 'beaker'. There were no visible human remains with the beaker, which was in a state of extreme disintegration.

Under the clayey part of the mound, the subsoil was found to be

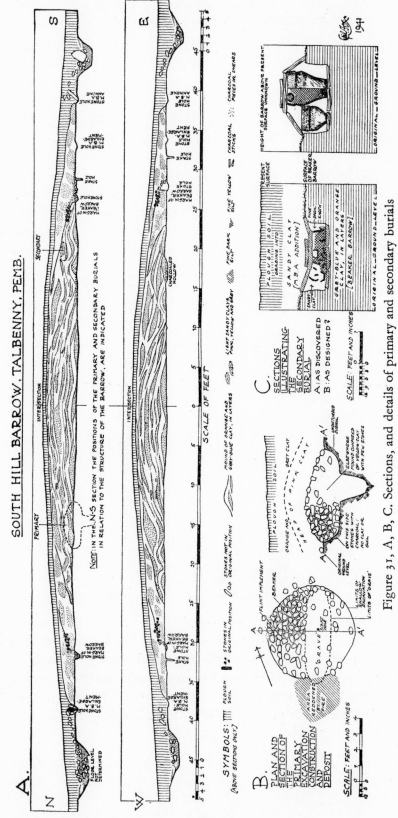

Figure 31, A, B, C. Sections, and details of primary and secondary burials

45

disturbed; further work disclosed a narrow elongated hollow or grave 6 ft. long. It was deepest in the middle (Inset B)—where there was a stake-hole, and nowhere more than a foot wide; it seemed to symbolize a grave, rather than to be intended for a human body. It contained clean soil with a few specks of charcoal. The original surface of the adjacent ground was hardened and reddened by fire over an area some 3 ft. × 3 ft.

*The Beaker.* The beaker referred to, when restored, was seen to be of our 'B' class, and is 6·5 in. in height; the breadth at rim and at base is estimated at 5·5 in. and 3·4 in. respectively (Figure 32). In colour the ware is red to brownish-black, with a black core; it is full of grits, ill-baked, and very rotten. The 'wall' ranges in thickness from 3 mm. to 7 mm. The surface

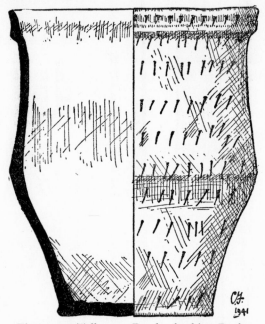

Figure 32. Talbenny, Pembrokeshire. Beaker

of the surviving portion of the pot—which includes most of the base and a complete section from base to rim—is rugged and disintegrating; it is thus difficult to make out the exact character of the ornament. This appears to consist of ten rows of impressed marks mostly cuneiform with broad end uppermost, each more or less diagonal, 0·2 in. to 0·3 in. in length, and covering the whole pot from rim to base. The impressions are up to

¼ in. apart; they are deepest on the rim. The vessel is a poor example of an important type (see p. 59 below).

*Implement* associated with the Primary Deposit (Figure 33, left). This implement—shown front and back—is of translucent dark flint worked on a flake; the cortex of the nodule is present on the left side. The upper half of the surface is carefully worked over to a point: sides and point are sharp. A flake struck from the (unfinished?) basal portion isolates a ridged spur on the left side, carefully worked over on its outward aspect.

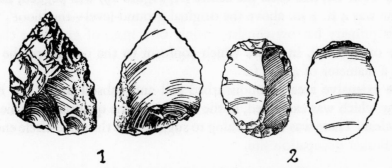

**1**        **2**

Figure 33. Talbenny, Pembrokeshire. Flint implements

*Posthole.* South-south-east of the primary deposit, a large stake- or post-hole, 4 in. in diameter, was found (see Figure 30, red). It was filled with grey clay showing that the post which it contained had been drawn immediately prior to the dumping of such clay—barrow material—on the site. There were no other holes in the central area.

*Hollows with Carbonized Wood.* Five shallow hollows made in the original surface were found, mainly filled with black earth and carbonized wood. All were within the stake-circle and may reasonably be regarded as holes from which boulders have been removed, and which were *ceremonially* filled up when the area was being prepared for the primary deposit.

The largest of these, a hollow 26 ft. south-east of that deposit, shown on the plan, will be described. It measured 4 ft. 9 in. in greatest diameter and 11 in. deep at the centre, was very irregular in outline and in depth, with firmly bedded stones on its margins; full of black earth, in which laminated (woody) masses and much small 'charcoal' was seen. Patches of re-set yellow clay also occurred. The filling did not rise above ground-level and the structure of the overlying mound gave no hint of its presence.

It is interesting, as showing that these hollows had no significance once (as we may suppose) the prescribed ritual was accomplished, that one of them should have been left outside the barrow when the circuit of this was planned.

*The Beaker Barrow: Its Character.* The two complete cross-sections of the barrow, Figure 31, show that the Beaker barrow extends to, and includes, the first ring of stone-holes: it is the hallowed area. It was designed as a true circle; its diameter is 59 ft. from north to south and 59 ft. 4 in. from east to west. On this basis the centre (A, Figure 29) was pegged; here the barrow was 4 ft. 8 in. above the original ground-level—the 'floor'.

This primary barrow consists mainly of a mass of grey-blue clay and clayey orange soil, in layers which conform to the outline of the mass: it has a diameter of 48–49 ft.

The extensive area of undisturbed soil and subsoil under the Beaker barrow which was examined, in the centre and the quadrant trenches, was quite clean. There was thus nothing to suggest that the stake-circle enclosed a pre-Beaker occupation site.

*The 'Beaker' Revetment.* Beyond the limits of the clay mass throughout the greater part of the circuit, and from 1 ft. to 1 ft. 5 in. above the 'floor' of the barrow is a close-set layer of stones, mostly small (Plate 9a). Though covered with later deposits this stony layer was originally exposed, as was indicated by the fine dark soil which filled the interstices between the stones: it terminated in a stoneless earth-face. The problem of its nature and function was solved when a continuous ring of stone-holes, some with packing stones still firmly fixed, was found at the bottom of this earth-face (Plate 9b): these stone-holes (shown also on Figure 29) evidently represented upright slabs or boulders, which with the stony layer formed a massive vertical-faced revetment to the Beaker barrow. The barrow type, thus known as 'composite', is widely distributed in Britain generally, and is common in South Wales. An example of slightly later date associated with an intrusive culture was strikingly illustrated by Professor W. F. Grimes in his study of Breach Farm Barrow in Glamorgan, described on pp. 91 ff., and we shall see others in this book.

*Reconstruction.* On the reconstruction, Figure 30, the stony layer of the revetment of the Beaker barrow is shown at its probable full breadth all round as are the stake-holes, the primary deposit, and two of the charcoaled hollows which were measured up. But I have only 'indicated' the 'stone-holes' and have not replaced the upright slabs, since we have no evidence of the size of these at any given point.

Lastly, the original barrow is crest-sited—on the skyline, that is—from the north-west, a point which will be taken up later (p. 59).

*The Second Phase: The Middle Bronze Age Enlargement.* In each of the quadrant trenches another series of stone-holes was found, *outside* the Beaker barrow, some with stones still in them. An extensive lateral clearance, illustrated on Plates 11b and 12a and Figure 29, was first undertaken in the north-west quadrant of the structure; it showed that, here, most of the stones which had evidently formed a continuous kerb to the enlarged barrow had been removed, but that a few, including two large and broad-based boulders, were still in position. The tops of these boulders were close to the surface and were scored with plough marks; the presence of no less than twenty-four such boulders on the margins of the field showed that the gaps were due to removals by the farmer, and were probably all fairly recent. In the course of later investigations, long stretches of the kerb were found to be fairly complete. The physical relation between the original and the extended barrow is well shown on Plates 11a and 11b. When undisturbed the stones were found to touch each other and so to present a continuous wall or wall-base. All those uncovered are shown to scale on the plan. Most of them must surely have come, originally, from the empty stone-holes of the Beaker barrow! The date of this development may be *c.* 1300 B.C.

*The Ditch.* Outside the kerb, and separated from it by a berm from 2 ft. to 4 ft. in breadth, was a small ditch (see plan and sections, also Plate 12b (left slope)).

*An Alteration in Plan.* While the determination of the limits of the enlarged barrow was in progress, it was observed that though the new stone kerb was only 7 ft. outside the revetment of the Beaker barrow in the *northern* half of the barrow it was over 12 ft. outside in the *southern* half. This eccentricity seemed strange, in view of the concentric character of the northern lay-out; attention was therefore directed to two intermediate hollows in the south trench. Lateral cuts (see plan, left and right, Figure 29) showed that these were stone-holes, on the circumference of the same circle as those in the northern half of the barrow; packing stones were occasionally found, firmly fixed, showing that kerbstones had actually been placed in position in the sockets. The circle was 71–73 ft. in diameter; it was practically concentric with the Beaker barrow. The discovery was followed up and the junctions with the later work disclosed. These junctions are illustrated, the eastern in Plate 12b, the western in Plate 12a, the former breaks sharply outwards to the new alignment, the latter gradually (see plan). The breadth of the extension, at the five points tested, was from 5 ft. to 6 ft.

The kerbstones of the western flank of the extension shown on Plate 12a are lying flat, having fallen outwards; they are plotted in their original positions on the plan. When the floor was examined a slight bedding hollow was found for one only; the others had merely been set upright on the ground—or possibly wedged into the turf. Examination of the adjacent stones showed that this slovenly work occasionally occurred also on the line of the true circle. Thus the gaps in the stone-holes of that circle, near the junction with the stones still in position, do not imply gaps in the structure, or that it was incomplete when the design of the structure was altered.

The ditch was, it appeared, not dug until this alteration in plan had been effected; stretches of its inner edge were examined at the junction between the old and the new work on each side, and it was seen to pass without any awkward angles from one to the other (Figure 29, left).

*The Barrow Material.* The material for the enlargement of the barrow was apparently dug from the same deposits as the filling-in of the Beaker barrow. The total thickness of these clays just outside the revetment of the Beaker barrow was at most 2 ft. 6 in.; and as there was about 7 in. of plough soil hereabouts, which rapidly increased to a foot or more as the outer stone-holes and kerbs were approached, there was little possibility of stratification. It was, however, seen that the clayey soil crossed the inner stone-holes without a break—the enlargement of the barrow had, it was clear, *not* been begun when the change of plan was decided upon.

The striking feature of the enlarged barrow was the quantity and wide diffusion of charcoal which it contained (and covered). Throughout the greater part of the circuit, close to the Beaker revetment and over this, the clayey soil was dark with it; it was blackest and most noticeable on the south side of the barrow—here, also, the floor was in places covered with charcoal in very small fragments. All this represented intentional deposit.

It is, I think, a relevant fact that many of the stone-holes of the Beaker barrow (Plate 9b, foreground) had been carefully and tightly packed up to ground level with small stones (and in one case, on the south side, with oak charcoal also) before the enlarged barrow covered them up. On the south side of the barrow, moreover, many small stones pressed into the surface soil extended in a layer for 4 ft. from the foot of the Beaker revetment.

These observations suggest that the dismantling of this earlier revetment was associated with ritual acts presumably designed to obviate any ill-effects on the well-being of the community resulting from the disturbance of earth-fast stones: *Life, not Death, that is, governed the action of those responsible.*

*The Discovery of the Secondary Burial.* Since the circular stone kerb of the enlarged barrow had originally been planned with some care, it seemed improbable that, when the strange decision to break that circle of kerbs, remove many of the stones, and extend the enlargement of the barrow, was arrived at, the two places from which the extension was to spring would have been casually chosen. Symmetry was, then, to be anticipated; each flank of the extension was likely to be the same distance from some spot which was of high importance; i.e. the intended place of the new interment. It was an easy matter to test this theory. The centre of the (destroyed) segment fronting the extension, and now represented by stone-holes, was found to be 51 ft. 6 in. from either end, and it was pegged. A 3-ft. trench was then dug, the axis of which was a radial line from the centre of the kerb circle, passing through the pegged point; and a secondary burial, obviously the one for which the extension was designed, was found on that radial line, sited just within the limits, on plan, of the Beaker barrow. This trench is shown in Figure 29; but the discovery is more strikingly indicated on the reconstruction (Figure 30). When the small size of the deposit in relation to the barrow mass is considered coincidence must be ruled out; and *it would thus appear that processes of reasoning and of mensuration*

51

*of the same order as those which enabled me to locate the burial, were employed by these barbarous Middle Bronze folk, over three thousand years ago, to fix the position of the extension in relation to the burial, and of the burial in relation to the new kerb circle.*

*The Character of the Interment: The Finds* (Figure 31, C). A saucer-shaped layer of slabby stone, measuring 3 ft. × 2 ft., covered the secondary interment. Immediately below this was a layer of fine dark soil through which appeared the rim edges of two pots; one, very small, inside the other. Further clearance exposed the overhanging-rim, partly disintegrated, of a cinerary urn, the photograph reproduced as Plate 10b being taken at this stage. The little vessel proved to be a pigmy cup (Plate 13), detail of ornament, Figure 34; it was resting on burnt bones. On the west side of the urn a third vessel was found; it was upright but contained no bones (Figure 31, bottom right). Surrounding the whole deposit, at the level of the overlying slabs, was reddened soil and charcoal. The bones were identified as adult and probably of one person; in the mass was a decayed bronze blade.

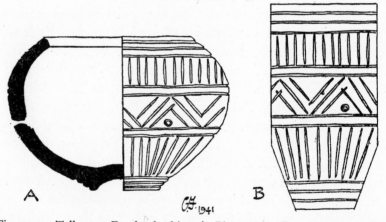

Figure 34. Talbenny, Pembrokeshire. A, Pigmy cup: B, pattern extended

We may attempt to reconstruct the procedure at the burial. A shallow hole having been made, charcoal hot from the pyre was dropped around it, and (probably) inside the urn, which was placed in the centre of the hole. The urn was then filled with the burnt bones, the bronze blade placed with them, and a pigmy cup upright on the top. A third vessel was placed beside

PLATE 13. TALBENNY, PEMBROKESHIRE: Pigmy cup

(a) First phase of excavation

(b) Last phase of excavation

PLATE 14. SUTTON 268′, GLAMORGAN

(a) 'U' cairn

(b) Pigmy cremation

PLATE 15. SUTTON 268', GLAMORGAN

(a) The rock-cut pit

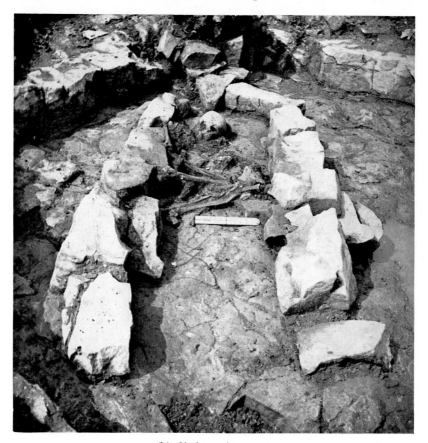

(b) Skeleton in grave

PLATE 16. SUTTON 268', GLAMORGAN

the first; if it had any contents they were perishable. A slab of stone was placed on the urn (an inadequate mode of protection frequently employed in South Wales in the Middle Bronze Age) and other slabs placed against it to form a rough roof. Clay and soil was then piled around and over this roof, which may have collapsed even before the completion of the enlarged barrow. Two sections (Figure 31, C) illustrate the character of the deposit as found, and my suggested reconstruction of the original set-up.

*The Pottery.* The urn containing the bones (Figure 35) proved on restoration to be 15·5 in. in height; it has a moderately deep overhanging-rim, the top of which though bevelled inwards is undecorated. There is a well-marked shoulder, that is, the urn is, in our phraseology, tripartite. The decoration on rim and neck—vertical zigzags and triangles—is elaborate, and incised with a fairly sharp point. The second vessel of overhanging-rim

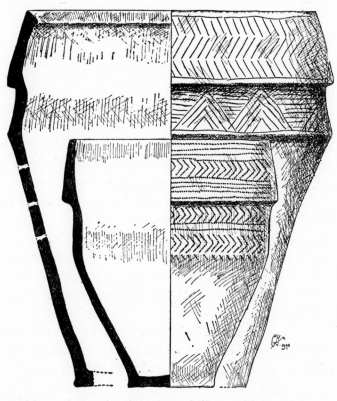

Figure 35. Talbenny, Pembrokeshire. Urn and associated vase

type in the same figure is smaller and has a weak shoulder; the rim edge is square-sectioned. It is decorated from rim to shoulder with impressed bands of > -shaped cord ornament. The pigmy cup is well-made; it is bowl-shaped with inbent rim and small footring, the base being markedly concave; it measures 2·2 in. in height and shows the usual pair of holes in the body. The triple band of linear ornament which covers it is incised with a smooth point. The purpose of these delicate little pots is unknown; the type, in south Britain, dates in Middle Bronze Age, *c*. 1400–800 B.C., and the associated urn with incised ornament, strongly shouldered, suggest that, here, it must be assigned to a fairly early date in the phase.

Six feet from the centre of the burial, 1 ft. 2 in. above ground-level, a plano-convex flint knife—that is, flint flake smooth on the bulbar face but trimmed to an oval by pressure-flaking on the other side—characteristic of the period, was found in a patch of charcoal (Figure 33, 2). It was probably contemporary with the completion of the roofing of the burial deposit.

*The Character of the Stone Rim of the Enlarged Barrow, and the Nature of the Present Ditch-filling.* The evidence for a continuous alignment of upright stones and massive boulders—a stone kerb—encircling the enlarged barrow, and for a complete ditch outside it with an intervening berm about 2 ft. broad, has been set out. The plan records a 'revetment of small stones' in the south-west quadrant of the barrow behind the kerbstones (Figure 36, C). It might then be supposed that the enlarged barrow had a stone rim of the same character as that which observation and inference have established for the Beaker barrow.

But in no area other than the one mentioned—less than one-tenth of the total extent of the barrow rim investigated—did the sections exposed justify such a reconstruction. Where complete clearances have been undertaken, such as those in the quadrant trenches, the number, condition, and positions of the masses of stones exposed in, and on the flanks of, the sections, demand a different explanation. Plate 11b, for example, shows kerbstones of the enlarged barrow, and the ditch full of stones: this photograph was taken after numbers of stones between kerb and ditch had been removed.

The nature of the problem will be more clearly envisaged if the evidence of the detailed sections, Figure 36, A and B, which deal with the same areas as those illustrated in the two photographs mentioned, is considered. The stones have evidently fallen forcefully downward and outward, from some point above the level of the kerbstone in each case; they reach across the ditch, and are rarely seen lying on the berm itself. Furthermore, such stones have been proved to extend downwards to the bottom of the ditch, usually in a close-set mass, in all four of the quadrant trenches.

Again, the matrix of the stones in the ditch has a bearing on the nature

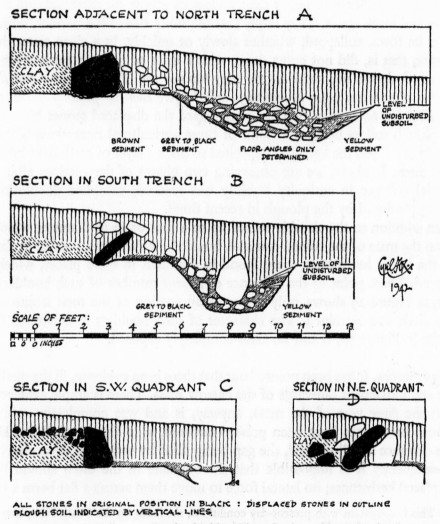

Figure 36. Talbenny, Pembrokeshire. Rim of enlarged barrow: details

of the structure and its collapse. When such a stony mass as that shown in Plate 11b was struck with pick or spade, it quivered like a jelly; the stones were found here (and in every ditch section) to be enveloped in the finest wet silt, black in colour, drying out grey. Such silt was evidently the result of secular decay of organic matter—plants—growing in a wet or damp ditch.[1] The curious fact was observed that the upper level of this silt was never horizontal but on a gentle slope from kerbstone to counterscarp. On the counterscarp indeed a different character prevailed, doubtless under the occasional influence of heavy rain; wedges of yellow silt extended into the grey and black zones. They imply that the stony rim of the barrow, what-ever its form, collapsed, whether slowly or quickly, in a clean state; the stones, that is, did not come down with a mass of moving earth behind them; *the barrow was stable but the stony rim was not. They also imply that the process of ruination began in antiquity, indeed before even the 'primary silting' of the ditch had taken place.* We can only regard the displaced stones high up in plough soil as being the result of those agricultural operations which partly destroyed the kerb and deposited so thick a layer of earth over berm and ditch. In short, we are observing two phases of destruction; after a partial collapse in antiquity stability was reached, complete dissolution being produced by the plough in recent times.

In addition to the sizeable stones up to a foot or so in diameter which form the mass of the ruined material, boulders or slabs, comparable in size to the larger kerbstones, were found in the ditch in three places, widely spaced. These point to the existence of a large number of such boulders, for, as Figure 29 shows, only a very small portion of the total length of the ditch was examined. The character of such boulders is illustrated in white in Figure 36, B and D: areas completely exposed.

*Reconstruction.* It has been pointed out that there is no evidence, in the ditch, for any movement outwards of the barrow mass. There is ample evidence that the *lower* part of the mass, anyway, is and was completely stable. Where kerbstones have been pressed outward, as in Figure 36, B and D, the clay face is still vertical, the gap being filled by soil fallen from above. Consequently it is impossible that the boulders in the ditch should be displaced kerbstones; no lateral force to move them across a flat berm 2 ft.

[1] This is consistent with present-day conditions; the fields on the South Hill plateau have large areas of standing water throughout the winter.

wide can be envisaged. Moreover, the third of these slabs, that shown in Figure 36, C, on the right, is confronted by an unbroken stretch of kerbing still in position, 13 ft. in length. Such boulders then must, like the smaller stones, have been displaced and projected outwards from some point above the line of kerbstones. One fell vertically downwards, and the kerbstone afterwards collapsed on to it: see section, Figure 36, D. Only one explanation covers all the facts, and had we been dealing with a hill-fort instead of a barrow it could have been taken for granted! The mound of earth was surrounded by a wall whose base was a continuous kerb of boulders or upright slabs, generally earthfast. On these slabs, and bedded also on the clayey barrow material behind them, and rarely (as in Figure 36, D) on stones set on the ground, or on a layer of small stones (C), rose this dry-stone wall, to which, we may surmise, boulders and slabs such as those found in the ditch formed a capping.

The numerous kerbstones that lean outwards provide one very good reason for an early collapse of the wall; set as they were in shallow holes they provided no adequate support, and a touch would send the whole crazy structure, forwards and downwards, into the ditch.

'The whole structure': can we say how high it was? Not with any certainty; but fifty stones were counted in one foot-broad section from kerb to counterscarp of ditch, and allowing for the loss of at least half as many by removal during ploughing and for the existence of a (lost) capping slab, a wall averaging 3 ft. thick and as much as 4 ft. in total height is probable. Two sketches, Figure 37, show the appearance and character of the wall thus envisaged.

The reconstruction, Figure 30, shows the plan of the enlarged barrow, as finally completed, in black; with the wall reconstituted as indicated

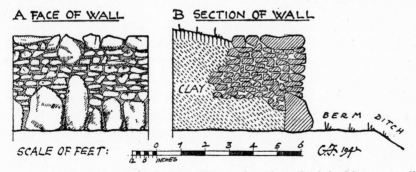

A FACE OF WALL    B SECTION OF WALL

CLAY

BERM    DITCH

SCALE OF FEET:    0  1  2  3  4  5  6    G.F. 194-

Figure 37. Talbenny, Pembrokeshire. Face and section of original barrow wall

above. The ditch is represented as unbroken, which is highly probable. It will be observed that the monument showed little sign of the change of plan—just one awkward angle on the east side. This introduces the question of the appearance of the structure. Since there was, *ex hypothesi*, absence of lateral thrust against the wall, the earth mound was not a high one—very little if at all higher at the centre than before the enlargement. It was, I think, a *low grassy dome like an inverted saucer, to which the retaining-wall formed a well-marked rim.*

*The Axial Plan: Inferences Therefrom.* In the preceding section we have seen reason to reconstruct our enlarged barrow as a flattish mound with a massive encircling wall. Had it any other notable feature? The discovery of the secondary burial, by alignment from the carefully ascertained centre of the mound, suggests that in the Middle Bronze Age that centre was known and obvious; one is therefore inclined to suspect the former presence here of an upright monolith, crowning the whole, a monolith which was erected for the Beaker barrow, and retained by the Middle Bronze Age builders. The remarkable density of the central mass of layered clay (Figure 31), the care which was taken in its construction—and it was not, as we know, directly over the primary deposit—is in favour of the view that it was intended to carry something important and heavy, which was to be exactly central to the structure as defined by the stone revetment. There is now no trace of a hole at the top of the barrow, but my section shows that it has been heavily ploughed down.

There is evidence that in western Britain at the dawn of the Bronze Age monoliths were associated with mound burial. Indeed, in the almost contemporary barrow at Linney, on the coast only 7 miles from Talbenny as the crow flies, built by folk who were probably of Beaker race, and who certainly were culturally akin to the South Hill settlers, a stone was—as we know—set upright on the covering slab of a cist, which contained a crouched burial and a 'debased beaker'.

An inhumation burial in the parish of Llanfachreth, Merionethshire, is similar in date and structural character, but here a great stone, bedded in the mound above the cist, was exposed to view. Since it interfered with ploughing operations it was, in 1873, dragged down by a team of horses. The Llanfachreth monument, then, provides exactly the evidence that is required; that such monoliths are rare today is probably because they so often 'interfered with ploughing operations'; apart from active destruction, the reduction in the height of a mound which always follows cultivation would soon render any central monolith unstable.

I would add that the famous cairn of New Grange, Ireland, which has a stone kerb, had a monolith on its summit.[1]

The plan of the enlarged barrow at Talbenny, and the position of the burial, indicate that the ceremonial approach to the site was from a direction opposite to that of the Beaker folk: from the south-east, not from the north-west. This suggests that the Beaker settlement had been given up, and that another group of people controlled the district, from dwellings on the other side of the little plateau. Whether a monolith existed on the mound or not, the annexe and the associated burial provide us with an axis which can be prolonged into an alignment representing the direction of approach demanded by that axis; *this alignment takes us, as Figure* 28 *indicates,* to a spring by a rill opposite to that referred to in the introductory paragraph of this record. Hereabouts, were I free to do so, I would search for the dwelling-place of the Middle Bronze Age chieftain whose ashes were inurned in so dignified a setting.

### THE TALBENNY BARROW: COMMENT

*The Barrow, the Beaker, and the Enlargement.* (*a*) It has been noted that the barrow was sited on a 'false crest' line, on the west side of a plateau close to the highest point thereof. The siting of the barrow was, I am convinced, a matter carefully thought out, and the governing idea may have been that it should be seen on the skyline from the settlement of its builders. If this be so the Beaker folk of South Hill lived on the seaward side of the upland, and probably used the landing-place of Mill Haven. This view receives support from the inference *that the 'entrance' to the wattled fence was on the north-west side* facing the hollow wherein the Mill Haven brook rises (p. 44 above).

It is perhaps worth mentioning that there is no evidence in the barrow structure to suggest that these Beaker folk regarded Preseli Top as a

---

[1] In 1699, as appears by a letter written by Edward Lhwyd: 'A stately mount . . . having a number of huge Stones pitch'd on end round about it, and a single one on the Top.'

sacred mountain, as apparently did their fellows on Salisbury Plain (Map C).

The primary deposit in the barrow, and its associated constructions, yield evidence of interest. The beaker is, as we have seen, of poor quality; but its shape and decoration deserve attention. With its flared rim and simple zonal ornament, it falls into the group called $B^1$ by students of the period; it has a well-defined body-angle, a feature which seemed to me in 1940 (p. 69, below) important enough in British archaeology to justify the creation of a sub-type $B^1\beta$.

This $B^1\beta$ beaker-type acquired a collar below the rim, probably in the middle Thames valley region, and thus equipped, has been found as we shall see (Sutton 268′, Pl. 17) on the South Wales littoral: also in the Herefordshire–Brecknockshire area—and now in West Wales. The possession of such a feature by the South Hill beaker is important, for it fixes the settlement as a Lowland offshoot, and not as an independent colonization from Brittany *via* the Land's End seaway. This view is indicated on the distribution map, Figure 38.

As for the enlargement, the inadequate protection afforded to the secondary burial by its stone 'roof', and the collapse of the plinth of the enlarged barrow shortly after its erection, illustrate the decay of the fine traditions of craftsmanship in the structural use of unwrought stone, inherited by our bronze-using folk, as the Bronze Age developed. Nevertheless, the enlargement of South Hill barrow was a fine conception, and it must have been an impressive monument when completed.[1]

The secondary burial provides the exact relationship, so rarely recorded in Wales, between a pigmy cup and its cinerary urn. It also confirms the infrequent association in one burial, in Middle Bronze Age barrows, of vessels (empty when found) of overhanging-rim urn type, with (larger) cineraries of similar type.[2] This association has, I think, never been discussed; it probably represents a survival, not unexpected in the Highland Zone, of the food-vessel association carried on into the cremation burial mode. It should be added that the contemporaneity of these two overhanging-rim vessels, one with a strongly marked shoulder (tripartite), the

[1] Marginal constructions: *Antiq. Journ.*, xxi, Pls. xxiiib and xxvii; *Archaeologia*, lxxxvii, Pl. xlix.

[2] As Greenwell, *British Barrows*, p. 72. '*Protective*' association is common; this occurred at Rhoscrowther (Pemb.) and probably at Llanboidy (Carm.). Also cremation 2 in the barrow on Kilpaison Burrows, and cremation 1 in barrow No. 1 at Crosshands.

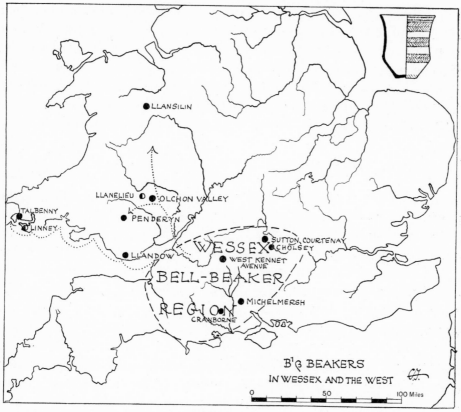

Figure 38

other with a weak shoulder (approaching the bipartite form) shows that these features do not represent a clear-cut typological succession, at all events in the Highland Zone. For we have a Phase ii urn associated with a vase representing the beginnings of Phase iii (Figure 35)—both probably made at the same time, in the same shop, for the interment.

Two somewhat unusual elements in the decoration of the overhanging-rim vessels—the peaked triangles of the larger, and the short diagonals of impressed cords on the shoulder of the smaller—reflect the decoration of an overhanging-rim urn in a cairn at Simondston, Figure 53, and illustrate again the community of culture along the southern coast of Wales. Striking a balance between the conflicting indications provided by these vessels, a date of 1100 B.C. for the South Hill burial might be suggested. But the most important vessel of the group is undoubtedly the pigmy cup, and this must be taken into consideration before we come to a decision. The

61

hollow base and the footrings point to a metal prototype, almost certainly Irish. The well-known gold bowls of the Bronze Age in Denmark, probably of Irish gold and Irish inspiration, show similar bases and also radial ornament: Bröndsted[1] dates one *c.* 1000–800 B.C. This derivation of our pigmy cup from a metal vessel, if it can be substantiated, represents a new fact in the history of early ceramic in the west.

The pigmy cup from Llywel, Brecknockshire (Figure 25), for the drawing of which I am indebted to Mr. G. C. Dunning, F.S.A., provides, however, a warning against too hasty a conclusion. In it the South Hill footring and hollow base seems to be in process of assimilation to a native type of cup; but the source of the feature in this cup may have to be sought in Wiltshire, in vases of a hollow-footed class.[2] A Flintshire bowl-shaped cup in the National Museum is, on the other hand, a direct debasement of the South Hill form.[3] A biconical cup from Betchton, Cheshire, illustrates another aspect of the devolution of the South Hill foot; the rings are represented by faint lines, the hollow base is a mere dimple. It is figured in *Prehistoric Cheshire*[4] and is associated with a local overhanging-rim urn-type which the authors of this work regard as the immediate precursor of the cordoned urn, and which they would date 900 B.C. and later. On the whole, then, the date suggested for the secondary burial seems to suit the character of the pigmy cup, and we may definitely fix the Middle Bronze Age enlargement of the barrow to *c.* 1100 B.C.

The diffuse scattering of charcoal in the course of the construction of the Middle Bronze Age barrow contrasts strongly with its absence in the Beaker ritual which seems to have made use of living sprays of oak in similar contexts. This free 'ritual use' of charcoal is, as will be seen, not uncommon in burials of Middle Bronze Age folk in South Wales. I have little doubt that our Middle Bronze ritualists hereabouts had taken the same sea-road as their Early Bronze predecessors; that is, that the sequence Wessex–South Wales–West Wales was repeated.

## SUTTON 268′: LLANDOW, GLAMORGAN, *c.* 1500 B.C.

The primary burial and cairn construction at the Talbenny barrow can be

[1] Fig. 109, *Danmarks Oldtid*, ii.
[2] As Winterbourne Stoke, Piggott, *loc. cit.*, 1938, Fig. 15,3, and pp. 75–6.
[3] Grimes, *Guide*, National Museum of Wales, 1939, p. 94, Fig. 38, *no.* 9.
[4] Varley, Jackson, and Chitty, 1940, Pls. ii and iii.

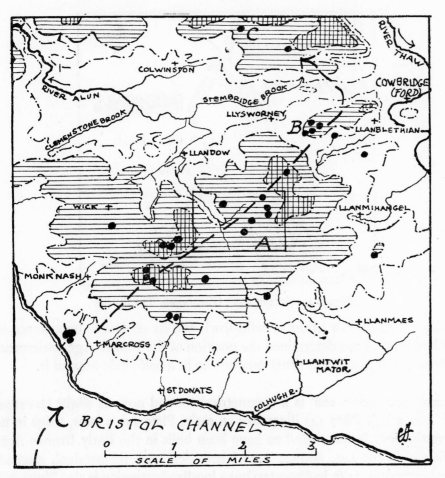

Figure 39. Sutton 268', Glamorgan. The region

better understood by reference to the burial customs, at a slightly earlier date, in Glamorgan, of the same Beaker folk. The barrow in the Vale of Glamorgan called Sutton 268' from (*a*) the nearest farm, and (*b*) its height in feet above sea-level, was excavated in 1939. It is the most westerly of a group of six lying well below the 300-ft. contour in the centre of a Lias limestone plateau west of Cowbridge: these are enclosed in the rectangle 'A' on Figure 39. This countryside is on the whole well-drained, the limestone being close to the surface; Sutton 268', however, is adjacent to an extensive marshy flat, fed by numerous springs, the sluggish outflow from which joins the Alun near Llandow village. This marsh (Figure 40) is

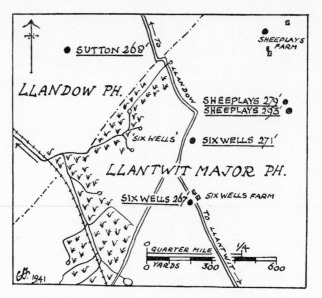

Figure 40. Sutton 268′, Glamorgan. The district

today a well-known haunt of wild-fowl, and its economic importance in antiquity may have determined the position of the Bronze Age settlements whose burial-places and ritual mounds lie in a half-circle around it.

*Description.* Sutton 268′ is a symmetrical mound now of slight elevation (+ 2 ft. 9 in.). Plate 14a illustrates an early, Plate 14b a later, stage in its investigation. It was found to have been built in the Early Bronze Age, enlarged in the Late Bronze Age: I here deal with the original, ditched, Beaker mound, 25 ft. in diameter: but a localized extension is also illustrated on the plan and sections, Figures 41 and 42.

The greater part of this little barrow was of material in which little or no stratification could be detected. A layer of hard-pan, produced by trampling, covered much of the floor. At the centre was a large U-shaped cairn, Plate 15a, mainly composed of small Lias stones in a soil matrix.

On removing the cairn it was seen that *its stony mass continued below ground level,* and further excavation disclosed a large rock-cut pit. The margins of this pit had been re-packed with the quarried blocks of Lias (interlocked with the stones of the cairn above) enveloped in the yellow clayey subsoil and shaly clay which had also been excavated; but the central area of the pit, which was between the horns of the cairn, was filled with surface soil—

64

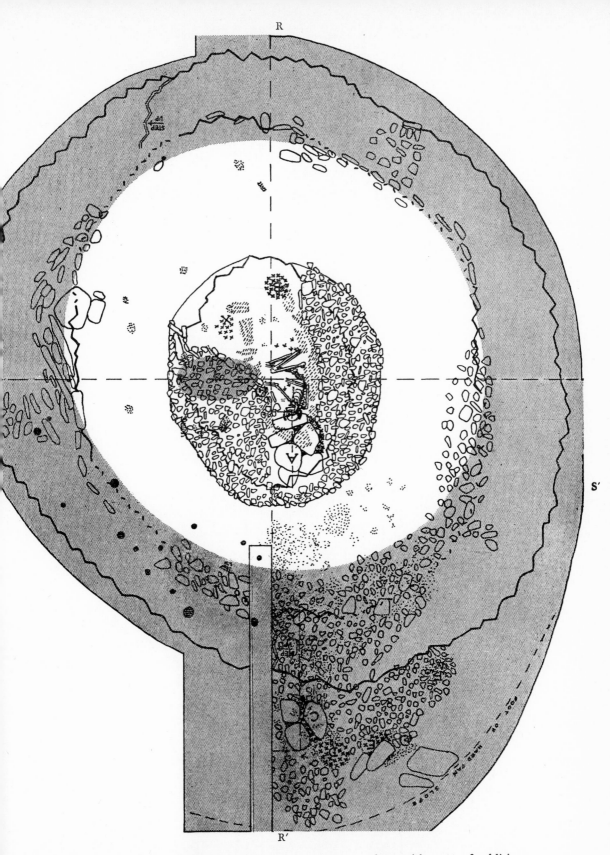

Figure 41. Sutton 268', Glamorgan. The primary barrow, plan, with part of additions. The hard-pan floor is shaded. Burials are lettered A–F. Section lines: see Figure 42. Zig-zag lines: limits of ditch and of grave-pit. R-R' is a north-south line

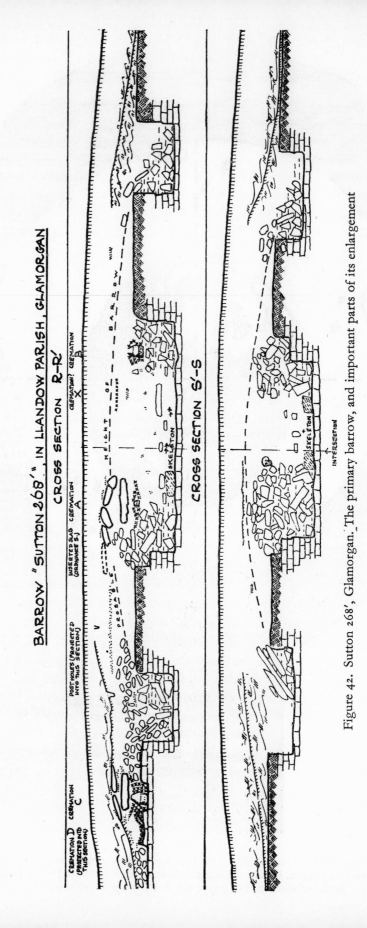

Figure 42. Sutton 268′, Glamorgan. The primary barrow, and important parts of its enlargement

a striking contrast. On the floor of the pit the soil-area was seen to be bounded on either side by a row of the above-mentioned quarried blocks; we were evidently isolating an inhumation burial (Plates 16a and b).

The dead person, a male in the prime of life, of round-headed—'Alpine'—type (Plate 21 and Figures 41, 42), lay flexed on the left side; carefully packed around his head were sherds of pottery, to one of which a flint arrow-head was adherent. Two other arrow-heads (and half a flint scraper) lay in the soil near the arms and four beyond the feet: there was evidence that the arrow-shafts had been broken before deposition. The quarried blocks—shaded diagonally on plan and section—formed a frame or cist, which was parallel-sided, 8 ft. in length and 2 ft. broad internally. The upper end where the head of the skeleton lay was rounded, the lower end was closed by small pebbles only.[1] The skeleton occupied less than half of the length of the cist, but the contracted body had been compressed with difficulty into its breadth. The reconstructed pot—a beaker—is seen on Plate 17 and the arrow-heads on Plate 20.

Clearance of the area around the cairn led to the discovery of the rock-cut ditch (see the zigzag outer line on plan and the outer trench on the sections) which completely encircled the cairn. Like the cairn it was oval, its *inner* diameter varying from 21 ft. to 26 ft. (Plate 18a and b). Bedding planes of the Lias rock formed the floor of the ditch, and as there was an eastward dip in the strata, the ditch was deepest (*c.* 2 ft.) along the north to south line, showing step-ups (to the next bedding plane) of nearly a foot. It was vertical-sided, and its breadth on the floor varied from $3\frac{1}{2}$ ft. to $5\frac{1}{2}$ ft. Slabs of stone were leaning against the inner edge of the rock-wall of the well-cut ditch; at some other points on the circle small stones formed, with a matrix of clayey soil, a similar tilted stony margin. This suggested that the original barrow ending on the ditch edge all round was, as it were, continued below ground-level by a stony slope. Conversely and more correctly, we can study a barrow springing from some 2 ft. below the ground, visible in a 4-ft. wide ditch! I know of no parallel to

[1] The resemblance to the gunwale plan of a stern-board canoe (*Antiq. Journ.*, 1926, p. 135, Fig. 6, Brigg) was noted at the time. The small round stones occupied the position of the stern-board. Compare the boat-shaped grave at Frocester, Glos. (*Proc. Prehist. Soc.*, 1938, pp. 214–17): it is of the same period as ours. Since Preseli, Pemb., blue-stones were probably transported in Neolithic and Early Bronze times to Salisbury Plain by sea along the coast of Glamorgan, and since this Bronze Age South Wales culture spread by sea along the north shore of the Severn estuary, the similarity may be significant.

such a structure, but how admirably it prevented involuntary trespass on sacred ground!

There is another significant feature of this ditch. At two points carefully sited in relation to the positions afterwards occupied by the horns of the cairn—as can be seen on the plan—there was a carefully placed layer of weathered (not freshly quarried) Lias stones which filled it up to ground-level and *formed causeways across it*. The causeways will have provided ceremonial access to the central (hallowed?) area and are surely to be associated with participants in the burial ritual: compare the procedure at Ysceifiog (p. 6, above).

Another point arises, when this barrier is being considered. It may, in a more permanent manner, have the same function as the stake-circle round the Beaker burial at Talbenny: that of preventing, shall we say, involuntary trespass on a sanctified area. Stake-circles will be shown to persist down to the Late Bronze Age in South Wales barrows.

*Comment*. Most of the features of the Beaker burial and its attendant constructions are elsewhere on record, but seldom is the known setting of such an interment so spacious, so dignified, so monumental. The unusual size of the grave-pit, enabling many persons to be associated with the last rites, is particularly notable—more officiants could be accommodated than at Ysceifiog (p. 8). The disparity between the space occupied by the contracted body and the size of the cist has been noted in burials of the period in northern Britain. Its 'bridges' or causeways, on opposite sides of a ditch, have been recorded also at a Beaker burial near Stonehenge; an expression in miniature of the same idea as is illustrated in Thornborough Rings and other similar works.

The variety of type of arrow-heads (Plate 20) found with the Beaker skeleton at Sutton 268′ is curious, but all the types have previously been recorded with Beaker burials. Features of the burial for which no parallel has yet been found are the breaking of a beaker and the careful packing of its sherds round the skull; and the form of the cairn. It is tempting to regard the U-shaped cairn as a survival of a most important part—the forecourt—of a long cairn of Cotswold type. But it has already been noted that this cairn was an above-ground expression of a design inaugurated over 2 ft. below ground: for the flanks and one end of the pit were filled with stone, the centre with earth. Until and unless a primary

(a) Beaker

(b) Pigmy cup

INCHES

INCHES

PLATE 17. SUTTON 268,' GLAMORGAN

(a) Rock-cut ditch—east side

(b) Rock-cut ditch—north side

PLATE 18. SUTTON 268', GLAMORGAN

(a) Revetment of enlarged barrow

(b) Cremation 'C'; the urn disclosed

PLATE 19. SUTTON 268', GLAMORGAN

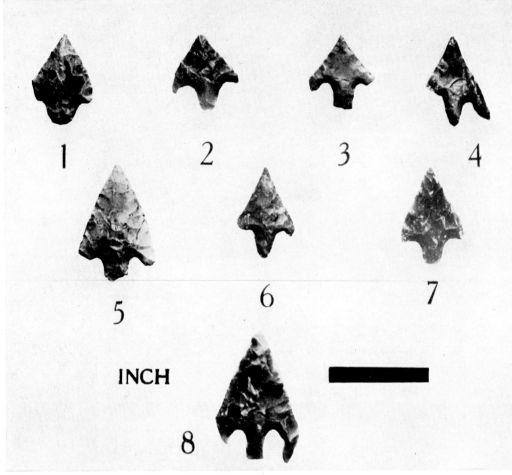

INCH

(a) Arrowheads from Beaker burial and cremation 'C'

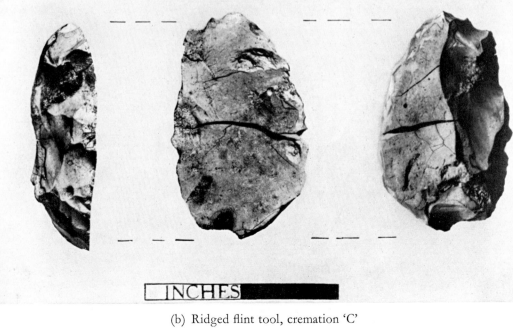

INCHES

(b) Ridged flint tool, cremation 'C'

PLATE 20. SUTTON 268', GLAMORGAN

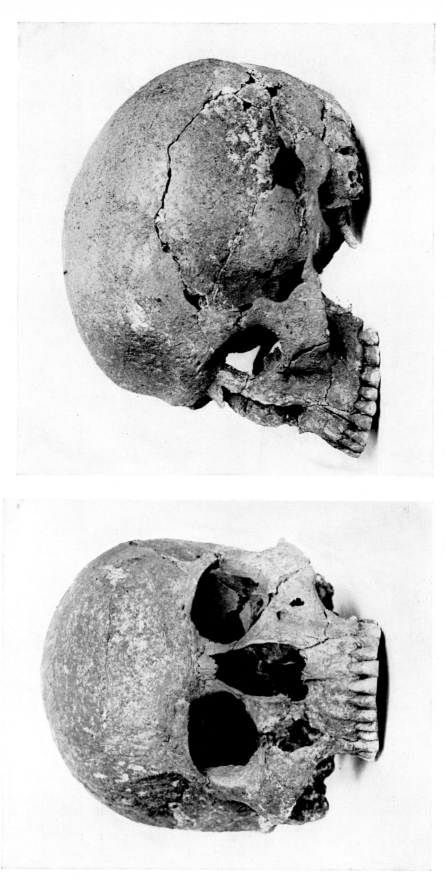

PLATE 21. SUTTON 268', GLAMORGAN: Beaker burial: the skull of a 'round-head'

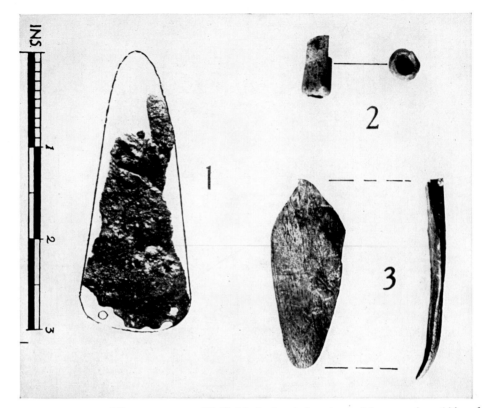

PLATE 22A. SUTTON 268', GLAMORGAN: Knife-blade, bead, 'netting rule': cremations 'A' and 'C'

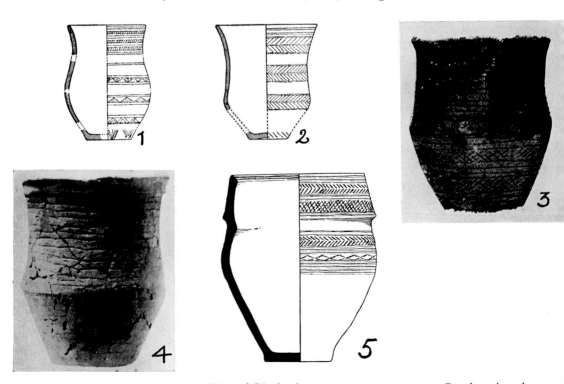

PLATE 22B. WILTS., HANTS, BERKS.: B¹α and B¹β beakers. NORMANTON, WILTS.: Overhanging-rim urn

Neolithic burial is found below the forecourt of a horned cairn in Britain, we must regard Sutton 268' as providing a type of cairn without known precursors in these islands.

When the sherds of the beaker were cleaned and hardened, they were found to represent a complete vessel 6·5 in. in height, the paste brownish-red externally with a black core. As Plate 17a shows, there is a well-marked cordon at the rim, with deeply impressed diagonal hyphenated ornament thereon. Below are two zones of hyphenated ornament, each consisting of six horizontal lines, and one series of diagonals centrally placed. The craftsmanship is poor and careless.

The Sutton beaker is of the 'B' class in form (which accords with its poverty in decoration). Like the Talbenny example (p. 60), it belongs to the angular group, B¹β: an almost identical beaker was found in a cist in the Olchon valley, Herefordshire, with a flint arrow-head resembling No. 5 in my series. Intermediate forms are not difficult to find in the Wessex area in which B¹ beakers normally occur, and examples from

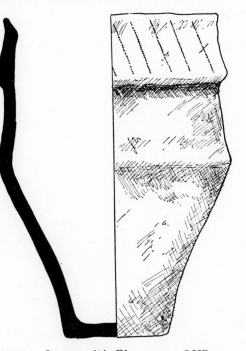

Figure 42a. Sutton 268', Glamorgan. OHR urn,
Cremation C, p. 103

Michelmersh, Hants., and Sutton Courtenay, Berks., are illustrated on Plate 22b, 3, 4. Figure 38 illustrates the presumed expansion of beaker-users in Central and South Wales from Wessex: a similar movement from the east coast to North Wales is highly probable.

The Wessex beakers on my Plate have hyphenated diagonals, separated by horizontal lines: except Sutton Courtenay, which has horizontal lines only. The evolutionary process is a reduction of the flare of the rim, the emphasis on this part of the beaker being retained by means of a rim cordon; weakening and raising of the body-angle; and coarsening of paste and decoration. Rim cordons are frequent in beakers from the Rhineland, but are not a common feature of beakers in this country. These probably developed in the upper Thames valley, and the expansion of the Bell-beaker folk across the estuary of the Severn shown on the map will have been late in their history.

What dates, then, are we to assign to Sutton 268' and Talbenny? The problem was analysed at length in the original paper and I concluded that *c.* 1500 B.C. was reasonable for these somewhat debased examples on a periphery of the Beaker culture.

# 4

## THE 'FOOD-VESSEL' PHASE OF CULTURE IN BRITAIN

Iᴛ has already been shown (p. xv) how necessary it is, if the reader is to gain a clear idea of the pottery sequence in British barrows from my book, to include one with 'food-vessels' of the classic, north-eastern type, not represented in Wales, and the kind permission of the excavator of Quernhow Barrow in the North Riding of Yorkshire, Mr. D. M. Waterman, has been mentioned. The Society of Antiquaries, in whose Proceedings the record was published, confirm this permission.

### QUERNHOW: A BARROW IN THE NORTH RIDING OF YORKSHIRE, c. 1500 B.C.

Quernhow—the second syllable signifies a burial mound—is situated beside the Great North Road in the Vale of York, near Ainderby Quernhow, on a gentle slope above the River Swale, north of Ripon. It represents food-vessel-using folk of the limestone hills of north-east Yorkshire: its region can be considered as part of that wherein this pottery-type was evolved. The *primary mound* is shown in Figure 43, the complete structure in Figure 44: sections, in Figure 45, define the successive deposits. The early pits 1, 3, and 4 are shown in Figure 46, and the six food-vessels in Figure 47. They are here associated with the rite of cremation. The photograph, Plate 24b, was taken when clearance was completed.

I quote from Mr. Waterman's summary, with my own references. At the centre of the site selected, a double pit (No. 1, Figures 43 and 45) was first excavated, evidently not for purpose of burial, but to fulfil a ritual function, in connection with which a considerable amount of charcoal was deposited before the whole excavation was refilled with a homogeneous deposit of large cobbles and sand. The principal burial, Cremation 1 on the plan, with Food-vessel 1 was sited a foot to the east of this pit. All the

71

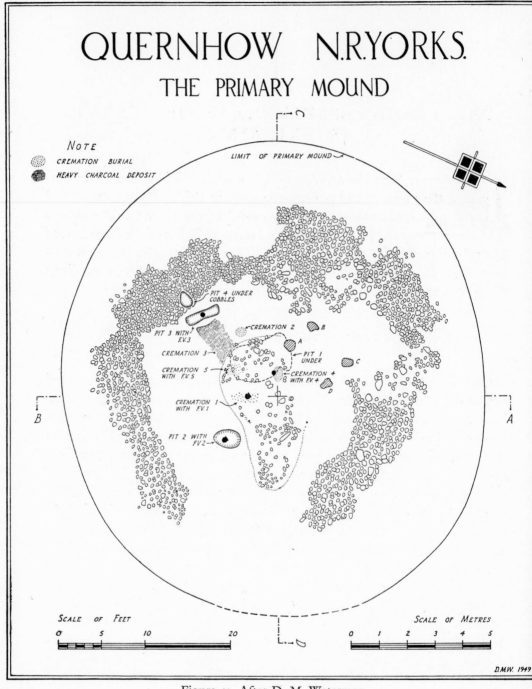

QUERNHOW N.R.YORKS.

THE PRIMARY MOUND

Figure 43. After D. M. Waterman

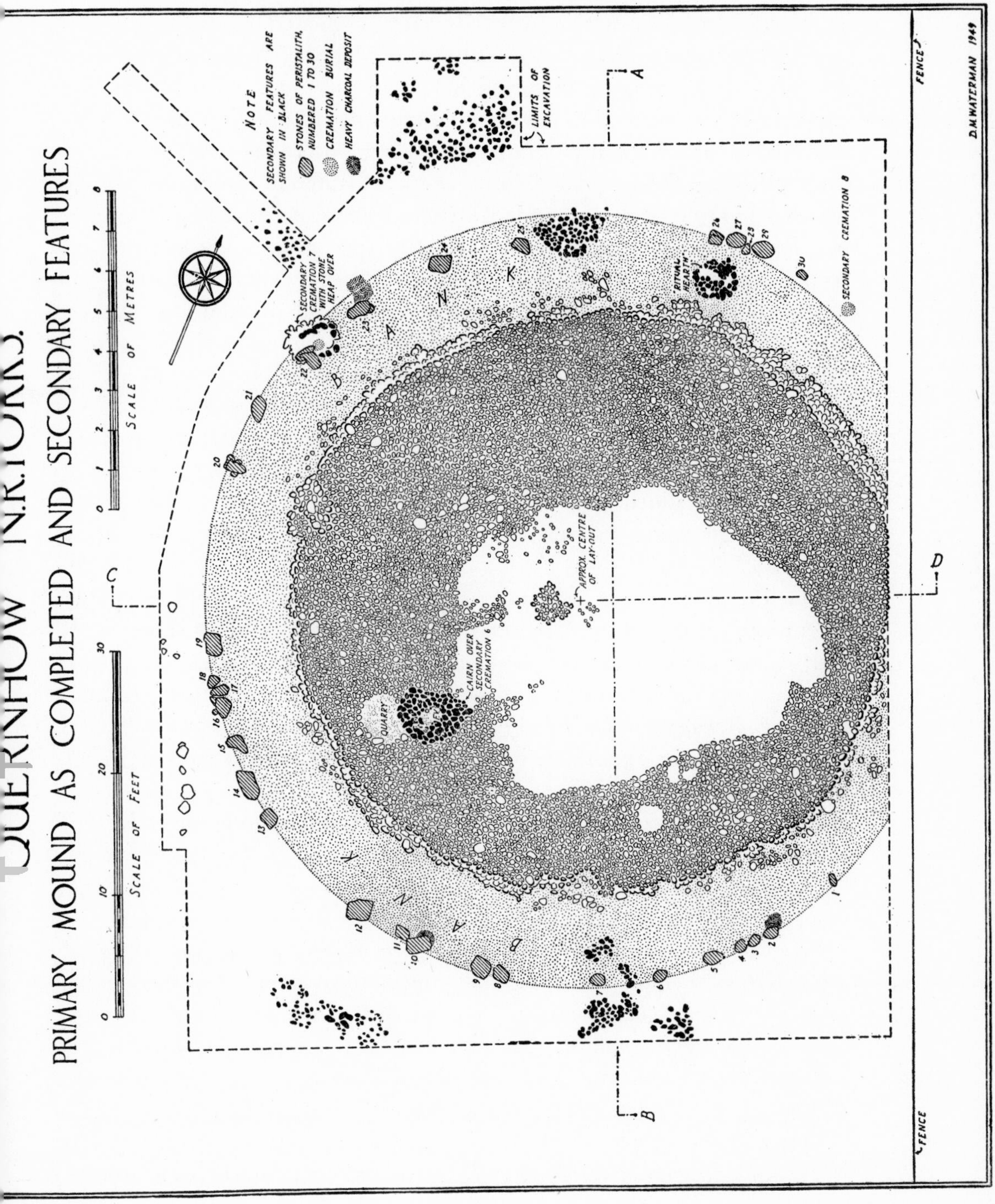
QUERNHOW N.R.YORKS.
PRIMARY MOUND AS COMPLETED AND SECONDARY FEATURES
SCALE OF FEET
SCALE OF METRES
NOTE
SECONDARY FEATURES ARE SHOWN IN BLACK
STONES OF PERISTALITH, NUMBERED 1 TO 30
CREMATION BURIAL
HEAVY CHARCOAL DEPOSIT
LIMITS OF EXCAVATION
SECONDARY CREMATION 7 WITH STONE HEAP OVER
RITUAL HEARTH
SECONDARY CREMATION 8
APPROX. CENTRE OF LAY-OUT
CAIRN OVER SECONDARY CREMATION 6
QUARRY
BANK
FENCE
D.M.WATERMAN 1949

Figure 44. Barrow, Quernhow, N.R., Yorkshire. Mound as completed and secondary features (by D. M. Waterman)

burials with 'food-vessels' in the barrow were cremated: we are dealing with a late phase of this north-eastern culture. In some the bones were cleansed before disposal, in others interred hot from the pyre. To continue: Presumably at the same time as the primary burial, and similarly of ritual significance, three shallow scoops were dug, one to the east and two to the south-west: food-vessels (Nos. 2 and 3) of different type to No. 1 were deposited in two of them, and in the other three small cobblestones spaced in a line along the length of the pit. After the filling of the central pit a rectangular setting of boulders was erected to the north, and the whole disturbed area covered by a low irregular mound of sand and cobbles. Two unaccompanied cremations, an adult and child respectively, were in turn placed at the foot of this central mound on the south-west, and on the summit two further cremation deposits, each with a food-vessel, Nos. 4 and 5, representing three individuals, one adult. The burial complex was finally concealed by heaping sand over and around the central mound, to occupy an ill-defined area about 20 ft. in diameter; in the course of this work one cremation was displaced and the associated food-vessel (No. 5) broken.

The burial area was next enclosed by a penannular wall of cobbles (Figure 43), roughly and irregularly constructed, with an opening to the east; its surface was thickly covered by burnt material which may have resulted from further observances associated with the ceremonial closing of the tomb. It was then concealed beneath the material of the barrow mound, 50 ft. in diameter and $2\frac{1}{2}$ ft. in height, of loamy sand (Figure 43, circle showing boundary).

A stone cairn was finally added to envelop the mound completely. This cairn was flat-topped, with a poorly constructed face that required a retaining bank to preserve its stability. The base of the bank was marked by a stone curb, enclosing an area 64 ft. in diameter (Figures 44 and 45).

Later on, the site was again required to accommodate further burials after cremation. Bank and curb were concealed by deposits of sand and an adult burial (to reconsecrate the monument?) introduced on the north-western margin (cremation 7, Figure 44). Over a large area in the centre the cairn stones were removed and placed in heaps around the perimeter of the barrow: the resultant clearing has been suggested as a ritual area, devoted to the obsequies of an adult and child, whose cremated bones, intermingled, accompanied by a food-vessel (cremation 6) were interred

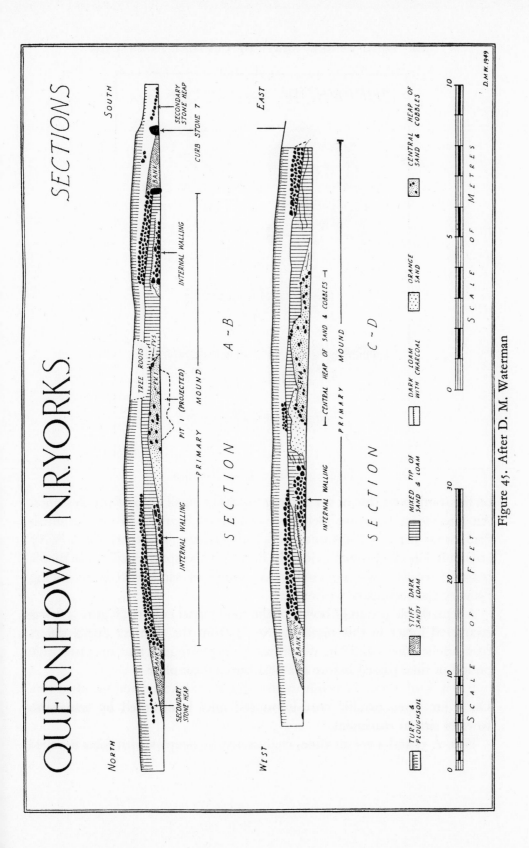

Figure 45. After D. M. Waterman

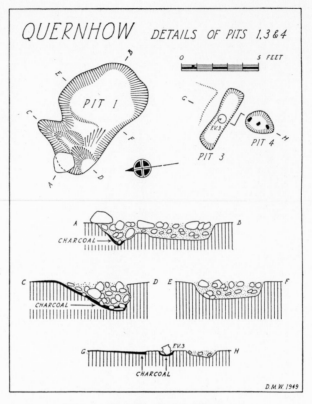

Figure 46. After D. M. Waterman

on the south-west side of the barrow beneath a small heap of cobblestones. An interesting structure identified as a ritual hearth was on the north flank of the barrow. Flagstones were laid with care, and there was a heavy accumulation of charcoal evidently burnt on the spot. Finally, the whole barrow structure was covered by a mound of sand, effectively sealing primary and secondary work alike.

A remarkable group of bowls of the food-vessel culture (Figure 47) was recovered intact in this research. No. 1 from the primary burial differs from all the others, and Mr. Waterman's record suggests that an appreciable period of time passed before the next burial took place.

It is a bowl 4·7 in. in height with a slightly thickened and bevelled rim. On it are three parallel cord-impressed lines interrupted by transverse rows of similar ornament.

Nos. 2, 3, and 4 are all alike, characteristic examples with their bevelled rims, hollow necks, and well-marked shoulders. No. 2 has on the outside below rim a row of nail impressions, with two further rows on the shoulder. The neck is encircled by four rows of twisted-cord ornament: there is another row below the shoulder, and two on the slightly bevelled rim. No. 3 is distinguished by a shoulder groove interrupted by four oval stops. (These are unperforated: the type normally has holes to thread a cord, doubtless for lowering the vessel into the grave.) The outside of the rim has round impressions, the internal bevel similar ornament bordered by cord-impressed lines. Above the base are two rows of jabbed impressions framing a row of oval incisions. The base has a rudimentary footstand, formed by a circular groove scooped out with the finger: it is ornamented with the same jabbed impressions.

The interested reader will not need more analyses: he can visualize the character and ornament of the remaining vessels from these descriptions: but it should be pointed out that the shape of No. 5 and its double raised moulding is approaching that of a Bronze Age cinerary urn, though the ornament is of food-vessel character.

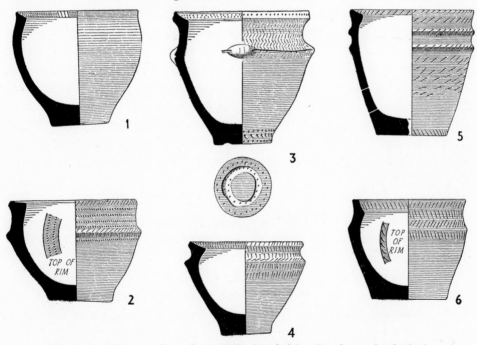

Figure 47. Barrow, Quernhow, N.R., Yorkshire. Food-vessels. Scale ¼.
After D. M. Waterman

The Yorkshire 'food-vessels' in general (as illustrated on Figure 47) have been regarded as a local development, in part based on the Neolithic traditions of the East Riding.[1] A bowl of this period from Goodmanham, for example, resembles No. 4 at Quernhow, but the fuller body it possesses brings our No. 1 also into relation with it. Our pots, then, are in an ancient tradition.

We turn now to the beginnings of the cremation culture of the Vale of Glamorgan, represented by Simondston Cairn, Coity, wherein enlarged food-vessels are used for the ashes. It was the only structure of this character that came my way and was in the same part of the Vale as Sutton 268'.

SIMONDSTON CAIRN, COITY HIGHER PARISH, BRIDGEND, *c.* 1400 B.C.
*Introduction.* In the angle between the rivers Ogwr and Ewenny on the northern margin of the Vale of Glamorgan, east of the town of Bridgend, Brackla Hill (287 ft.) is the outstanding feature. Its grassy slopes are linked to higher ground on the north by a saddle, on the east side of which there is a gentle fall to a tributary of the Ewenny, and on the west to a rivulet flowing into the Ogwr: Coity village lies at the point where the saddle merges into the upland. I was asked to examine two mounds hereabouts, one, Simondston Cairn, being 190 ft. above sea-level, 700 yd. due south of Coity church, the other, Pond Cairn, in the basin-like hollow to the west of it, near a rivulet, at 125 ft. Both were investigated by me, with Aileen Fox's help, in 1937: the sketch-map, Figure 48, illustrates the relation of the mounds—which no longer exist—to the topographical features described above.

*Simondston Cairn*, on the saddle below Brackla Hill, was of scarcely perceptible elevation (18 in.). Plate 24a shows the site as seen from Brackla Hill, and Figure 49 its exact contours.

Under the turf there was about a foot of soil, the whole area having been arable until recent times. Below it was a layer of stones (Plate 25b). A trial trench revealed the ancient surface soil under the stones; under that again

---

[1] Abercromby, *Bronze Age Pottery*, Vol. I, 1912; also see M. Kitson Clark, 'The Yorkshire Food-vessel', *Arch. Journ.*, 1937, p. 43 ff.

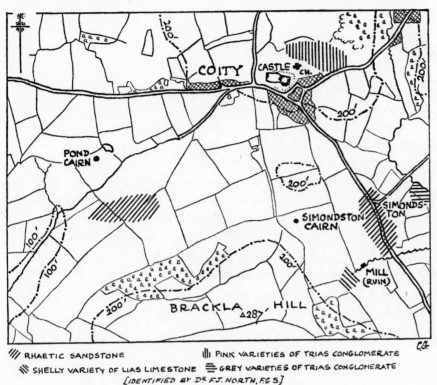

/// RHAETIC SANDSTONE     ||| PINK VARIETIES OF TRIAS CONGLOMERATE

\\\\ SHELLY VARIETY OF LIAS LIMESTONE   ≡ GREY VARIETIES OF TRIAS CONGLOMERATE

[IDENTIFIED BY Dᴿ F.J. NORTH, F.G.S]

Figure 48. Simondston and Pond Cairns, Glamorgan. Map. Scale: 4 in. to 1 mile

was a layer of clay, then rock. The rock here, as at Sutton (p. 67, above), is Lias, which 'here consists of alternations of limestone and shale'. The clay (which everywhere overlies the rock to a thickness of 3–18 in.) has resulted from the disintegration, *in situ*, of the limestone and shales. A trench carried well beyond the limits of the cairn showed that there was no surrounding ditch.

*The Primary Burials: Enlarged Food-vessels.* In the centre of the low mound (Figures 50 a and b) the large side-slabs of a cist ($3\frac{1}{2}$ ft. × $2\frac{3}{4}$ ft.), marking the primary burial, were visible at the centre of the stony layer, which was close-set, about 35 ft. overall. Practically the whole cairn had, it was clear, been carried away. The cover slab or lid had gone and the cist was filled with loam: removal of this soil disclosed two urns of 'enlarged food-vessel' type (numbered $A^1$ and $A^2$), placed, inverted, at either end of the floor (Plate 27a). That these had survived the removal of the greater part

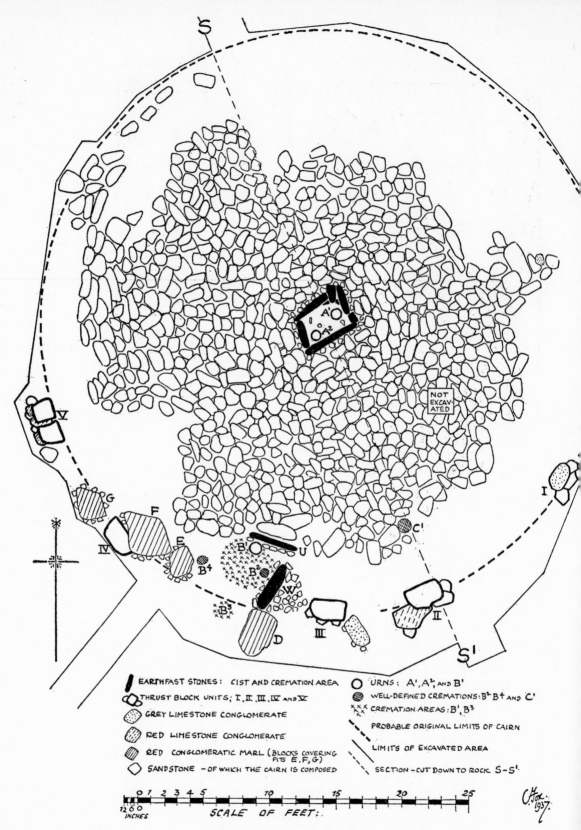

EARTHFAST STONES: CIST AND CREMATION AREA
THRUST BLOCK UNITS: I, II, III, IV AND V
GREY LIMESTONE CONGLOMERATE
RED LIMESTONE CONGLOMERATE
RED CONGLOMERATIC MARL (BLOCKS COVERING PITS E, F, G)
SANDSTONE - OF WHICH THE CAIRN IS COMPOSED

URNS: A¹, A², AND B¹
WELL-DEFINED CREMATIONS: B², B⁴ AND C¹
CREMATION AREAS: B¹, B³
PROBABLE ORIGINAL LIMITS OF CAIRN
LIMITS OF EXCAVATED AREA
SECTION - CUT DOWN TO ROCK S-S¹

NOT EXCAVATED

0 1 2 3 4 5    10    15    20    25
12 6 0
INCHES          SCALE OF FEET:

C. F. Fox
1937

Figure 50a. Simondston. Plan of cairn

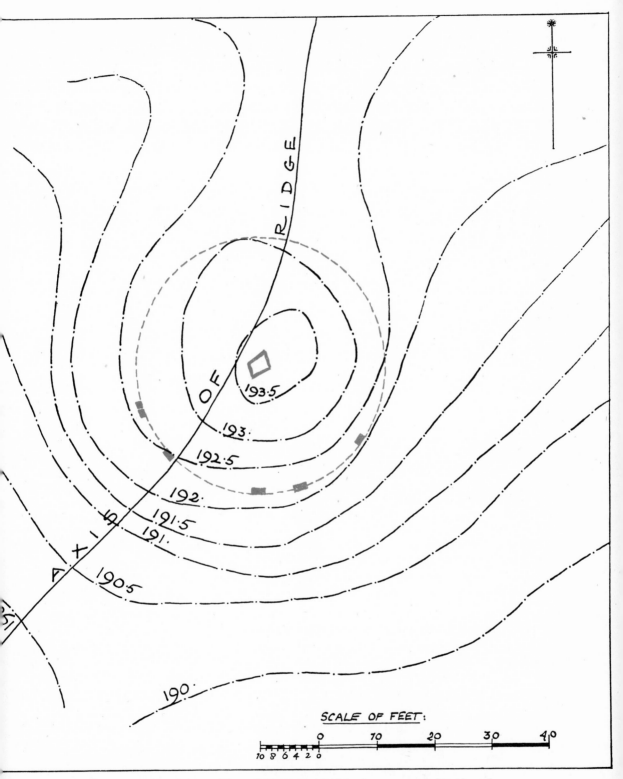

Figure 49. Simondston: Plan of site, contoured in feet; constructions in red

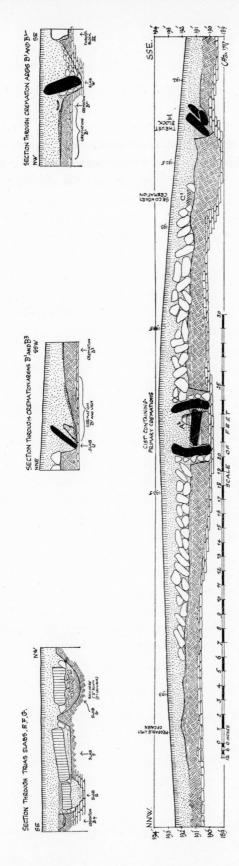

Figure 50b. Simondston cairn: Central cist, and thrust-block II: also minor sections

of the cairn is remarkable. The urns were ill-baked and had partially collapsed in antiquity: having been, moreover, exposed to an unusual degree of wet, they were in a condition of disintegration, having indeed less cohesion than the surrounding clayey soil. Both are illustrated on Plate 27 and Figure 51: they contained burnt bones. Mr. W. F. Grimes, who made the drawings, remarks: 'I suggest that the decoration may be finger- or thumb-nail impressions which have been dragged downwards over the pot. In some places (though rarely) the characteristic outline is distinct; in others an incised line in the bottom of the depression may be due to the finger-nail itself.'

The floor of the cist also was covered with burnt bones, which, mixed with fine earth, filled the crevices between side-slabs and floor.

Adjacent to the urn A[1] was a plano-convex flint 'knife'; a flake of unweathered flint showing the cortex in two places, chipped into an ogee outline by pressure flaking along the edges in imitation of a bronze blade. The type is characteristic of the Food-vessel culture in Britain and has a Neolithic background.[1] Adjacent to the urn A[2] was a flint fabricator whose rounded point shows the smoothed surface characteristic of that tool. (Both are shown in Figure 52.)

A third associated object is a small hemispherical cup 45 mm. in breadth (Plate 26b): it represents the oxidized surface layer of a nodule of marcasite[2] derived from the chalk, the nearest outcrops of which are in Wiltshire and Dorset. That Bronze Age man collected natural objects of striking form has several times been noted: the most famous example is the group of fossil *echini* in the Dunstable, Beds., burial recorded by W. G. Smith,[3] but these were of local origin.

The bones from the urn A[1] were those of one adult; the bones from the urn A[2] were of two persons, an adult and a child. We may have here the burial of a man and woman and their child; the three objects in the cist, the fabricator, the knife, and the cup, are certainly suitable to the character, age, or function of each.

The cist itself was made with the greatest care (Plate 25a) and was a very stable construction of weathered slabs of Rhaetic sandstone. The procedure

[1] See my figures and Gordon Childe, *Prehistoric Communities*, p. 123 and Fig. 34; and Stuart Piggott, *Neolithic Cultures of the British Isles*, pp. 174–5.

[2] Identified by Dr. F. J. North.

[3] Windle, *Remains of the Prehistoric Age in England*, Fig. 60, p. 144.

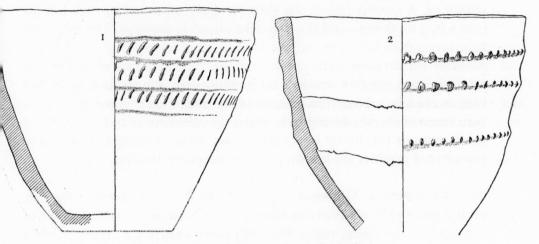

Figure 51. Simondston. Food-vessels. Scale $\frac{1}{4}$

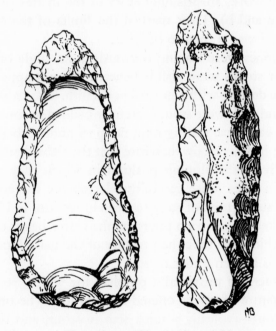

Figure 52. Simondston. Flint knife and fabricator.
Scale $\frac{1}{1}$

was as follows: A hole was made in the clay subsoil of such a depth as to bring the top edge of the floor-slab—which was very thick and heavy—up to ground-level. It was wedged up on one side with a small block of sandstone. A narrow trench was then cut down all round to rock level—here 1 ft. 4 in. down—and the side-slabs placed in position. The side-slabs were unwrought with one exception—that at the eastern angle, which was probably the last stone to be put in place: see Plate 25b. This small slab had probably been roughly squared; on its inner face five shallow holes had been pecked in a Neolithic manner (Plate 28a). Cup-marked slabs have been noted in chambered tombs in Wales (Pembrokeshire and Caernarvonshire), but not previously in a round cairn. Three isolated and undatable cup-marked menhirs are known on the Glamorgan borders.

*The Cairn Structure.* At distances of 20–21½ ft. from the centre of the cist, on the south side, six earthfast slabs were noticed, so spaced as to cover one-third of the circle, two (Plate 28b) being closely set. Their position was in every case tangential to the circle, and, having regard to the primitive character of the work, surprisingly exact in the matter of radial distance (see Figures 50a and b). They marked the limits of the cairn, and from them its diameter was shown to be 43 ft.

All the six stones were leaning outwards at an angle of approximately 45°, and smaller stones were visible beneath them; it appeared, then, that we could not be dealing with a normal peristalith. The slabs were therefore lifted out. Behind each were stones carefully bedded in rows and layers, the lowest layer in each case resting on a ramp of undisturbed clay subsoil at the same angle; it was certain therefore that the slabs themselves had been placed originally in the sloping position in which they were found. In many cases thin slabs were carefully selected for the under layers. On Figure 50b one such group of stones is seen in section. In Plate 28b the pair of slabs numbered V has been photographed after being cleared down to its bases; here thin slabs take the pressure of the main blocks, and a third layer of stones is hidden under these.

These constructions provided a problem for which, so far as we were aware, the literature of cairns offered no solution. The only valid reason for such a lay-out—typically a thick slab in front, and thinner flat ones behind set on a sloping face of undisturbed clay reinforced with small round stones pushed into it—was to resist pressure; and the pressure could only be that of the cairn itself. Each group of stones represents, in short, a *thrust block* or bedded buttress, in which the initial pressure was taken by the surface of the carefully chosen upper slab, and was extended outwards

PLATE 23. SUTTON 268', GLAMORGAN: Cremation 'B', urn

PLATE 24A. SIMONDSTON CAIRN, COITY, GLAMORGAN: General view; site from Brackla Hill

PLATE 24B. QUERNHOW CAIRN, N.R., YORKS: The remains cleared

(a) The cist with urns

(b) The cist cleared; cup-marked slab at left corner

PLATE 25. SIMONDSTON CAIRN, COITY, GLAMORGAN

(a) The southern complex

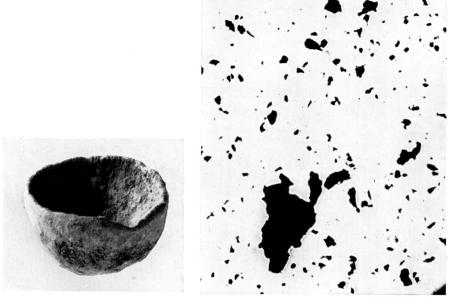

(b) Marcasite cup

(c) Coke from debris

PLATE 26. SIMONDSTON CAIRN, COITY, GLAMORGAN

(a) Enlarged food-vessels and urns—from secondary burial

(b) Urn from primary burial

PLATE 27. SIMONDSTON CAIRN, COITY, GLAMORGAN

(a) The cup-marked slab

(b) Thrust-block (right-hand slabs)

PLATE 28. SIMONDSTON CAIRN, COITY, GLAMORGAN

by the slabs (usually broader and thinner) below; each thrust-block played its part in rendering the cairn stable.

We thus determined the purpose of the peripheral slabs on the southern rim; *an explanation which accounts for their absence on the remaining two-thirds of the circumference of the cairn.* For if the contoured site plan, Figure 49, be referred to, it will be seen that the natural slope of the ground is towards the south, and that the thrust blocks are placed only where the slope, slight everywhere, is most marked: that is, only where the outward and downward thrust exerted by the weighty and high-piled cairn was in wet weather likely to cause movement of the clayey soil and so disturb the tomb structure. If so, we may justifiably consider that it had a cover of smooth slabs, carefully chosen. It is probable that thrust blocks at intervals are as effective as a continuous line; and it may be added that while the blocks cannot, as we have seen, have been continuous, the full number has not necessarily been determined owing to later disturbance of the ground on the southern periphery.

The whole cairn was removed: the floor was free from charcoal layers, traces of a pyre, or burning of any sort. The area around the cist bore no signs of trampling, or of any ritual acts. Furthermore, in order to determine whether any small filled-in 'ritual' ditch surrounded the cist,[1] a sectional trench was cut down to rock level (S–S' on plan, Figure 50a). The Lias clay subsoil was found to be entirely undisturbed (the variations in rock level shown in the section (Figure 50b) are quite normal). Finally, to see whether a rock-cut ditch surrounded the cairn, this section was extended outwards for 20 ft. beyond the cairn limits with negative results.

*Secondary Burials.* Two large earthfast slabs, prominent in the plan (Figure 50a) near the southern rim of the cairn, have not yet been referred to.

The thin slab of shelly limestone, marked U on the plan, set tangentially to the circle, 3 ft. 8 in. long, may first be considered. It was leaning outwards. Excavation showed it to have been set in a trench cut down to the rock and packed on the south side with small stones. The larger and thicker boulder marked W, set radially to the circle, which was also 3 ft. 8 in. long, was placed in a large hole, the more upright face of which was to the

---

[1] Bearing in mind my experience at Ysceifiog, p. 4 above.

west. A small area within the cairn boundary was thus protected on two sides against the thrust of the cairn structure: it was found to include a number of close-set cremation burials which are clearly later intrusions (Figure 50, B[1]–B[4] and C[1]). The position of these, on the south side of the cairn, is in accordance with the usage frequently noticed in the literature of barrows. One only is of sufficient interest for record here.[1]

Cremation B[1]. An urn was found which had been placed, mouth downwards, close to the thin slab of limestone, below natural ground-level (Plate 27b). It was surrounded by a layer of burnt bone, charcoal, and reddened clay: this was not itself a pyre, for the underlying yellow clay subsoil was unburnt. The urn contained burnt bones: it had been deformed and disintegrated under pressure set up by the leaning slab 'U'. Such deformation afforded proof that this slab was originally set upright, and it is so shown in the plan of the cairn.

The urn when restored (Figure 53) was found to be of different character from A[1] and A[2], being a 'collared' or 'overhanging-rim' urn of early type (Phase i)—possibly contemporary with the food-vessel culture. The rim is decorated with 'maggot' impressions herring-bone fashion, as is the shoulder, and the neck with incised lines of zigzag ornament. The large mass of bones inside it represents an adult and two children. The date will be c. 1300 B.C.

Some of the burnt material—the 'black layer'—was submitted to my colleague, Dr. F. J. North. He reported that while most of the fuel used was wood charcoal, there was an appreciable amount of coal. He adds that it resembles the coal which occurs along the southern margin of the South Wales coalfield, the nearest exposures being about $1\frac{1}{2}$ miles to the north of Simondston (Figure 48). This is probably the first recorded use of transported coal for fuel in Wales.

Lastly, mention must be made of slabs of rock, 'red conglomeratic marl', brought from an outcrop about half a mile away, grouped in the south-west margin of the cairn. These are lettered D, E, F, and G on the site plan; they were all lying either on, or a little below, the natural surface of the ground. They measured from $2\frac{1}{4}$ to $4\frac{1}{4}$ ft. in greatest length and from 9 to 12 in. in thickness: Figure 50b shows three of them in section.

Slab E was surrounded by packing stones, and covered a hole nearly

[1] Three other secondary cremations, of little interest, shown on Figure 50a, are referred to in the original report, *Archaelogia* 87, pp. 137–8.

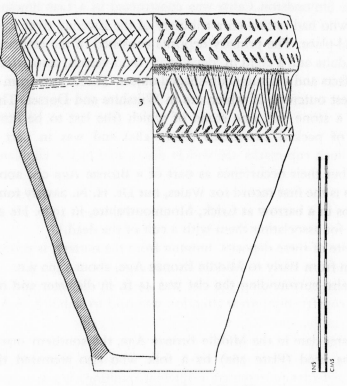

Figure 53. Simondston. Urn B[1]

2 ft. deep made by removing fractured blocks of Lias: the clayey soil which filled it was clean. Slab F, the largest, lay partly over thrust block 4 (Plate 26a), showing that it was later than the building of the cairn: under the lower edge black earth sloped down into the margin of slab E. Slab G had packing stones carefully placed round it, and it covered an oval basin-shaped smooth-sided hole made in the clay. It contained angular slivers of sandstone.

Let us see how we stand: Three of the four slabs were in carefully prepared positions, had packing stones round them, and were therefore in their original positions: the fourth, slab D, is doubtful. Two covered deep artificial holes dug, and refilled, for some purpose unknown to us; one partly covered a thrust block and was therefore later than the cairn construction. It may reasonably be suggested that the holes were 'ritual pits', the deposits in which contained perishable food, and that they were connected with the 'Secondary Cremations'.

*Summary.* Simondston Cairn was constructed in a Lias limestone region by folk who had settled on a tributary of the Ewenny river to the east of the burial-place. The primary deposits consisted of the cremated remains of two adults and a child in 'developed' food-vessels, associated with two flint artifacts and a natural cup-shaped object. These came from the Chalk, the nearest outcrops of which are in Wiltshire and Dorset. The deposits were in a stone cist, one stone of which (the last to be fitted in) had a series of pecked cup-marks (Plate 28a) and was in part artificially shaped. Such cup-marks are widely distributed in the Highland Zone of Britain, but their occurrence as part of a Bronze Age cist appears to be rare: this is the first record for Wales, but Dr. H. N. Savory found several such slabs in a barrow at Crick, Monmouthshire, in 1940. He gives good grounds for associating them with a cult of the dead.[1]

The date of these deposits, judging from the pottery, is probably in the transition from Early to Middle Bronze Age, about 1400 B.C.

The cairn surrounding the cist was 43 ft. in diameter and of straight-forward construction: great attention was paid to stability, as is shown by the earthfast buttresses on the lower (southern) side.

At a later date in the Middle Bronze Age, the southern margin of the cairn was used (Plate 26a) by a folk who also cremated their dead. Their burial rites represented a different tradition. We may note the free scattering of charcoal; the neglect of, or indifference to, sound construc-tional methods in the use of earth-fast stones; the digging of pits and holes in the area set aside for burial,[2] and their sealing with large slabs of red-coloured stone (from the Trias). The most important of these secondary interments was associated with a collared urn of early type (Phase i) which, on the conventional dating, was made about 1300 B.C. Coal (Plate 26c) was used as a fuel in the pyre of this burial: the earliest record for Wales. My colleague, Mr. H. A. Hyde, recorded the presence in the charcoal associated with this and other burials of ash, hazel, oak, and mountain ash —an interesting range.

It is of interest that there was found in 1901, at Candleston (Figure 54), close to the Ogwr-Ewenny estuary, five miles to the westward, a cremation

---

[1] H. N. Savory, *Archaeologia Cambrensis*, 1940, p. 186.

[2] Such occur freely in Neolithic long barrows (*Proc. Prehist. Soc.*, 1937, p. 174): many are recorded by Greenwell in round barrows on the Yorkshire wolds, in words which might have been used for the Simondston examples (*British Barrows*, p. 9).

in a cist associated with a 'dagger-knife' and a 'food-vessel'.[1] The cist-structure conformed to a Megalithic tradition, being similar to that found at Corston in Pembrokeshire (p. 23, above). That the Simondston folk represented a later generation of the group that settled in this estuary is probable enough, having regard to the geographical relationship: in other words, they migrated up the Bristol Channel, a sea journey likely to have been familiar to many family groups at this time.

The trading connections of the Simondston Cairn builders were, however, definitely with the east. The flint tools in the cist were not made from beach pebbles but from imported material; west Wiltshire and west Dorset are the nearest source for these, and for the marcasite cup.

[1] *Arch. Camb.*, 1919, p. 327, Fig. 1.

# 5

## COMPOSITE (EARTH AND STONE) BARROWS IN GLAMORGAN

### Early and Middle Bronze Age
### (c. 1350–900 B.C.)

WE now return to the plateau country nearer the Channel where barrow Sutton 268′ (p. 62, above) was sited. This region, lying between the river Thaw and the Ogwr-Ewenny river system, was well populated in the full Bronze Age: a landing place now under the Channel sea, near Nash Point, is to be inferred. Figure 54 shows no less than forty barrows in this region: of these nine were excavated on scientific principles by myself and others between 1937 and 1940.

*Note on the Wessex Culture.* Features of our Early Bronze Age barrows in the Vale will suggest connections with north Somerset and relationship to the 'Wessex Culture' (p. xvii, above) centred in Wiltshire and Dorset, and present in east Devonshire. (The initial phase in the matter of weapons is that of the flanged bronze axe and the flint arrow-head, at the close of the Early Bronze Age.) Ornaments of gold, from Ireland, a sceptre—or wand of office—of southern character, amber beads, pendants (and rarely a cup), from Jutland, developed bronze daggers, their finest hafts decorated with gold pins—the basic type being that found at Corston (p. 24, above), and beads of blue faience from Egypt, define the noble elements of the culture.

In the initial stage, moreover, it is contemporary with the food-vessel culture in the north. It is too novel to have arisen other than by the intrusion of a continental (Brittany?) group familiar with northern and southern trade—its personalities, its routes, and its 'know-how'—and anxious to take a hand, from a new and closer angle, a secure island base, in the Irish gold trade. This group assimilated the insular culture—and led it: their dead were buried in composite barrows of earth and stone such as we have seen: they promoted the culture of southern and western Britain in general as well as benefiting themselves. That they were few in number is suggested by the native products that got into their graves, especially towards the close.

BREACH FARM, LLANBLEDDIAN, GLAMORGAN, *c.* 1350 B.C.

Of the first two barrows to be considered that at Breach Farm already mentioned, Figure 54, was dug by Mr. (now Professor) W. F. Grimes. He remarks that the group in which this was found seemed wholly un-disturbed; if so, his choice was fortunate, for it is difficult to recall more significant burial-furniture of the period, in the Highland Zone of Britain. It dates, and introduces, a culture found in my own local barrows, and

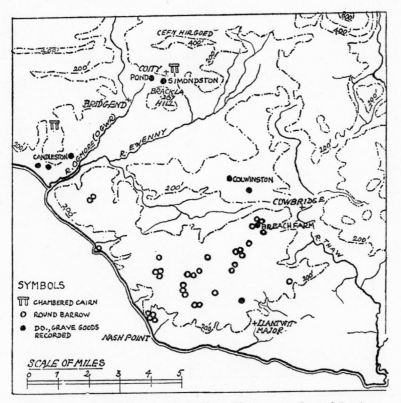

Figure 54. The Bridgend–Cowbridge, Glamorgan, Coastal Region

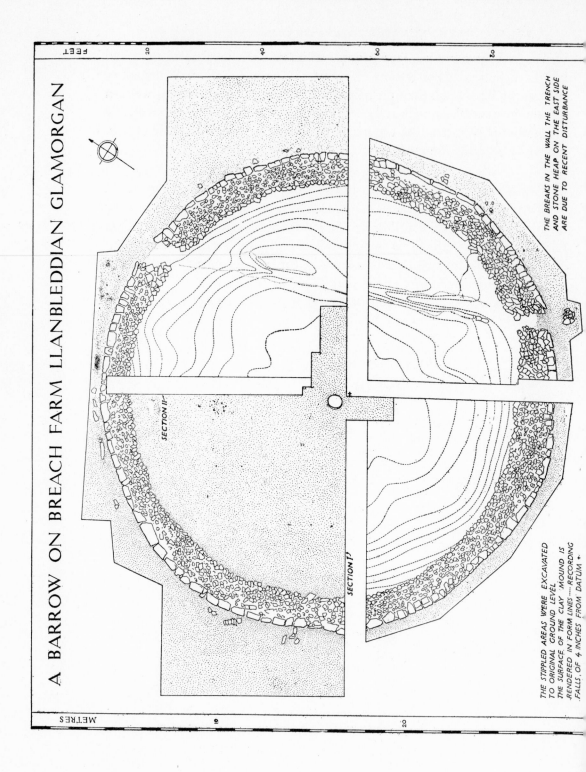

A BARROW ON BREACH FARM LLANBLEDDIAN GLAMORGAN

FEET

20

40

60

80

METRES

0

20

SECTION II

SECTION I

THE STIPPLED AREAS WERE EXCAVATED
TO ORIGINAL GROUND LEVEL
THE SURFACE OF THE CLAY MOUND IS
RENDERED IN FORM LINES ----- RECORDING
FALLS. OF 4 INCHES FROM DATUM +

THE BREAKS IN THE WALL THE TRENCH
AND STONE HEAP ON THE EAST SIDE
ARE DUE TO RECENT DISTURBANCE

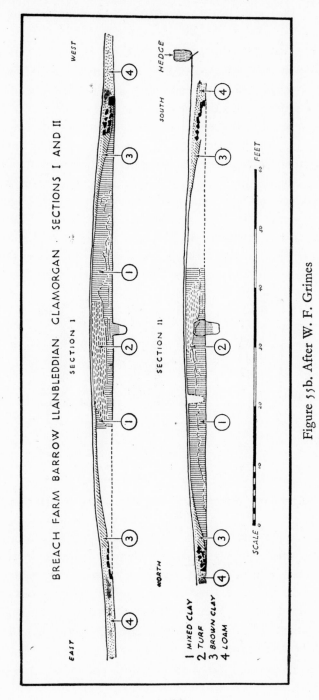

Figure 55b. After W. F. Grimes

93

their structure: I illustrate this barrow plan, the sections and principal finds.[1]

The barrow, excavated by the quadrant method, showed, at the margins, a ring of stones with heavy curbs, all Lias limestone. This is illustrated in Figure 55a. The sections, Figure 55b, show the hidden elements of the structure and their relation to the ring.

Three individuals are represented in the cremation pit: the associated objects were, firstly, four bronze axes (of which only the heaviest one had survived the corrosive action of its wet surroundings). This is slightly flanged, and dates the mound, as Mr. Grimes points out, to the 'turn of the Early and Middle Bronze Ages': it is illustrated on Figure 56, together with an unusual find—small blocks of sandstone, each with a central groove, regarded as arrow-shaft smoothers. The reason for this identification is very apparent in the next figure (Figure 57), a series of thirteen flint arrow-heads 'unsurpassed in this country' as the author remarks. The material

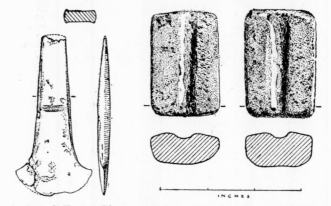

Figure 56. Breach Farm, Glamorgan. Bronze axe and arrow-shaft smoothers.
After W. F. Grimes

varies: Nos. 1 to 3, 10 and 11, are of pale yellow flint, sometimes with patches of orange, and these show slightly incurved sides. Moreover, they have finely serrated edges, which are accompanied by flaking of the highest quality. The uniform thinness of their sections is notable: three have horizontal terminals to their barbs, two, drooping barbs. The rest show slightly convex sides. The author praises particularly, and rightly, the exquisite group at the top of the figure.

[1] With his kind permission and that of the Prehistoric Society, who lent the illustrations.

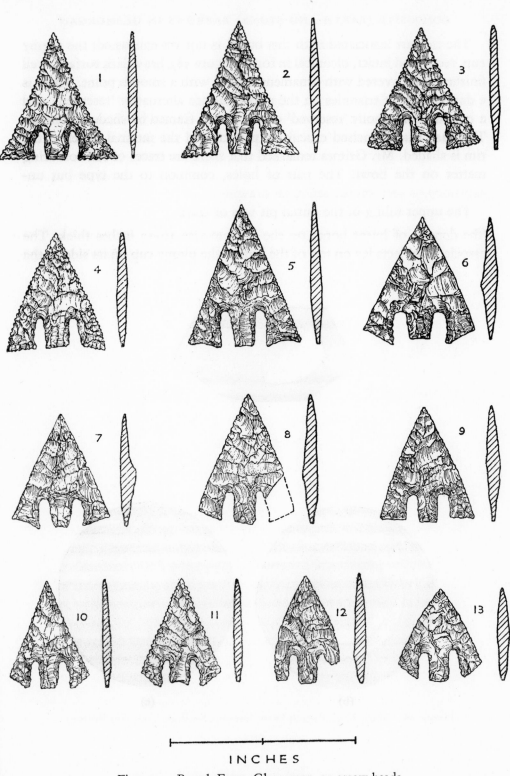

INCHES

Figure 57. Breach Farm, Glamorgan. 13 arrow-heads
After W. F. Grimes

The rich art associated with this burial is not yet exhausted: the pigmy cup, recovered intact, biconical in form (Figure 58), has a dark surface, well finished and covered with ornament incised with a smooth point. There is a double row of triangles on the upper surface alternately 'reserved', and a bar-chevron wholly 'reserved' on the lower, framed by shaded triangles. The base has an incised cruciform pattern and the internal bevel of the rim is shaded. Mr. Grimes remarked that there are traces of red colouring matter on the bowl. The pair of holes, common to the type but unexplained, is seen on the sectional drawing.

The upper filling of the burial pit was of clay:

'the deposit of burnt bones on the bottom was 10–12 inches thick. The associated objects lay on top of the bones, the pigmy cup on its side to the

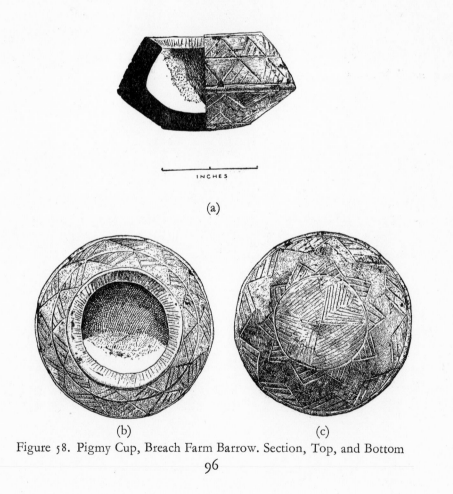

INCHES

(a)

(b)                                    (c)

Figure 58. Pigmy Cup, Breach Farm Barrow. Section, Top, and Bottom

west, with its base against the wall of the pit, the bronze and stone implements in a compact mass against the east side. With the latter had been
deposited a quantity of wood most of which had become a porridge-like
pulp.'

The whole of the central mound of clay though showing a contorted
section was a single deposit 'except in the middle part where a . . . heap of
what was probably turf was piled up before the last of the clay was added'.
This is interesting to me, in view of the large part turf plays in my own
Glamorgan barrows (pp. 129 ff., below).

The construction of the stone ring (diameters 81:79 ft.) offered features
of interest: it was built after the mound was completed, for a thin trace
of this extended beneath the facing stones themselves. These stones, of
Lias limestone, are pitted and weathered, showing that they had been
obtained by quarrying from the top of the bed rock (probably somewhere
in the immediate locality); the stones are not *all* set on a curve (the plan
shows the minor variations). The ring was probably three courses high,
and was intended to be seen. The date of the barrow will be *c*. 1350 B.C.[1]

I turn again, now, to my own work, beginning with Sutton 268' *in its
second phase:* it will be recalled that the primary 'Beaker barrow' was
discussed in an earlier chapter.

SUTTON 268', LLANDOW, GLAMORGAN: SECONDARIES, 1300–900 B.C.

The constructions marked A, B, C, D, on the plan (Figure 41) present
two main phases of secondary activity; the first comprises two out of three
burials (A and B) inserted in the Beaker barrow in the Middle Bronze Age,
the second burials (C and D) *outside* the Beaker barrow which were followed
immediately by the enlargement of the structure, part of which is shown.
The sections (Figure 42) show the relationship of the later developments
to the earlier structure; the extent of the enlargement is very apparent in
the photographs taken after the whole of the outer revetment had been
cleared (Plates 14b and 19a).

Cremations A and B were inserted in the original barrow, both at the
same level; A had covering slabs, visible on the surface of the barrow
(as my Section suggests). Cremations C and D are close together on the

---

[1] H. N. Savory, in *Arch. Camb.*, 1948, p. 79, presents a case for later dating of this
and other barrows.

north side of the barrow and outside its ditch, the former being protected by covering slabs. The original surface soil had been removed from the neighbourhood of these interments: the reason for this procedure, which I have not met with before in secondary deposits, is unknown.

Lastly, a 'hard-pan' layer, shown by shaded lines on either side of the sections, indicates a trampled zone extending, all round, from the margin of the original barrow outwards, over later burials. The plan shows how much of the 'hard-pan' was uncovered. It is enough to show that the trampling—we can, I think, now call it a dance—was round the ancient barrow in a belt from 12 to 24 ft. wide: the broadest part being that occupied by burials C, D (and E). When the 'ritual act' took place, then, the enlarged barrow was only partly built; the trampled area was lopsided because the placing of the new burials, C, D, and E, was off-centre.

The rite then was practised here some time *after* the deposit of the secondary burials A and B. It was *not* a consecration of the enlarged structure of the barrow which with its stone ring is much more extensive, and much higher (Plate 14b).

*A Description of the Secondary Burials. Cremation A.* A prominent mass of slabs at the base of the 'U' of the original burial, on the inner side of the curve (Plate 15a), were placed over a cremation burial (Plate 15b) which was *at* the original ground-level but over the filled-up pit. In the centre of the burnt bones was a pigmy cup (Plates 15b and 17b) empty and inverted, and near the margin a bronze knife, without central rib or side grooves, in an advanced state of decay, but originally some 3 in. in length (Plate 22a). A fractured bone bead (Plate 22) was also found among the burnt bones, and there was a spread of charcoal under and around the deposit. The covering slabs referred to overlaid earth, not cairn stones (cross-section R–R'): I consider their position represents the original barrow crest. The burnt bones are those of a male over 18 years of age.

The knife, as we have seen, is small and flat; such tools are frequently associated in this culture with the larger grooved dagger; the flat dagger grew smaller as the grooved type came into fashion. The knife then provides no reason for assigning a particularly early date to the burial.[1]

The cup (Plate 17b) is a fine piece of craftsmanship, well formed, well

1 The various types of knives and daggers of the Age are illustrated in *Archaeologia*, 43 (ii), Pls. xxxii–xxxv, part of a well-known paper by John Thurnam.

baked, and covered with carefully wrought *cord* ornament. In Wessex, cup types with exotic ornament are found as well as native (cord-ornamented) wares such as ours. An example of the former class was present in the Breach Farm barrow, it will be recalled (Figure 58): the fact is significant, for it may imply a somewhat later date for our burial. The two pierced openings have never been explained. They are a common feature, and show that whatever the purpose of the pigmy class, it was not to hold liquid, as indeed does the inverted position of our example in the grave.

The siting of the burial is remarkable: it is at the head (within the loop) of the U-shaped cairn, as the plan shows. The character of the original burial, then, was known to those concerned: we are dealing surely with successive obsequies of a local family of distinction.

*Inhumation.* At the foot of the inner slope of the eastern horn of the cairn was an inhumation; the skull (section S–S') and part of the skeleton were recovered, being those of a child about 11 years old.

*Cremation B.* This was close to the tip of the western horn of the cairn, on the inner side. The burnt bones were in an inverted tripartite overhanging-rim urn (Plate 23), partially sunk below the original ground surface; they were those of a woman with a newly born infant. With the urn were three flint flakes.

*The Later Developments.* To the above cremations, which complete the series of secondary deposits within the ditch, the general remarks applied to the first are relevant. We are now to consider the burials which caused the barrow to be greatly enlarged, from 31 ft. to 69 ft. in overall diameter with a low drystone wall instead of a ditch to define its limits. The only part of this on the plan and section is the zone which contained the later burials. Culturally we enter a different but to us familiar climate of ideas as to what a barrow should look like, but as we shall see, there is no evidence for a change in the ruling family!

In the northern part of the ditch of the primary barrow, then, a filling of quarried stone and clayey soil was found, in places occupying the whole hollow; the tilted slabs defining the inner margin were disturbed. Masses of small stones filled the ditch, rose above it, and extended both outwards and inwards (section R–R', Figure 42, and upper part of the plan).

The northward extensions covered a large area (Plate 14b). Our excavation showed that prior to their deposition the whole of the soil and subsoil had in places been removed, the rock floor being exposed (section R–R', left). In the north trench the replacement material—stone—was set in a loose matrix of charcoal-impregnated soil.

*Cremations C, D, E, and F.* Hereabouts four secondary burials by cremation were found, the most important of which was cremation C. Under a series of slabs (plan, Figure 41, top) disposed in the same manner as in the case of cremation A in the cairn, was an inverted tripartite overhanging-rim urn, of the same character as that in cremation B. Its base was near the original ground level, its rim on the rock floor; it had thus been placed in a shallow hole (Plate 19b and Figure 42a). Around it was a layer of charcoal, on the northern edge of which lay a flint arrow-head (Plate 20a). Among the burnt bones in the urn, which were those of a child under seven, were a ridged (plano-convex) flint tool with secondary pressure flaking at both ends—coarse work, a Middle Bronze Age type (Plate 20b) and a tongue-shaped piece of smooth bone (Plate 22a).

In the neighbourhood of this cremation were the three others; each consisted of a mass of charcoal and burnt bones, set in hollows between the stones, without urns or grave-goods. They proved, like C, to be of children; one was 12 years or under, one under 7 years, the third indeterminate. An adult human skull placed close to cremation E completes the series of interments in this part of the barrow.

Overlying all these later deposits, structural and burial, was a turfy soil, stained orange and black with iron oxides, and with patches of grey clay. In or immediately under this was an unbroken layer of hard-pan. This is an iron-impregnated concretionary deposit that may develop within soil at a level where there is a change in the 'relative permeability of the material from more porous above to less porous below'.[1] Trampling is an obvious (and the most likely) means whereby permeability may have been locally reduced; and in the present case we may conclude that the addition to the Beaker barrow was thrown up in two stages, and that what was the surface at the end of the first stage was rendered compact (by trampling) before the remainder of the material was placed on top of it. The hard-pan,

[1] My colleague, Dr. F. J. North, was most helpful in working out this problem.

(a) The mound in a field

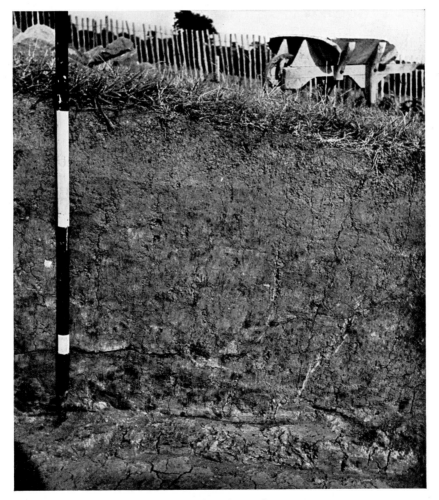

(b) Turf stack: section

PLATE 29. POND CAIRN, COITY, GLAMORGAN

PLATE 30. POND CAIRN, COITY, GLAMORGAN: Wholly cleared, looking north-east

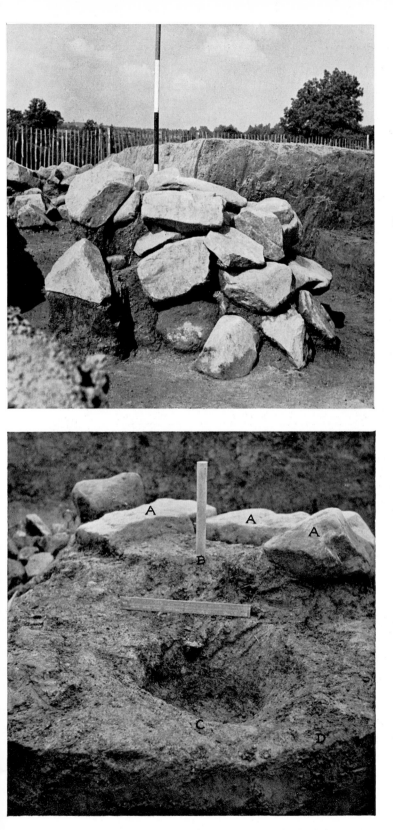

(a) The central stone-heap and burial

(b) The central burial—basin

PLATE 31. POND CAIRN, COITY, GLAMORGAN

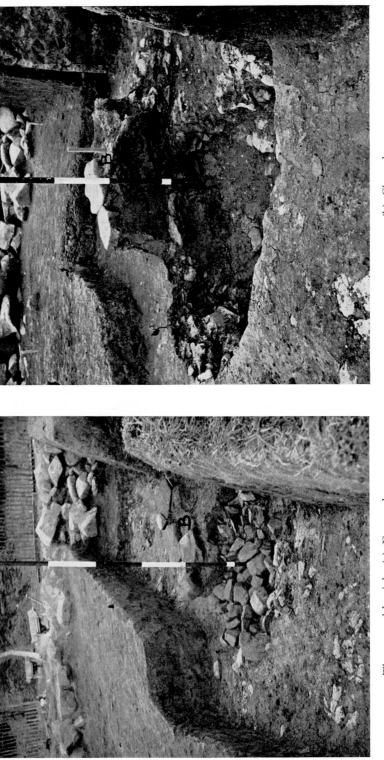

The central burial:   (a) Exposed                        (b) Cleared

PLATE 32. POND CAIRN, COITY, GLAMORGAN

of course, developed by slow degrees on the plane of the trampled surface after the completion of the barrow. It is well seen in both my sections.

The hard-pan layer sloped upwards and inwards, fading out on the margin of the central portion of the barrow. Its inner edge thus overlay the rock-cut ditch and the stony mass which in places defined it, at from 1 ft. 2 in. to 2 ft. 1 in. above the original ground-level (see plan and sections): stake-holes were found in it—two are shown—but no pattern could be demonstrated.

The boundary of the enlarged barrow was easily determined, being marked by a drystone wall of Lias in places still 11–12 in. in height, and of from one to four courses (Plate 19a): its diameters, then, were 73 ft. (north–south) and 60 ft. (east–west).

It should be noted that the double protective covering of cremation C is so similar to that of A and the pottery type of C so similar to that of B (see section), that whatever may have been the interval of time, a single family group or *gens* was probably concerned in all three burials.

The position of the hard-pan is significant in this connection. It covered the whole of the stony mass on the north side except the flat slabs of cremation C which were exactly on its level (section R–R'). Similarly, the margins of the hard-pan, where it dies out on the central area, are at approximately the same level as the top of the slabs of cremation A (a straight-edge suitably placed along section R–R' will demonstrate this point). Moreover, fine charcoal deposits lie on the slabs of cremation C, and extend from one burial to the other. These features show that burial A was not ignored when the works following on burial C were carried out.

The trampling implied by the hard-pan layer marked by a shaded line on the section was regarded as a ritual movement[1]: *the small patch of hard-pan[2] in the centre of the barrow* (see section S–S and plan) *may have been the point of ritual control.*

Turning to the outer limits of the hard-pan (and the turf mound) it is to be noted that the trampled area extends at one point at least so close to the dry-stone wall (N. side) as to suggest that at this stage the limits of the enlarged barrow were marked out; a good thickness of turfy soil is needed to provide this ferric concretion, and experience in other barrows will show that this tends to fade out on the thin edges of the mound.

[1] See pp. 131, 146.
[2] Some turf must have been placed here.

We have now to consider when the remaining secondaries were inserted. Cremations E and F are covered with the hard-pan which here as elsewhere forms an unbroken layer; they are therefore approximately contemporary with cremation C. Unless one is prepared to admit the likelihood of a number of youngsters of an important family dying in quick succession, they must with cremation D be, I think, regarded as sacrificial deposits connected with cremation C, the most important in the area. Thus four children were, it seems, selected to accompany the noble child to the other world.

I cannot offer any explanation of the inhumed skull of an adult unaccompanied by any long bones, near cremation E: but it was under the hard-pan and therefore contemporary.

Cremation B alone remains; for its relationships there is no stratigraphical evidence; the only evidence then available to us is typological, which places it within a few years of C.

Immediately thereafter the barrow was completed (Pl. 14b). More turf and soil were brought to heighten the structure; a dry-stone wall of Lias boulders and slabs, probably collected from the fields and pastures of the settlement (or from neighbouring watercourses), strongly reinforced behind to prevent slip, was constructed. Finally, the front of this revetment wall was in chosen places hidden by a sloping mass of small stones, rammed hard. Turf, in places of some thickness, still survives above the hard-pan slopes (see sections), and we may assume that the structure was originally not less than 7–8 ft. in height at the centre.

Soil was used not only for the centre of the barrow, but as a foundation on which the stone packing behind the dry-stone wall-facing was built up.

*The Dating of the Secondary Burials.* The Beaker barrow has been dated (p. 69) to about 1500 B.C.: we have now to consider whether approximate dates can be assigned to the later burials. These certainly belong to the Middle Bronze Age in general. Cremation A, a heap of burnt bones associated with a pigmy cup and with a flat bronze knife, is of course representative of that Middle Bronze culture which we have already seen at Breach Farm (p. 91) and in West Wales. Certain of the decorative features on our cup, the triangles on the body and the quadrant pattern on the base, are not unlike those on the Breach Farm cup, though in a later technique: the two burials are probably not far apart in time. It is to be noted that in both barrows the pigmy cup culture is 'pure', as in Wessex; that is, the cups were not associated with overhanging-rim urns. I suggest that a date of *c.* 1300 B.C. for cremation A is reasonable.

We now turn to the second Middle Bronze phase: in particular to cremation C, in which the burnt bones were placed in an inverted over-hanging-rim urn. This vessel was very badly baked, and had telescoped. It was found impossible to restore it, but it could be measured, with a close approximation to accuracy, and, as the drawing (Figure 42a) shows, it had a broad rim with diagonals of impressed cord pattern, and a well-marked shoulder. The stratigraphical evidence suggests, as we have seen, that it was later in date than the pigmy cup burial; but how much later? The writer worked on the problem of such urns in 1940 and defined three phases of development.[1] His dates were too high, but the phases stand. Our urn is of Phase ii, and for a variety of reasons, detailed in the original paper, *c.* 1150 B.C. will now be suggested as its date.[2] The associated worked flint, in such a setting, illustrates the decay of this craft.

It should be emphasized that the interment of cremated bones in an urn represents a variety of burial ritual distinct from the pigmy-cup association, where the bones are spread on the ground. This ritual seems to have originated in Wessex and probably came to the sea-plain of South Wales as a separate inflow of cultural ideas. Whereas in Wales generally pigmy cups and overhanging-rim urns are found in association, as at Talbenny, the notions they represent for a time remained separate in the minds of these 'Glamorgan' folk. Or, more probably, the use of the pigmy cup hereabouts lasted but a short time, and urn burial reasserted itself.

Cremation B, which we must now consider, was in an urn inverted like cremation C, but was not protected by overlying slabs. This urn is an ill-made 'Phase ii' specimen which represents a later stage of development; the shoulder is weaker, and the neck flatter: it has unusual finger-tip ornament. I see no necessity for an earlier date for this than *c.* 900 B.C.

Lastly there is the dry-stone revetment. This as we know is paralleled at the Breach Farm barrow; the feature recurs in our series, and is discussed on p. 147, below.

[1] *Archaeologia*, 89, 1940, pp. 105–7; see also Varley, Jackson, and Chitty, *Prehistoric Cheshire*, pp. 92–4.
[2] See H. M. Savory, *Arch. Camb.*, 1948, p. 80, for a lower time-scale.

*Summary*. Let us not forget the archer who was buried here, in a last look at the structure. The culture this man inherited was of Breton origin: it had lasted in southern Britain some 200 years when he practised it, and was in decay when his family built the barrow.

The neighbours of this archer (at Breach Farm) adopted new conventions and ideas, one of which was related to the disposal of the dead—by cremation instead of inhumation. Pigmy cups, and thereafter overhanging-rim urns, replaced beakers, and bronze knives were in use. The *proximate* source of the new cultures was in all probability the same as that of the old: the opposite coasts of the Bristol Channel. The successor of the Beaker colonist adopted the new pigmy cup fashions, but the pots his women made were of native design and decoration. When he died, probably not later than 1300 B.C., his ashes (cremation A) with bronze knife and pottery cup rested in the founder's barrow; its construction was still in memory, and a position of dignity was chosen for the interment exactly at the base of the hidden cairn. A child's body, reminiscent of the ancient burial rite, was inserted at the foot of the cairn overlapping this cremation; human sacrifice was evidently part of the ritual.

The interest then shifts to the outside of the ditch, on the north. The death of a child presumably of the same *gens* but after an interval of perhaps a century and a half was the occasion for another cremation, in an inverted tripartite overhanging-rim urn; a finely flaked arrow-head, perhaps symbolic of the craft the noble youngster would have mastered, lay beside it (cremation C). The slabs that covered the deposit, like those covering the first cremation (A), are held to have been taken from the rim of the Beaker barrow.

Cremation C was associated with elaborate ritual, for the ground in the neighbourhood was cleared down to the rock and a mass of stones deposited all round; these filled the ditch where it was not already levelled up and extended on to the barrow itself. Again child sacrifice is in evidence, for three adjacent cremations of children placed in hollows between the stones without grave-goods can hardly be natural deaths. They are certainly contemporary, for at this stage the enlargement of the barrow was undertaken. Originally an oval 29–33 ft. to the external edges of the ditch, the new bounds gave an oval 69–73 ft. in diameter; the material chosen for the enlargement was mainly turf. This formed a ring, rising from ground-level on the new margin, covering the new deposit of stones, and surrounding the ancient barrow. But the traditions of the founder's folk seem to have been respected: the Beaker barrow was of soil, and mixed soil, not turf, was tipped into the centre of the *new* structure, making a large flattened area whose height was approximately that of the crest of the original barrow. The slabs covering cremation C were intentionally visible on the slope of this new structure, and the top of the slabs covering cremation A were still to be seen by those taking part in the ceremonies on the central flat. The turf slope all round (and the turf flat on the north side) were then heavily trampled; we may envisage a ritual movement which completed the ceremonial of cremation C and had some reference to the older interments.[1] These ceremonies should be dated not later than *c*. 1150 B.C.; the ridged flint knife was a survival of the food-vessel period.

### POND CAIRN, COITY, GLAMORGAN, *c*. 1100 B.C.

The second mound at Coity, though correctly described as in a hollow in relation to the major topographical features, is actually on a slight hummock in the pasture fields extending towards the rivulet which runs into the Ogwr (Figure 48). This is seen in the panorama, Plate 30, where the fall of the ground to the south-west is apparent: Coity village forms the greater part of the skyline (A, A').

The Lias rock is, in the neighbourhood of the mound, close to the surface, and two shallow quarries probably of medieval date lie within a stone's throw. One of these (marked on Figure 48) has now become a pond and has given its name to the cairn, being the only identifiable feature in the immediate neighbourhood.

The appearance of the mound is shown in Plate 29a. It was about 3 ft. above natural ground-level at the centre, and gave promise of being undisturbed save by the plough. It was necessary in this case to locate the primary burial as quickly as possible after the opening of the mound to avoid a definite risk of irresponsible interference. A north to south line was taken to include the highest point of the mound (line A–A' on plan, Figure 59) and a section trench cut. At both ends beneath a layer of top soil 4–15 in. in thickness, a mass of stones was encountered; as the centre was approached the stony mass was replaced by loamy soil. Underlying all, as at Simondston, was Lias clay overlying Lias rocks (Plate 29b). We

---

[1] A ritual dance, on a larger area, is envisaged at Pond Cairn, below.

were cutting, it was evident, into an earthen mound surrounded by a ring of stones (Figure 60 and Plate 32a).

From this trench, after the examination of the central deposits, the mound was cleared outwards (westwards). This was the first stage. Thereafter, such portions of the second half of the mound, the eastern, were cleared as were needed to ensure that all the facts bearing on the meaning and the history of the structure were obtained.[1] Plate 30 shows the completion of the work.

*The Central Stone-heap and Urn Burial.* When the centre was reached, a small pile of stones was disclosed (Figure 61). This stone-heap consisted of blocks of Rhaetic sandstone, the largest 2 ft. in diameter, piled up round a central space some 16 in. × 16 in. in area (Plate 31a). Some stones had collapsed into this space, and the upper part was filled with fine earth like the interstices of the rest of the heap. There was here a thin slab of red Triassic conglomerate (from near Coity village), tilted sideways. From the earth of the central space, from the more clayey loam near the floor, and from the spaces between adjacent stones, much burnt bone and fragments of a cinerary urn were recovered: one basal angle was in position showing that the cinerary had been placed upright on an earth floor (Plate 31b, B). All the fragments were as soft as the soil which enveloped them. Treatment at the National Museum showed that the urn was of overhanging-rim type with broad collar and well-marked shoulder, originally over 14 in. high (Plate 38a). It has short shallow diagonal impressions drawn with a blunt point on rim and shoulder. The burnt bones were those of an adult.

This urn was typologically more advanced than that deposited as a secondary at Simondston, but it is *not a late example*. Its character points to the cairn having been built about 1200 B.C., in the Middle Bronze Age.

*The 'Basin'.* When the stones of the heap were removed a circular black discoloration was noted on the east side of the urn. This was found to be the charcoal-lined wall of a shallow basin (Plate 31b) cut in the clay floor.

[1] Since the reader can hardly fail to notice differences between the technique of the work carried out here and that at Simondston, I may be permitted to mention that while Simondston was a 'rush job' carried out at a time unsuitable for field work, and when the writer had other pressing duties, the Pond Cairn was examined under the best possible conditions.

The charcoal was in the form of long sticks laid more or less vertically downwards to form a lining to the hollow, and there was a well-defined extension to the north-east in which the sticks were laid horizontally. This charcoal was wholly oak. Inside the layer of charcoal was a zone of red or pink clay (coloured doubtless by the action of hot charcoal), and within that again a centre of greyish-yellow clay.

Plate 31b shows the basin when cleared down to the red clay, the charcoal here and there exposed. On cutting a section through it, the floor was found to consist of 5 in. of solid charcoal 'paste' resting on the Lias rock (section, Figure 61, inset). Burnt human bone and one molar of sheep or goat were found to be incorporated in this charcoal paste: portions of human teeth and digits were also recognizable. The small quantity of material (3 oz.) does not permit certainty, but since nothing identified in the urn burial is duplicated here, it is probable that it all comes from the funeral pyre.

In considering the significance of this basin, regard must be paid to the fact that while the floor-stones of the stone-heap on the west side of the urn were carefully pressed into the clay floor (three are shown in Plate 31b), those on the east side, and over the basin, lay haphazard on the surface; that is, the former were placed in position before the deposition of the urn. The person officiating, then, at whatever ceremony the basin indicated, stood on the east side of the urn, facing west. The plan, with the projection (Figure 61) is certainly singular; there was no doubt in my mind when removing the charcoal that it was intentional.

Extending outwards and northwards from the basin was a layer of reddened clay overlaid by a thin layer of charcoal. Only heat could have produced this appearance, but the area was not large enough, nor the intensity of reddening sufficient, to suggest that it was the site of the pyre. Two areas covered with a thin layer of charcoal trodden into the floor were also found, partly under the stone-heap, and extending outwards; they are planned on Figure 61.

*The Central Pit.* Evidence of disturbance having been noticed in the neighbourhood of the stone-heap, the trench already made was deepened down to the Lias rock. On the south side the clay subsoil was found to have been relaid to a depth of 7–10 in., covering a shallow pit cut in the rock. When the clay was completely cleared away (Plate 32a) it was seen that a number

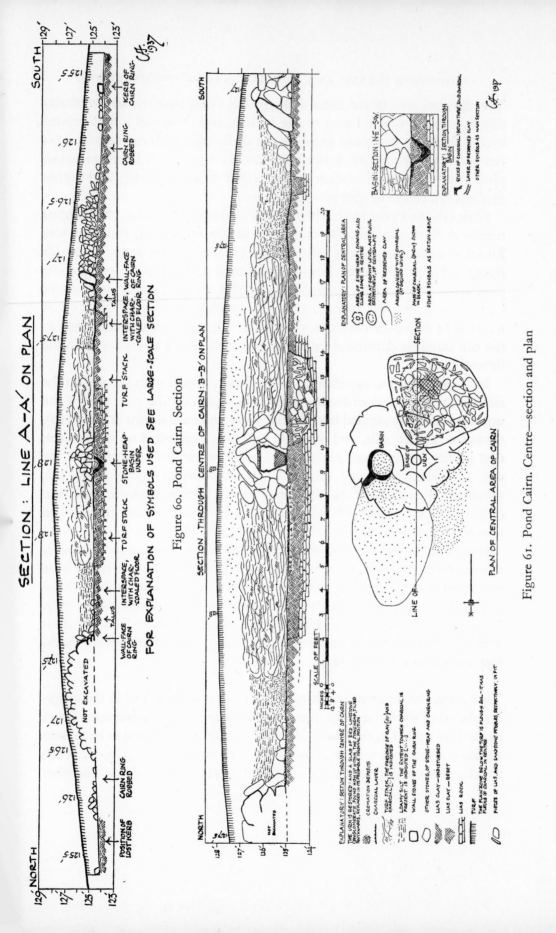

SECTION: LINE A-A' ON PLAN

FOR EXPLANATION OF SYMBOLS USED SEE LARGE-SCALE SECTION

Figure 60. Pond Cairn. Section

SECTION: THROUGH CENTRE OF CAIRN: B-B' ON PLAN

Figure 61. Pond Cairn. Centre—section and plan

(a) The south-west quadrant and original wall-face of cairn ring

(b) Sillstones, and (left) four courses of dry-walling

PLATE 33. POND CAIRN, COITY, GLAMORGAN

(a) The cairn-ring face, north side: cleared—sillstones

(b) The interspace: charcoaled floor

PLATE 34. POND CAIRN, COITY, GLAMORGAN

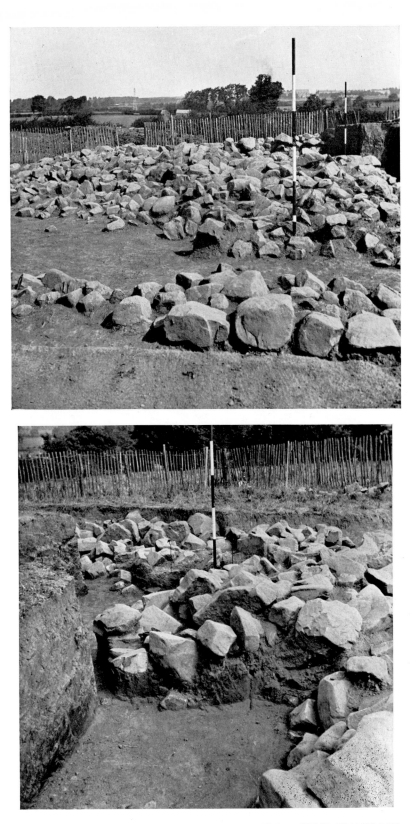

(a) Kerb-wall defining cairn ring, in foreground

(b) The east stone heap, projecting into open circle

PLATE 35. POND CAIRN, COITY, GLAMORGAN

(a) The east pit: firehole marked by ring-headed pin

(b) The east pit: approach

PLATE 36. POND CAIRN, COITY, GLAMORGAN

of large sandstone pebbles had been tossed into the hole, and that small fragments of Lias rock were disposed around them. The stone filling was the same down to the bottom. Fine earth occupied the interstices of the upper layers; this got more loamy, even clayey, as the clearance progressed, exactly as in the stone-filled pit under Trias slab G at Simondston (p. 87). Near the top there was an animal bone 3 in. in length pointing downwards between the stones: it is probably a portion of the metatarsal of a red deer. At the same level tiny fragments of burnt bone were noted; these became more numerous as one got lower, and tended to be concentrated in one part of the pit, but nowhere showed any sign of careful deposition. The total quantity of burnt bone was 1½ lb., and it probably represented the remains of a child under 7 years. On the floor of the pit was a flint flake— a fresh spall of good material, unburnt.

The pit measured 4 ft. × 4 ft. at ground-level, and was 15 in. deep. (See Plate 32b, and the plan and section, Figure 61.) It lay in part beneath the stone-heap, and clearly antedated the urn-burial. Its contents—a scatter of burnt bones—preclude the idea that it is the primary burial for which the cairn was raised; rather, it would seem to represent something in the nature of a dedication, a sacring, of the site.

*The Turf-stack.* We may now turn to the earth-mound enveloping the stone-heap. From within a foot of the surface down to the original ground-level it presented peculiar features. It was free from stones and very variegated, orange-black (iron-stained) stripes and layers contrasting with grey-blue clayey patches (showing occasional scraps of shell from the Lias), and with yellowish soil and dark earth; there was an occasional flake of charcoal. The pattern of colour was irregular, almost fantastic, a feature which Figure 61 attempts to reproduce symbolically, since the photographs do not bring it out.

Every observer on seeing it said 'Turf!' And there can be no doubt that this is its nature (Plate 29b) and that it was derived from a moorish or peaty site. The grey-blue clay formed, we may suppose, the underside of thick turves. At a variable distance above the natural ground-level, a continuous and sinuous orange-and-black layer, harder, thicker, and grittier than elsewhere, was seen. The patches of clay seem not to be present below this deposit.

Analyses of the material from immediately above and below this ferruginous layer indicate that the whole was of common origin; that the slightly higher content of iron in the lower layers was due to local segregation of ferruginous material *in situ*, and that the ferruginous layer is to be regarded as incipient iron-pan.

The difference between the earthy material of the mound and the present soil of the immediate vicinity may be accounted for, in my friend Dr. F. J. North's opinion, by supposing that damper and more acid soil conditions formerly prevailed. A small affluent of the Ogwr river traverses the area, and even after centuries of agriculture there are ponds in the vicinity which indicate that the drainage is to some extent impeded. Such areas could readily have yielded turf of this moorish, peaty character.

Some of the outer stones of the central stone-heap appeared to rest on the turf structure (Plate 31a, left). This suggests that the stone-heap and turf-mound were erected contemporaneously, the stones settling down into the surrounding turves as they were being piled up.

The variegated colouring of the turf-mound faded out into the surrounding brown loamy soil, but the margins were vertical, even overhanging. *We are, then, justified in speaking not of a turf-mound but of a turf-stack.*

*The Cairn Ring: Inner Face.* The loamy deposit referred to in the previous paragraph cannot be explained except in relation to the outer stone structure which impinged on it; we will therefore next consider this structure, massive enough to justify, in spite of the central turf-stack, the description of the monument as a cairn (Figure 59).

Clearance of the western half of the mound, then, disclosed a mass of stones forming a semicircle round the turf-stack. This mass was about 2 ft. in height on the inner edge, but towards the outer margins (having been robbed) it thinned out to scattered and single stones. These features are shown in the panorama (Plate 30) taken from the south-west and in the photograph of the semicircle from inside (Plate 33a). At one or two points on the inner curve there were indications of a wall face; clearance quickly demonstrated that there was a continuous dry wall, from which, when it was higher than it is now, much stone had fallen, forming a talus at its foot. Plate 33b shows the north side, what we may now call the cairn ring, partly cleared. The dry-wall construction was of varied character, and for the most part of poor quality. At many points of the circuit there was, however, a well-laid foundation course of stones, carefully chosen for their squareness (Plate 34a). Rarely a stone is set on end: in such a case no attempt is made to fix it firmly in the earth. Examination having been made of all doubtful cases, and two sections cut through the ring, it can safely be asserted that there is no earth-fast stone in Pond Cairn.

Occasionally, a very large boulder is used, and is bedded with an outward slant, as in the section, Figure 61. Occasionally again, the inner wall-face is so badly built of small stones that only the well-constructed portions adjoining enable one to be certain of the line. Much of the apparent inadequacy of the walling is, however, due to the instability of the structure as a whole. The wall, with rare exceptions, is ill-designed to resist the inward thrust of the cairn mass, which was found on section to be completely structureless, merely a pile of stones; the thrust must therefore have been considerable. Many of the surviving stones of the wall-face are pushed forward for distances up to a foot, and precariously balanced.

*The Interspace.* It will be recalled that the outer margins of the central turf-stack faded out into loamy soil. The talus of fallen stones in front of the wall-face of the ring was enveloped in this soil (Figure 61), which was full of flakes and flecks of charcoal, especially near the turf-stack.

The original ground-level below the loamy soil was found to be covered with charcoal; it was hard, as though heavily trodden. The charcoal was in places a thin skin, in places a thicker deposit; sometimes (on the south-west side of the ring) it formed a gritty black mass fully an inch in depth, in certain places on the north-west side the ground in which it was embedded was slightly reddened, as though the charcoal had been scattered when hot. Its composition was studied, oak, hawthorn, and hazel being identified.[1]

The margins of this charcoal layer were definite. On the inner side it ended at the turf-stack, on the outer side it extended right up to the wall-face of the cairn ring at all points; indeed, flakes of charcoal were found here and there on the stones of the wall and in the spaces between the sill-stones as though it had been tossed in showers on to the ground. The

[1] Both Mr. H. A. Hyde and Dr. F. J. North examined this charcoal; no coal was present in it.

charcoaled floor, moreover, in many places rose up in a curve to reach the wall: not much, half an inch to an inch, but sufficient to be noticeable (see section, Figure 61, south side). The layer did not extend under the wall; the fact recorded above was sufficient to prove this, and it was confirmed in the two places where the cairn ring was removed.

One must conclude from these facts that a narrow circular interspace—it was from 3 ft. to 6 ft. in breadth—was left between the turf-stack and the cairn ring; that a certain amount of dust and soil (from the stack?) blew on to this floor and settled against the sill-stones of the wall, before the charcoal was scattered on it—no doubt by the master of the ceremonies on top of the stack—and trodden in by an orderly movement of persons—mourners(?) round him and it!

The lowest stones of the talus of the ring rested on the charcoaled floor of the interspace, showing that the collapse of the structure started soon after it was built; in Plate 34b, three stones have been turned over to show the charcoal staining their undersides (the wall face, here of three courses, is shown on the left of the footrule).

The talus nowhere extended under the turf-stack. The fact confirms the sequence of construction here suggested. The limits of the stack in relation to the talus at one point are shown in the *foreground* of Plate 33a by two white pegs; here no stone of the talus has been touched by the workmen.

We are now in a position to interpret the loamy deposit which envelops the talus and fills the interspace. The view that it is a natural silting, derived from a *wall-sided turf-stack* after the ceremonies were completed and the cairn deserted, has everything to commend it. Decay, naturally, began immediately thereafter; the inner wall face of the cairn ring was pressed forward by the weight of the structure, and its upper stones fell on to the floor; more slowly the turf-stack disintegrated, its outline changing from that of a squat gas-holder to a dome. A difficulty in this interpretation led to an extended, but I think reasonable, conception of the charcoal ceremony. The difficulty was this: if the loam filling were the result of natural processes, why and whence the heavy load of charcoal it carried? Clearly, charcoal and plenty of it was in the forefront of the orders for the day; it would have been scattered as freely on the top of the turf-stack as on the floor—the top was indeed the obvious and only point of vantage for the leader (Figure 59), who will have cast the charcoal, in clouds, downwards, on to those circling the ring! And as the charcoal-smeared and well-trodden top decayed, the (finely comminuted) charcoal would be thickest in the silting exactly where it was found, nearest the stack and nearest the bottom.

*The Cairn Ring: Outer Edge.* The circularity of the inner face of the cairn ring and its diameter (p. 109) having been determined, attention was directed to its outer edge. Further clearance showed that the external irregularity seen in Plate 30 was due to stone-robbing at a comparatively recent date. The whole of the outer part of the cairn ring had been removed for a quarter of its circuit, and an intermediate zone had been removed round the rest of the structure. Much of the material thus collected remained on the site in a heap!

The clearance brought to light the original kerbstones of the cairn ring, large stones laid to present plane faces outwards (see Plate 34a). On the north-east side two courses were found in position, showing that these kerbs were really the base stones of the outer facing of the ring. Some of the upper stones oversail the lower and were obviously pushed forward by the pressure of the cairn mass; but two or three were in their original position. These show a pronounced batter, even a curved face; and this suggests that the whole external surface of the cairn ring was originally composed of stones chosen to present, whether on top or sides, as smooth an appearance as possible; looked at from a vantage point it would, I think, have seemed a three-dimensional, coarse, mortarless mosaic. The ring then was, in essence, a rubble core with stone facings. This is illustrated diagrammatically in the reconstruction, Figure 62.

It is relevant to mention that at the point on the rim of the cairn where the outer facing survived (Plate 30) there was a spill-over of stones (removed before the photograph was taken). The talus thus formed had preserved the wall.

The care which seems to have been taken over the *surfaces* of the cairn ring made the casual deposition of its mass very noticeable. Sections of the mass showed that while the stones were closely packed, there was no attempt at dealing with the dynamics of the problem. Obviously it was no use leaning the stones inwards as at Simondston; this would have made the inner wall more insecure even than it proved to be. But since these Middle Bronze Age folk had given up the ancient and well-proven notion of opposing thrusts by the inertia of earth-fast slabs, their only line of

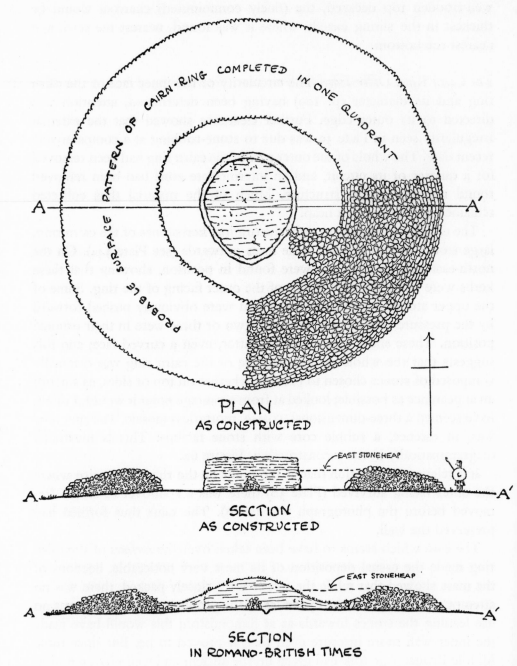

PLAN
AS CONSTRUCTED

EAST STONEHEAP

SECTION
AS CONSTRUCTED

EAST STONEHEAP

SECTION
IN ROMANO-BRITISH TIMES

Figure 62. Pond Cairn

action was careful dry-stone walling throughout, and this was obviously too laborious and difficult.

*The Lithology of the Cairn Ring.* The material used by the builders of the cairn ring, Dr. F. J. North reports, 'contrasted strongly with that used in the Simondston Cairn, in that, whereas in the latter quarried blocks were used, the stones of the Pond Cairn were surface gatherings'. This accounts for the stones being more varied in size and character than at Simondston. The source of the Rhaetic sandstone of which the cairn is mainly composed, as determined by Dr. North, is shown on Figure 48; it is different from the Simondston source.

*The East Stone-heap and Pit.* There was one interruption in the symmetry of the cairn ring, a stone-heap projecting inwards on the east side of the monument (Plate 35b). At the point where the photograph was taken it completely blocked the interspace and was higher than the existing portions of the ring. On investigation it was found to be composed of similar material to that of the cairn ring with some Lias nodules in addition. The western angle where it touched the turf-stack was vertical, built of sandstone and Lias slabs selected for their squareness, but its remaining edges were not so carefully defined. Over 1 ft. of laid stone had been removed from the western angle when photograph 35b was taken.

In clearing, it was found that the bottom stones in the centre of the heap had partly sunk into a grey-black greasy mass filling a shallow oval pit (Plate 36a and b) to cover which the stone-heap had been raised. The pit was basin-shaped, 6 ft. × 3 ft. in area and 10 in. in depth, dug into the clay subsoil. Its eastern edge cuts into the inner wall of the cairn ring, the line of sill-stones being interrupted. One sill-stone was undercut when the pit was made (Plate 36a, right-hand side) but remained firmly fixed in its original position! The pit then must have been a later construction than the cairn ring; but since the turf-stack—an unstable structure—was still vertical-sided when the stone-heap was erected over the pit, the lapse of time may be regarded as insignificant. On the bottom of the pit sticks of charcoaled wood were seen to be pressed into the clay, which was reddened in places—the bottom was soft and had not been trampled on. The central area of the pit everywhere contained the greasy mass already referred to; at the sides this mass became more earthy, until it reached the clay wall. In general, it contained carbonized wood (a few large sticks at the top and the east end, but mainly twigs and roots) and bits of reddened clay: a quantity of grains was also noted on the surface of the mass by Aileen Fox. There was no bone, human or animal, burnt or unburnt. In the centre of the mass, lying flat, was a thin slab of grey shelly Liassic limestone, $12\frac{1}{2}$ in. in length, from a site on the slope of Brackla Hill (see Figure 63, section).

Some of the top layer of grey-black material and a sample of the grains extracted therefrom were sent to Professor John Percival, who found wheat, probably bread wheat (*Triticum vulgare*) or possibly club wheat (*T. compactum*) with numerous caryopses or grains of cheat or chess (*Bromus*), 'a common weed,' he remarks, 'of cereal crops, abundant in ancient times, as now, in some places'. There were also a few grains of barley, see Plate 37b, series a, b, and c. In his view the cereals were deposited unburnt in the pit, but my colleague Mr. H. A. Hyde considered that the carbonization of the wheat grains from the pit was due to heat and not to slow spontaneous chemical change.

The amount of carbonized wood in the mass, sticks and twigs of appreciable size, was considerable. Much was picked out and submitted, together with a general sample of the material, to Mr. Hyde; he identified no less than eight species. The list in order of determinations is gorse (38), hazel (9), oak (6), hawthorn (4), bracken (3), mountain ash (1).

The following points then are established. The grey-black deposit in the pit consists largely of charcoal sticks and ashes from a fire, mainly of brushwood, some collected while still hot. Cereals and cultivation weeds presumably in the form of sheaves—whether burnt or not is debatable— were placed with the carbonized mass, mainly on the top. A delicately patterned (fossiliferous) slab of stone was placed in the middle of the deposit.

*The Ramp and Fire-hole.* The soft floor of the pit merged on the east side into a hard-trodden slope. It was reddened; further investigation showed that the redness had its source in a shallow hole (marked by a pin in Plate 36a). This was filled with fine charcoal 'paste' with a 'piece of red clay looking like burnt daub' in the centre. Evidently a fire had been lit here and the flames licked the ramp of trodden clay.[1] Above the fire-hole

[1] A sample of the ash was handed to Dr. North; he finds 'there is no appreciable amount of coal present'.

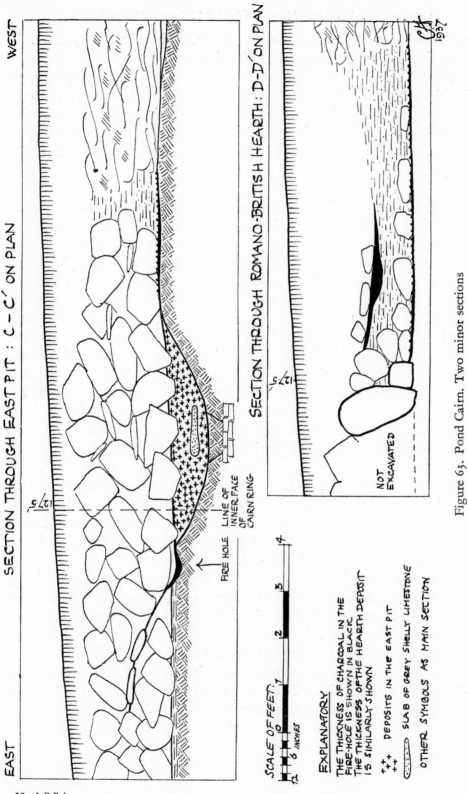

EAST

WEST

SECTION THROUGH EAST PIT : C – C' ON PLAN

1917'5

FIRE HOLE

LINE OF
INNER FACE
OF CAIRN RING

SECTION THROUGH ROMANO-BRITISH HEARTH: D–D' ON PLAN

1917'5

NOT
EXCAVATED

C.H.
1937

SCALE OF FEET.

12   6 INCHES   1   2   3   4

EXPLANATORY

THE THICKNESS OF CHARCOAL IN THE
FIRE-HOLE IS SHOWN IN BLACK.
THE THICKNESS OF THE HEARTH DEPOSIT
IS SIMILARLY SHOWN

+ +
+ +     DEPOSITS IN THE EAST PIT

⬭     SLAB OF GREY SHELLY LIMESTONE

OTHER SYMBOLS AS MAIN SECTION

Figure 63. Pond Cairn. Two minor sections

was a floor of small stones, tilted upwards, set in a hard dirty earth. All these features are shown in section in Figure 63.

The ritual meaning of the series of acts which have left their mark in this area of the cairn is difficult to determine. The significant element of the deposit in the pit is surely the cereals. Due weight must be attached to the breaking of the cairn ring, and the importance of the deposit is attested by the raising of a stone-heap over it. The fire in the hole on the ramp suggests a ritual act connected with the pit.

*East Entrance* (?). Bearing these points in mind, it seemed possible that the cairn ring might have been broken down to construct some sort of ceremonial entrance east of the fire-hole, and the investigation was there-fore extended outwards—with little result. The excavation yielded no trace of flanking sills or dry-walling, or of paving or cobbling. The soil at the original ground level was found to be dirtier and harder in this area than in the section cut in the south side of the ring, but there are reasons for holding that the cairn was built by folk approaching it from the east, and the traffic would be heavier on this side. All one can suggest is that the inner wall of the cairn ring was broken down sufficiently to make standing room for the persons or person officiating at the fire-hole, and at the filling of the pit, and that if there was an approach from the east at this point it went over the ring rather than through it. That is, any constructional work was destroyed when the upper portions of the ring were removed by farmers.

*Romano–British Hearths*. A later occupation of the site remains to be considered. On clearing the inner wall of the cairn ring, reddened clay and charcoal were met with at several points in the angle formed by the wall and the east stone-heap, over an area some 8 ft. in length and 3 ft. in breadth (Figure 63 and Plate 38b).

Three centres of intense or prolonged burning were located, consisting of grey ash surrounded by hard reddened clay; beyond the centres there was much charcoal. Further examination showed that two of these centres belonged to one hearth, A + B; a base of clay daub burnt to a brick red, between them, suggested the remains of a hearth wall. The fire in hearth C, where the burning apparently was less intense, had been put out by dropping a flat oval piece of Lias rock on to it (Plate 37a). (It has not been cleaned: the whiteness is the result of weathering, *in situ*.)

Food grains were noticed in the charcoaled surface soil beside all these hearths; in particular around hearth C there was a heavy deposit, in places a continuous layer. In the photograph of this hearth, the grains lie mainly between the foot-rule and the stone. Professor Percival, who reported on these grains, found barley in the material from hearths A and B; and both 'bread wheat and barley grains in that from hearth C, the latter being the more abundant' (see Plate 37b). Mr. H. A. Hyde found wheat grains in the material from hearths A + B also; and he has found chess (*Bromus secalinus*).

Charcoal from hearth A + B yielded to Mr. Hyde's analysis slight remains of hazel; from hearth C there was a hazel nutshell, but the fires were lit with hawthorn, no less than twenty-one determinations of this tree being obtained.

The date of the hearths can fortunately be fixed, for a Romano–British potsherd—a portion of the rim of a black bowl, its outer surface scored with a smooth point—was found in charcoal-stained loam beside hearth C. My late colleague V. E. Nash-Williams recognized it as a type commonly occurring on fortress sites in South Wales and dating from the 2nd century A.D.

The stratigraphical position of these hearths is important, since they show *the exact amount of silting* that had taken place between *c.* 1100 B.C. and *c.* A.D. 150. They lie on the loamy filling of the interspace; the outer margins of A + B and C respectively touch each other, and they are therefore strictly contemporary.

The surface of the silting here slopes downwards from the large slabs of the wall of the cairn ring towards the centre, as is shown in Plate 38b (left-hand pin, hearth C). Under the silting lies the talus from the cairn ring; while over the hearths lies a mass of stones, representing a later ruination of the ring. The silting had reached a depth of 8–12 in. when the squatters settled there. They chose a sheltered corner, where the east stone-heap joined the cairn-ring. The sequence of events is shown in the section (Figure 62).

*The Dimensions and Appearance of Pond Cairn.* As the plan (Figure 59) shows, the length of the kerb-wall of the cairn ring which has been preserved is about two-thirds of the circumference. Since the monument is not truly circular or concentric in any of its parts, a just measure of its dimensions can best be obtained by taking two diameters, each where the kerbs are present at either end, and as far apart as possible. The following measurements comply with this requirement, and are taken through what is obviously the centre of the structure, the point where the urn was placed.

*The Mean of Two Records, at Right Angles*

|  | ft. | in. |
|---|---|---|
| Turf stack—diameter | 17 | 9 |
| Interspace—north of urn | 4 | 10 |
| „     —south of urn | 4 | 10 |
| Central area—diameter, being total of above | 27 | 6 |
| Cairn ring, thickness—north of urn | 17 | 0 |
| „     „     „     —south of urn | 17 | 0 |
| Cairn, overall—kerb to kerb | 61 | 6 |

The evidence for the original appearance of Pond Cairn has been set out at length in the preceding pages. It is summarized in the form of an ideal reconstruction, in Figure 62. Here the plan of the cairn—with the flat top of the turf-stack, and the rounded hump of the carefully built-up cairn ring, with the projecting east stone-heap—is shown. These features can be more readily appreciated in the section shown in the same figure. Directly the monument was finished decay set in. The upper portion of the inner facing of the cairn ring, and the top of the turf-stack, slid into the interspace. Stability came when the turf-stack was a grassy dome and the interspace a grassy hollow. This was the state of the monument when the squatters settled on it; the cairn ring stood up rather rugged and ruined, but substantially as it was built. This condition is illustrated by the second section on the same figure. These two sections can be compared with that on the plan which shows its condition in the 20th century, and with Plate 30 taken when the work of excavation was completed. Here the standing figure gives the scale: the site of the urn-burial is on his right hand, between the two 'islands' left to illustrate the character of the turf-stack, and to show the ground-level prior to excavation. The kerb in the foreground is well shown; also the zone robbed of its stone in modern times which now divides the cairn ring into two.

In this connection it is pertinent to inquire how and why the cairn ring, an exposed heap of stones in *c*. A.D. 150 as in *c*. 1100 B.C., obtained its existing covering. The stones lying on the Romano–British hearth A + B (Plate 38b) suggest that soon after that period destruction by man of the monument began—the levelling down of the cairn ring or removal of its stones; for no stones had fallen from the inner wall in that area since the period of 'rapid silting' some 1450 years before, and the structure must have been completely stable.

Organized stone-robbing, as we know, accounts for certain features of the cairn ring as seen today; but it will not account for the overlying soil. That from 4 in. to 12 in. of earth should accumulate over the stones of the ring between *c*. A.D. 150 and A.D. 1937, though none had so accumulated between *c*. 1100 B.C. and *c*. A.D. 150, is a particular instance of a general and still unsolved problem. The lowering of the dome of the turf-stack can account for some but not all of this soil.

I have elsewhere suggested that such soil is mainly dust blown from arable fields on to areas which by reason of their unsuitability for cultivation have been allowed to grow bushes and scrub. When clearance takes place, all stones sticking through this accumulation of soil are removed by the farmers; and ultimately, when ploughing the mound is attempted, every stony obstacle within a few inches of the surface is hooked out; until at length coulter and share meet no obstacle at all and the very nature of the structure is forgotten.

If this is a correct explanation in this instance, then we must infer that extensive arable cultivation of the Coity region did not begin until the Christian era. This is very likely to have been the case.

*Summary*. Pond Cairn is a hybrid construction; an earthen centre surrounded by a stone ring. The diameter is ± 61 ft. It was erected over the ashes of an adult personage at the beginning of Middle Bronze Age B (*c*. 1100 B.C., on a revised dating), to judge from the cinerary, an overhanging-rim urn of the archaeologist's 'Type 1, Phase ii'. There were no secondary burials.

The sequence of events at the cairn provided at its date, 1938, one of the completest records of Bronze Age burial ceremonial published in Britain. In detail the meaning of the ritual which the remains indicate is obscure, but the general significance can hardly be in doubt. I shall, then, include in this summary a measure of interpretation.

The site chosen for the burial-place of the high personage to be com-
memorated was first dedicated. A child's body was burnt; a pit was dug
and the burnt bones, washed clean of charcoal, were scattered in it; at the
same time the pit was being filled with stones. It was then sealed with
clay. The body of the dead personage was subsequently burnt (not on the
site). Flat stones defining the place where his (or her) ashes were to rest
were then firmly set, and a small deep basin-shaped hole with a shallow
extension, phallic in outline, made in front of the urn-site and the flat
stones. The inurned ashes of the dead having been placed in position, with
a slab of pink stone atop, ritual was performed which involved the filling
of the bottom of the basin with charcoal from the pyre, and the lining of
the upper part, and its extension, with hot charcoal sticks, also presumably
from the pyre. The basin was then filled with clay.

A small stone-heap and a turf-stack—the latter material brought from
neighbouring marshy ground—were raised in rapid succession over and
around the urn. This closes the first phase.

A complete ring of stones, some 16 ft. thick and probably 5 ft. high,
rubble-cored but with an inner facing wall and a carefully finished outer
surfacing, was then built. The second phase of the ritual was then carried
through; wood-ash was scattered on the turf-stack and the floor of the
interspace between stack and ring; the trodden floor of the interspace
suggests a ceremonial movement (of men, or both sexes) round the stack.

The third phase is perhaps the most interesting of all; it seems to
represent the dedication of the monument as a whole. The inner face of
the cairn ring, which was a complete circle, was broken into at one point
where a shallow pit was dug. The point selected was on the side of the
monument (the east side) from which, to judge from the relation between
urn and basin, the ashes of the dead man were brought. A sloping ramp
was made in place of the vertical wall-face of the cairn ring at this point,
and a small hole dug at the eastern end of the shallow pit. This was
dedicated by fire[1]; much charcoal—some sticks, hot enough to redden the
bottom of the pit in places—was thrown into it and a fire was lit in the
hole referred to. Then an offering of the fruits of the earth—sheaves of
wheat and barley with their associated weeds from the cultivated fields
of the settlement—was placed on top of the mass of material, which now

[1] Thus the person carrying out the dedication faced west to the setting sun (?), as did
the person concerned in the ritual of the urn deposition.

stood high above ground-level.[1] One slab of stone, selected for its colour and pattern, was placed in the centre of the mass of charcoal and cereals. The whole offering was then carefully enclosed, weighted down, and covered high with stones.

The ceremonies connected with Pond Cairn, which may have taken a year or more to complete, were thus ended.

It is for students of comparative religion to assess the significance of the manifestations of ritual here discovered. The cumulative importance of (*a*) the child-burial (sacrifice?) in the rite with which the work was begun, (*b*) the employment of the symbol of fertility in the central rite, and (*c*) the choice of vegetation (corn in particular) for the act which must be regarded as the final dedication, is evident. Fire played a part in each of the three main phases of the action. The facts, then, suggest that the person whose ashes were in the urn occupied a position of exceptional importance in the economic life of the savage community which then occupied the area. Was he a 'corn king'—an embodiment of the corn spirit?

*General Considerations.* The student of prehistory in his barrow-digging is driven to scrutinize every aspect of the structures he examines, in order to see whether the differences they must show are likely to be within the same culture or not. We have now carefully examined Simondston and Pond Cairns. They are situated in one parish 5 miles from the sea and a convenient estuary, at a modest elevation (100–200 ft.), by no means the highest available in the immediate neighbourhood, but are different. Simondston is certainly the earlier. Its primary (cremation) deposits in 'enlarged food-vessels' indicate a date at the beginning of Middle Bronze Age, round about 1400 B.C. Its carefully wrought construction shows that, in cist and cairn alike, stability and permanence were the chief aims. The absence on its floor of any trace of ritual practices emphasizes its classic simplicity. The only structural elaboration presented by it was a cist-stone cup-marked and pecked.

Pond Cairn is later—its OHR urn dates about 1100 B.C. It provides evidence of a dramatic and prolonged ritual; it was a showy and indeed fantastic erection; its constructional technique was superficial and unsound; its material was casually collected; in brief, it is grotesque and odd: baroque.

[1] It was densely compressed by the weight of the stone-heap and yet was of considerable thickness.

Finally, though cairn construction dominates, it is in part earthen barrow—a hybrid form.

On the whole the lithology of the cairns was similar, the mass of the material in each case being Rhaetic sandstone. But whereas the sandstone of Simondston was quarried—i.e. levered out along bedding planes and joint planes, and of even sizes—the sandstone at Pond Cairn consisted of weathered boulders and pebbles, varying greatly in dimensions and evidently picked up from the surface.

It might be thought that nothing can be gained by discussing two such different structures in one section of this book. But there is a link. Subsequent to its erection Simondston Cairn was used as a cemetery, the approximate date of which is fixed by the occurrence of a collared urn similar to, but typologically earlier than, that at Pond Cairn. In this 'cemetery', the simplicities characteristic of the primary burial have no place. Holes are made in the ground and afterwards filled with earth or stones; charcoal and burnt clay are widely scattered around the most outstanding interment; coloured slabs of stone are prominently displayed.

Now these features are paralleled at Pond Cairn. We recall (Figure 60) the central pit with its stony filling, the remarkable scatter of charcoal in the interspace, the slab of grey fossiliferous limestone placed in the centre of the deposit of cereals in the east pit, the piece of red Triassic conglomerate covering the open mouth of the urn. This was the only piece of red Trias at Pond Cairn, and it had to be fetched from some distance.

There are, of course, special features at Pond Cairn, but nothing culturally inconsistent with those associated with the Simondston secondary interments. We may then regard the folk who erected Pond Cairn as the same people who were using Simondston Cairn as a cemetery. Pursuing the same train of ideas, we may say that the differences between their culture and that of the *builders* of Simondston Cairn are so profound that we must regard them as intruders in the Coity district.

Consideration will now be given to the sources of the two cultures.

In Britain generally, unbroken stone rings in barrows are distinctly rare. Occasionally a circle of separate stones or boulders is found within the mound, but these are probably typologically connected with the stone circle proper, or with cairn peristaliths; the only close parallels which came to light were on the other side of the Bristol Channel. Wick barrow, near Stogursey, excavated by Mr. H. St. G. Gray, revealed a circular wall surrounding the primary burials.[1] Again, on Blackdown, Mendip, circular stone heaps or walls formed part of the structure of the three cairns or barrows excavated by members of the Bristol Spelaeological Society.

In searching through these Somerset records we were, as children say, 'getting warm'; for the true parallels, in abundant measure, are in Devon. Here it is recorded that 'Composite barrows, partly of earth and partly of stone, the materials separate, are numerous'. The methods of arrangement of earth and stone vary; characteristic forms are figured in the *Report* of the Barrow Committee of the Devonshire Association, from which the quotation is taken.

Of these 'Hameldon', one of a number on Hameldown, 1,737 ft., at the eastern edge of Dartmoor, springs to the eye as providing a counterpart of the essential structure of Pond Cairn. 'The margin of the barrow is built of stone'; it is indeed a ring of stones heaped up; there is a small central cairn; the rest of the structure is 'peaty earth'.[2]

One of the later reports of the Barrow Committee yields a yet closer parallel. A round barrow of the Chapman group at Parracombe excavated in 1905 shows a central stone heap covering an interment pit containing a cremation burial; a barrow of 'heaped turf', quite certainly, from the figure, a turf-stack of Pond Cairn type; an 'interspace'; a ring of heaped stones. Charcoal was 'extremely plentiful in the turf-mound'.

The positions of the structures mentioned in this survey are shown in the sketch-map of south-western Britain, Figure 64. All the known hybrid cairn barrows in South Wales, it will be observed, are close to the coast, and the facts we have marshalled point to one conclusion only. The men who buried their dead with novel rites in the margins of Simondston Cairn, and who constructed Pond Cairn, were settlers hailing from the other side of the Severn sea. Their Middle Bronze Age culture was that developed in Wessex.[3]

It is not yet certain where the collared urn, this distinctly native type of pottery, was developed from the Neolithic B bowl; but the large number of early forms in Wiltshire and Dorset, and their associations, render

[1] *Proc. Som. Arch. Soc.*, liv (ii), 1908, pp. 1–77.

[2] A cremation burial eccentrically sited was associated with a gold- and amber-hilted knife-dagger of the Wessex culture. Thus the structural form represented at Pond Cairn was present in Devon at an early date.

[3] Stuart Piggott, 'The Early Bronze Age in Wessex', *Proc. Prehist. Soc.*, 1938, pp. 52–106.

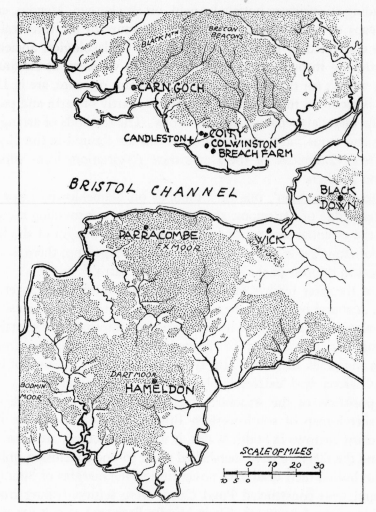

Figure 64. Map, south-western region

Abercromby's view that the type 'apparently began in the area south of the Thames'[1] still acceptable. The universality, then, of the type in Britain is something of a puzzle. Did its use spread from south England by peaceful means, representing merely a change of fashion in matters appertaining to burial? Or was it spread by conquest? Our text-books speak of the Middle Bronze Age in Britain generally as an age of peaceful development. This may well be doubted. Rapiers and spearheads were not ornaments but

[1] *Bronze Age Pottery*, ii, 23.

weapons; and we are at liberty to picture the ebb and flow of internecine strife as contributing largely to the uniformity which marks this period. At all events the Coity cairns have provided us with definite evidence of the spread of the collared-urn culture into one particular area by the migration of family groups, or a tribe.

The discovery of wheat and barley grains is a valuable addition to our knowledge of the Bronze Age in South Wales. Records of food grains in such a context are extremely rare in this country. The only one that is well known represents an accidental occurrence. Three grains of wheat were found (still connected together in the husk) in the fractured core of a food-vessel in a barrow on the Yorkshire Wolds, accompanying an inhumation burial.[1]

What may be more to the purpose is the finding of a wheat grain in a round barrow with a cremated burial at Upton Pyne, near Exeter, Devon, in 1870.[2] For it is possible that the South Wales littoral received from Devon the first bread wheat to be grown thereon; Professor Percival identified the wheat found in Neolithic pits at Hembury,[3] the only Neolithic wheat as yet found in Britain, as probably *Triticum vulgare*—using almost the same qualified terms of identification as in the case of Pond Cairn.

Be this as it may, Pond Cairn provides what is probably the first scientifically controlled record of wheat for the Middle Bronze Age in England and Wales, and of barley for any period prior to the Early Iron Age.[4]

[1] Mortimer, *Forty Years in a Moorland Parish*, pp. 111–12.

[2] *Trans. Devon Assoc.*, 1870–1, p. 646: 'We observed a grain of . . . wheat lying in the debris of the heap (of ashes and burnt bones).' 'Without doubt it found its way into the barrow when the mound was heaped up.'

[3] Liddell, 'Hembury', *Proc. Devon Arch. Explor. Soc., 3rd Report*, 1932, p. 180.

[4] A study by E. Cecil Curwen of 'The Early Development of Agriculture in Britain' (*Proc. Prehist. Soc.*, 1938, pp. 27–51, esp. pp. 40–1), should be consulted in this connection.

# 6

## TURF BARROWS IN SOUTH WALES

*Middle and Late Bronze Age*

### INTRODUCTION

THE four round barrows to which the above description applies are in the northern part of Llantwit Major parish in the Vale of Glamorgan, close to Sutton 268′ (Figure 40). Being nameless like Sutton, they are defined by (*a*) the nearest farmstead, and (*b*) the height of their crests above sea-level. The excavation of three was carried out during the severest winter weather of modern times (1939–40); alternations of frost and thaw played havoc with sections and floors, and prolonged delays ate into the time available. I started, in fact, without experience of excavation under such conditions. In a frost, for example, a floor cannot be studied for stake-holes or other features: the conditions destroy colour contrasts. In a thaw the floor (with its stake-holes) comes away on one's boots: vertical sections disintegrate and collapse. The only way to deal with the difficulty that I could discover was to examine and record all floors, sections, or deposits *immediately* on exposure: but the limitations which this imposes on the study of difficult problems—such as that of 'mortuary houses'—and on overall planning are obvious. Aileen Fox worked with me most of the time, and skilfully overcame many of our troubles.

The two 'Sheeplays' barrows (Sheeplays 293′ and 279′) are close together on a crest-line as viewed from the margins of the marshy flat previously referred to; the two 'Six Wells' barrows, 267′ and 271′, are nearer to the marsh. This haunt of wildfowl may have determined the settlement of the folk who built the barrows, but its site has not been found.

The barrows are alike in having been heavily ploughed down: they proved to be structurally similar, as the title of the chapter shows, but they fall readily into two groups, the earlier of which shows a central burial:

the later a central deposit, here termed a ritual deposit. 293′, 279′, and 267′ are assigned to the Middle Bronze, 271′ to the Late Bronze Age. 293′ has a secondary of the latter period.

There are two barrows in the 'Turf-stack' Group, erected primarily as 'mortuary houses': Sheeplays 293′ and 279′, on the same farmland. Sheeplays 293′ is the more elaborate: 279′ can be summarily treated.

## SHEEPLAYS 293′, c. 1000 B.C.

Around a primary cremation burial of the Middle Bronze Age were four or more concentric circles of stake-holes, the two inner representing a circular hut with roof supports. Within and without the structural frame which inner holes imply, a turf-stack of peculiar form was erected. Subsequent to partial collapse, a casing of soil was heaped up against the stack, completing a structure of which the basal portion survives today.

The barrow structure will first be described, because the evidence for the stake-holes cannot be understood without reference to it.

*The Turf-stack and the Primary Burial.* The central portion of the barrow (below the plough-soil) was composed of clayey turf, grey and orange and black, of the same character as that seen in Pond Cairn. The plan (Figure 65) and sections (Figure 74) indicate its contours and area; the turf is clearly seen in the background of Plate 40a. The deposit differed from that at Pond Cairn in showing on the margins and on the original ground-level larger masses of grey-blue clay; this may have been in order to give greater stability to the structure. Neither grey clay nor the orange and black layers have any parallels in colour in the neighbourhood; the soil here is loamy, grading downwards into yellow or purple-yellow Lias clay, the Lias rock having been demonstrated at 6 ft. But, as Dr. F. J. North has shown,[1] the appearance of such turf-stacks is due to changes taking place subsequent to their erection; they are physically identical with the adjacent soil and subsoil. Our turf-stack, then, is of local origin.

As the plan shows by means of stippling, the stack was approximately circular, with two curved wings on the south side. The main mass— defined by the 28-ft. circle—is steep-walled—wellnigh vertical on the

[1] The reader interested in geology will find the demonstration in *Archaeologia*, 89, 1943, pp. 118–25.

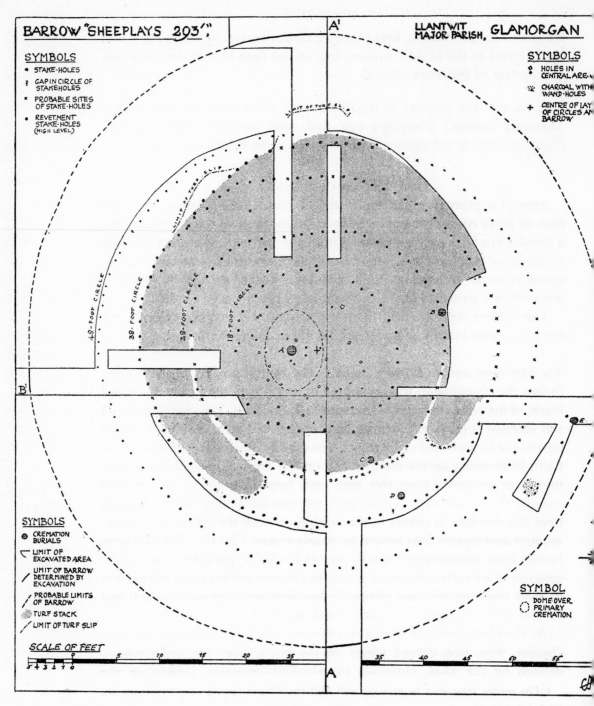

Figure 65. Plan

south side (section A–A', Figure 74)—while the curved 'wings' are low; indeed at their tips they fade out almost imperceptibly, and therefore sloped downwards. Section B–B' shows one wing near its tip, the other near its point of mergence with the main mass; the difference in height is striking. At the tips the wings are structurally separate from the mass—that is, the gap, filled by soil, extends to the original ground-level, in future called the floor of the barrow. The wings, like the margins of the stack, are very clayey.

It will be noticed that the sections record a layer of hard-pan under the turf-stack, as at Sutton 268': the plan shows most of it. This, it will be recalled, is a ferric concretion normally occurring in turf barrows of the Vale of Glamorgan, deposited at any level in the structure which has been rendered (*by constant treading?*) comparatively impervious to the seepage downwards of water impregnated with iron oxide. The deposit is usually on the floor of the barrow—as in the present case—sometimes in stake-holes (Plate 40b): the thickness of the hard-pan in general seems to be directly related to the mass of the turf-stack; here it was unusually thick, 2–3 in. in places, needing a blow of a pick to break it (it resembled decayed iron plating!). That the stack was originally a high one is thus probable. By contrast, the hard-pan was very thin under the curved wings, and was a mere orange stain near their tips.

*The Primary Burial and the Central Stake-holes*. In the centre of the barrow (see plan) a large hummock was found from which the overlying turfy soil came away cleanly, showing that it had been consolidated before the turf-stack was built (Plate 39a). It was covered with criss-crossed black material like long strips of bark. Below this thin layer (see section, Figure 66a) was clayey turf with lumps of charcoal; then another stripy layer of bark-like material. This overlay yellow Lias clay containing lumps of charcoal; in the centre a patch of loam was then disclosed, and below the patch a brown circular stain on the ancient ground surface. The bark-like material represented, in part at least, decayed and flattened tree branches laid on a clay surface. Now the quality of the workmen allotted to me—I always asked for two, mainly for the hard work of removal of the mound structure—for this war-time service on the great Llandow air-field on behalf of the Ministry of Works, varied greatly. At Sheeplays 293' my potentially best dirt-shifter was bored with the finicky trowel-work to

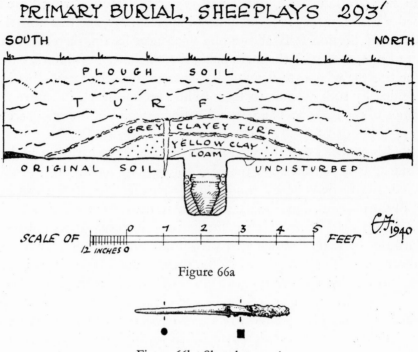

Figure 66a

Figure 66b. Sheeplays 293'.
Bronze awl. Scale $\frac{1}{1}$

which the activity had declined—and showed it. Now I had promised the C.O.—to whom I was careful to commend the research—that when the primary burial was reached I would send for him. At this point then I called the worse workman, and gave him a note—which I read to him—for the Adjutant's Office—saying that I would await the C.O. before disclosing the burial. My man looked at the ground (no different, to him, from what he had been scraping for three days), sniffed, and departed.

When the C.O. arrived I touched the loamy soil which formed the circular stain with a trowel, and to my own surprise and everybody else's, it vanished: disclosing a neat round hole $13\frac{1}{2}$ in. in diameter with an over-hanging-rim urn inside, the rim 5 in. below the ground surface (Plate 39b): the fall of earth barely covered it. When cleared, the space between the wall of the hole and the pot was just wide enough to insert one's fingers under the rim and to lift it out—or put it in! This space had been filled with a black deposit from the pyre, small stones being fitted round the upper part to keep the urn upright (Figure 66a): the hole was 18 in. deep.

(a) Hearth 'C'

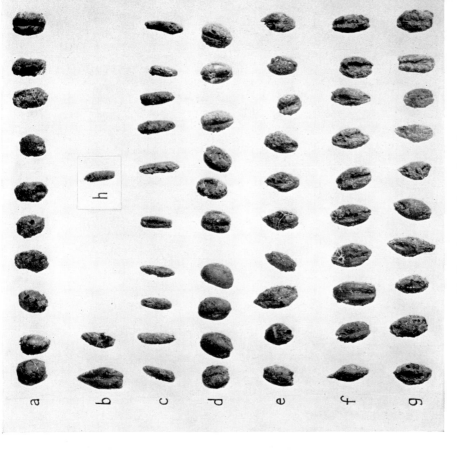

(b) Cereals, etc., from the cairn

PLATE 37. POND CAIRN, COITY, GLAMORGAN

(a) The collared urn of the primary burial, restored

(b) Romano-British hearths

PLATE 38. POND CAIRN, COITY, GLAMORGAN

(a) Dome over primary burial

(b) Primary burial—urn visible

PLATE 39. SHEEPLAYS 293', LLANTWIT MAJOR, GLAMORGAN

(a) 28-ft. stake circle

(b) Three of these stake-holes—open

PLATE 40. SHEEPLAYS 293′, LLANTWIT MAJOR, GLAMORGAN

To my recalcitrant digger, this foreknowledge of mine was almost miraculous: thereafter I had no fault to find and he became my foreman.

The urn contained, in the upper 4 in., soil, charcoal, and many needle-like objects. Below this were clean burnt bones; in them, near the bottom, was a bronze awl, and an unworked flint flake which had been calcined. The bones were those of a youth 18 years old or under. The urn (Plate 41a and Figure 67) was a beautifully proportioned vessel, and well-made; c. 1000 B.C. would, in the present state of our knowledge, be a reasonable date to assign to it. It is 12·2 in. in height with incised herringbone decoration from collar to angular shoulder, and it was recovered without damage of any sort.

The awl (42 mm. long) is circular in section, having a square-sectioned tapering butt, a type recognized as of the Middle Bronze Age. It is well preserved, with a rich blue-green patina (Figure 66b).

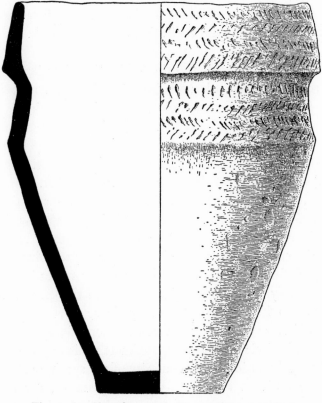

Figure 67. Sheeplays 293'. Urn—primary. Scale ⅓

*The Casing of Soil.* A peculiar feature on the northern margin of the turf-stack was noticed, patches of turf being intermingled with soil (Figure 68, left), very unlike the clear-cut face seen on the south side. The hard-pan ceased abruptly well within this irregular turf-face—marked 'limit of turf-slip' on Figure 65—and this led to a satisfactory explanation. A partial collapse of the stack took place in this segment before an addition was made to the barrow, but the fallen turf was not sufficient in bulk to create hard-pan.

The addition referred to was a casing of soil—a loamy deposit with occasional Lias pebbles—obtained from the immediate locality; it butted up against the turf-stack everywhere, and covered the 'wings' and the hollows between wings and stack (sections A–A' and B–B', Figure 74). It faded upwards into plough soil and in places was very difficult to recognize as an artificial layer; only after long study of the cross-sections under varying conditions was it possible to determine with certainty the outer limits of the casing and therefore of the barrow. This measured 64 ft. in diameter from east to west; and 66 ft. from north to south.

*The Stake-circles.* The turf-stack and the 'casing', as the plan shows, cover an elaborate series of stake-holes; a large area of the barrow being cleared to the floor, four rings of such holes, approximately circular and concentric, were demonstrated (Figure 65). These circles were smaller than that at Talbenny (p. 42, above), being roughly 18, 28, 38, and 48 ft. in diameter, and these mnemonics are for convenience applied to them (Plate 44B).

The '28-ft.' circle (range of diameters 26 ft. 9 in.–28 ft. 9 in.) is entirely within or on the edge of the turf-stack, where the floor of the barrow is covered by hard-pan (p. 131). On the floor being scraped, a circular ring is seen, dark brown to black or orange on the periphery and of various colouring in the centre. This centre is usually the grey-blue of the clayey element in the turf-stack which on the decay of the stakes had slipped into the hole. Frequently the hole remains unfilled in the centre, as is shown in Plate 40b; such holes are outlined by dense hard-pan and seem to represent the diameter of the stake after peripheral decay had set in.

To uncover this circle once the approximate radius was known proved a mechanical task, because of the regularity of the spacing of the holes (see plan, and Plate 40a). In the south-western quadrant, for example, the distances from centre to centre of seven stake-holes in succession was exactly 17 in.; the eighth and ninth stake-holes were 16 in. apart. In the north-eastern quadrant of the circle the distances from centre to centre of the 18 stake-holes varied from 12·5 in. to 18·5 in. The average of twenty-six such measurements in this circle is 15·61 in.

The stakes were certainly driven in, for no disturbance of the soil was detected outside the ring described above.[1] The subsoil here is very yielding in wet weather, and in such conditions no difficulty would be experienced in driving 3–3½-in. stakes 10–12 in. into the ground—which is the range of depth of the holes in the 28-ft. circle which were tested.

The evidence for the massive stakes of the 28-ft. circle is not confined to the floor of the barrow. In the northern half a black, orange, and brown 'pipe' was frequently seen to extend upwards from the floor to the present much denuded top of the turf-stack, and indeed was faintly traceable in the overlying plough soil 1 ft. 9 in. or more above the original ground-level. Sometimes a cylinder representing a section of the stake thus transformed detached itself from the workman's spade.[2] We note then that this circle of stakes was at least 2 ft. high, and that it was left in position when the turf-stack was built. It will be observed on the plan that the circle coincided with the southern face of the turf-stack and with the notch between it and the wings.

It was noted in certain places in the northern quadrant of the circle that the distance between the stakes was exactly the same, 2 ft. up, as on the floor, which suggests that there was a lateral tie—almost certainly an interlacement. For no such rigid parallelism in comparatively slender stakes, driven into the ground, would be possible unless they were thus held. *The orange-and-black staining described above should, then, represent close-hurdling or wattle-work.* It is likely that there was no wide gap or entrance in the circle; 57 holes out of an estimated total of 64 were plotted; the missing 7 are widely distributed under my balks, as the plan shows. Nevertheless, we are studying a hut of some sort.

[1] A ditch surrounding the barrow was searched for by extending the north–south trench in both directions, but no evidence of such was obtained.

[2] Stake-holes of exactly this character '3–4 inches in diameter outlined by a ring of oxide-impregnated soil' and '8 inches to a foot deep' were found in Wales by H. Noel Jerman in a Bronze Age barrow on Caebetin Hill, Kerry, Mont., in 1931 (*Montgomeryshire Collections*, 1932, pp. 176–81). The circle was from 17 ft. 4 in. to 19 ft. 6 in. in diameter; there were 36 holes, from 15 to 32 in. apart. From the fragmentary remains of pottery the present writer judged the barrow to 'be contemporary with the first phase of the overhanging-rim urn'.

The '38-ft.' circle (range of diameters 37 ft. 11 in.–40 ft. 4 in.) was almost completely uncovered, 79 stake-holes out of an estimated total of 96 being plotted. The spacing of the stake-holes is remarkably even; 66 measurements from centre to centre of the holes were taken, and the average distance between the stakes was 1 ft. 3 in. No staining of the turf-stack indicative of wattling between these stakes was observed. It will be seen on the plan that while the northern half of the 38-ft. circle comes within the area of the turf-stack the southern half is outside it. Here, then, there was no staining or hardening of the soil composing or ringing the stake-hole as is the case where hard-pan is present; and only the closest scrutiny of the probable alignment enabled the holes to be found.

The '48-ft.' circle (range of diameters 48 ft. 7 in.–48 ft. 11 in.) was detected because on the north side it was near enough to the turf-stack for a few holes to be iron-stained (sections A–A' and B–B', Figure 74). Assuming that it was another circle, its radius was measured and clearing along its probable line began; confirmation was obtained through the occasional appearance of a vertical hole in the barrow, and soft dark circular stains on the floor at regular intervals. These were only 1–1 $\frac{1}{2}$ in. in diameter, and the circle must have been of wands rather than of stakes. The determination was ultimately certain; but had not those two iron-stained holes been found, the sustained and close examination needed to prove a fourth circle would never have been initiated.

Twenty-five measurements from stake-hole to stake-hole in the circle were taken; the extreme variation was from 1 ft. 2 in. to 1 ft. 6 in. and the average interspace 16·0 in.

We now return to the central part of the barrow, where the 18-ft. circle (range of diameters 17 ft. 11 in.–18 ft. 11 in.) is irregular; there are wide gaps where it is certain stakes were never driven into the ground, and the distances apart of those holes which are in series show a variability so wide as to render the striking of an average useless. The type of hole seen in the other circles—evidencing a stake driven straight in—is seen here, but two other types occur: an angular dug hole, in the centre of which the stake is placed, and a cone-shaped hole, the stake being screwed in on its point. The depth is similar to that in the case of the other circles—about 1 ft. Most of the stake-holes were of the same size as those of the 28-ft. and 38-ft. circles; the rest were definitely larger—a significant fact.

Lastly, it should be said that the circles appear to have been struck from the same centre, the nearest approximation to the position of which is shown on the plan by a cross; but they were most probably measured off circle by circle, each from the one within it. The final form of the barrow (its greatest diameter is north–south) appears to have been influenced by that of the turf-stack, rather than by the circles.

*The Revetment Stakes: Repair Work.* In clearing the north-western quadrant of the barrow a series of stake-holes was found which were related not to the hut and other stake-circles but to the margin of the turf-stack (which —see plan—here extends outwards from the line of the 38-ft. circle to touch the 48-ft. circle). They were first seen high up in the barrow immediately below the plough-soil, and on being followed downwards were found to curve inwards (Plate 40a, outer row). *Clearly they represented stakes thrust out by pressure; and, since they were on the edge of the turf-stack, this pressure must have been exerted by the stack itself.* Moreover, their ends were found to rest in the grey clay—already mentioned—which here formed the basal portion of the turf-stack, not in the ancient surface soil as do all the circle stakes. As there was in this area a spill-over of turf from the stack into the zone of the loamy soil which surrounds it, the only possible conclusion is that the stack, being here insecure, was revetted or reinforced before the soil addition was made which completed the barrow structure.

Figure 68 is a drawing of the west face of my trench A–A' at the north

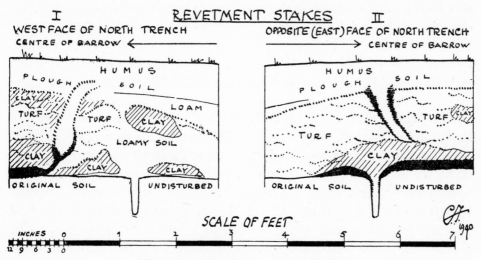

Figure 68. Sheeplays 293'. Stake-holes

end (Plate 40a), together with a sketch made on the opposite side of this trench. In the first section hard-pan (black, horizontal) is seen merging into the foot of the revetment stake-hole set in the clayey base of the stack; this stake-hole is bent outwards, has an orange and black border and base, and a greyish centre. Lumps of greyish clay, with orange and black turfy material, mingle with the casing of loamy soil on the right of the stake-hole. Deep in the floor of the barrow, one of the stake-holes of the 48-ft. circle is shown.

In the opposite section the whole turf-stack is seen to have collapsed outwards and spread itself to the angle of rest, prior to the addition of the loam casing (which therefore is not seen in the drawing). The revetment stake had its foot in the clay base of the turf stack and is bent outwards more heavily than its neighbour; one of the 48-ft. stake-holes here comes within the limits of the hard-pan and consequently was clearly visible as an orange-and-black circle on the surface thereof. It had a grey clayey core.

These two sections are thus variants on the same theme; they show how different in detail the effects of a given cause may be at closely adjacent points.

It is remarkable that, measured at their fairly high surviving level, these stake-holes are as constant in their distances apart as are the stake-holes of the circles in the ground. Fifteen distances, measured from centre to centre of the holes, vary by only 3 in.—from 1 ft. 2 in. to 1 ft. 5 in.; it follows that large stretches of these revetment posts bent and broke without changing their lateral intervals—that is, they were tied together by some form of wattling. And it is equally interesting to observe that the average distance between the posts is 15·7 in.; they represent then the identical technique used in the construction of the stake-circles.

*The Secondary Burials and the Charcoal Deposit.* There were four secondary burials by cremation, only one of which was in an urn; none had any grave-goods. Of these two are in the turf-stack and two in the soil zone of the barrow (see plan, Figure 65). Only the outermost, cremation E, needs mention here. This is an interesting example of one of the cordoned-urn types of the west (Plate 41b and Figure 69), to be dated in the Late Bronze Age: it is a small vessel, 9·0 in. high, of poorly baked ware. The rim-angle and shoulder of the earlier overhanging-rim urn have developed into a succession of hollow curves and ridges. One cannot speak of

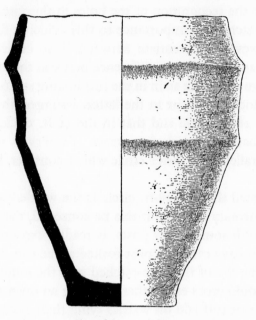

Figure 69. Sheeplays 293′. Urn—secondary

debasement; a new type, with its own character and values, has arisen. A similar urn in the National Museum of Wales comes from Towyn, Merioneth.

*Commentary.* A major problem of Sheeplays 293′ is the interpretation of the stake-circles. It will be recalled that the 18-ft. stake-holes were irregular in spacing and size—sometimes large, but the regularity of the 28-ft., 38-ft., and 48-ft. circles was remarkable and the same technique was clearly employed in the construction of all of them.

The average distances between the centres of the stake-holes in these circles were respectively 1 ft. 3·6 in., 1 ft. 3·3 in., 1 ft. 4 in. Some standard system of wattling or interlacement which provided for a given number of verticals in a given length of construction must be invoked to account for this almost mathematical accuracy. These 28-ft., 38-ft., and 48-ft. circles again were probably alike in showing no portal of entry. The 28-ft. circle was completely examined except where balks crossed it; five-sixths of the 38-ft. circle was also examined and there was only one missing stake-hole. Nearly a third of the 48-ft. circle was examined; there were two missing stake-holes; but the recognition of the holes in this circle was so difficult[1] that I cannot attach great importance to this evidence for a gap.

We can, however, differentiate between these circles. The 48-ft. was but a ring of wands; whilst the difference between the 28-ft. and the 38-ft. is that the orange and black stain in the turf linking stake-hole to stake-hole in the former does not occur in the latter. I suggest that there was close wattling in the 28-ft. circle and that in the 38-ft. circle the wattling was open—a mere band of interlacing weave at intervals to hold the stakes upright and parallel. This latter circle will, I consider, have been a fence, 4 or 5 ft. high.

I have suggested that the 28-ft. circle is the wattled wall of a House of the Dead,[2] a mortuary hut: and if this be conceded, the inner 18-ft. circle, irregular, and with some larger posts, is readily explained. Every hole of this circle would have carried a post forked at the top, supporting a rafter set radially; at the top of the high-pitched roof the longest of these brush-wood rafters would cross each other, forming an open network, wigwam fashion. Heather or turf laid on wattles tying these rafters together would form the roof.

The holes may seem small to accommodate posts capable of supporting such a large roof. In this connection a remark made in a letter from my friend T. C. Lethbridge, F.S.A., is relevant. 'In the Viking houses' (in Iceland), he says, 'there are rows of posts marking aisles. I saw three cleared ones, and was interested to see how small the post-holes were. They could hardly have had anything in them much bigger than a prop for a clothes-line, and yet one of the houses was huge, 100 feet long inside at least.'

The turf-stack provides problems hardly less interesting than that of the circles. In the first place, since the shafts of the stakes have in many cases been traced to the present top of the stack (the surface soil, that is, of the barrow), it is certain that no decay of these stakes had set in when it was built, and that the turf-stack is part of the original design.

Now since the 28-ft. circle was almost certainly a complete wattled and roofed hut and the 38-ft. circle a close 'fence', it is difficult to see how the

[1] A dark smear on the ancient surface, freshly exposed with the polished blade of a spade applied horizontally, is the primary indication.

[2] Compare the Ritual Hut at Cassington, Oxon, *Oxoniensia*, 1946–7, pp. 5 ff., and see *Early Cultures in North-West Europe*, 1950, p. 61. Mortimer (*Forty Years' Researches*, pp. 154 ff. and Figs. 397 and 400) describes a hut of this sort in a Yorkshire barrow.

stack could have been constructed at all. We must, I think, assume that gaps were made in the 'walls' (and fences) above ground-level, the posts being cut short. The inconveniences resulting from building a stack by carrying, or passing, turves into a hut, and also by making a ramp immediately outside it, conforming to its curve, are I think reflected in a curiosity of the construction, the dip between the ramps and the main mass of the stack—*which is the exact line of the wattled walls*: the turves here could not be packed tightly enough! They were, however, packed more tightly in the northern quadrants, for the posts (and the wattling in places) remained upright. This tight packing was essential, as we shall see; for there was a high external platform on this side to be supported.

In the course of this work the floor of the hut was heavily trampled like the rest of the area which was being covered by the stack, providing the impervious stratum needed for the formation of hard-pan.

A remarkable feature of the stack is the lack of correspondence with the plan of the circles in the northern segment, where its margin moves outward from the 38-ft. circle. This lack of correspondence caused us much mystification in the course of the investigation. Since the whole foundational symbolism consists of circles, the introduction of an elliptical turf barrow on the circle basis, destroying the correspondence between the hut and its envelope, seemed inexplicable. But when it became probable that the wings of the turf barrow formed rising ramps which curved round the outside of a wattled hut wall, a serviceable explanation dawned. It may first be recalled that at Pond Cairn there was evidence for a ritual movement of men round the turf-stack, controlled, it was thought, from the flat top of the stack (p. 112).

*The ramps at Sheeplays, then, provided ways for those persons who were controlling ritual*[1] *to reach the flat top of the stack.* The greater part of this top, however, was occupied by the upper part of the sacred hut; and there would have been, if correspondence with the 38-ft. circle was to be adhered to (see plan), a space only 5 ft. wide from hut wall to stack edge— hardly broad enough for dignity—or action! *The stack was therefore extended on the north side of the hut*, making a platform 11 ft. wide. It was in this very area that, as we have seen, the turf-stack was in danger of collapse, and

[1] As well, no doubt, as serving the practical purpose of providing a means of dumping turf into the hut from the top, after filling from the bottom had reached the limits of practicability.

was propped up by revetment stakes. The extra weight—of men on the stack—would suffice to account for the collapse, and the care taken in the matter of repair attests the importance of this part of the structure; these considerations render my explanation of the elliptical form of the stack offered above the more probable.

The soil barrow now claims attention. It is prehistoric, for secondary cremation burials were in it. But the question as to whether it was part of the original design still remains open. On this it may first be said that the wattling of the revetment stakes, though necessarily of soft sapwood, was still undecayed when the soil addition stopped further movement of the turf-stack, for the lateral distances of the stakes were constant from their bases upwards, though they were bent and broken. This is a pointer: the question is settled by the fact that stake-holes of the 38-ft. circle in the south-east quadrant could be detected high up in the soil barrow. They were vertical, hence no decay had set in in this circle where it was covered with soil; again, this circle existed contemporaneously with the inner circles (28-ft. and 18-ft.), for it was covered by the turf barrow throughout part of its circumference.

I conclude that the extent of time intervening between the construction of the turf barrow and the addition of the soil barrow was no more than long enough to allow for the partial collapse and reinforcement of the former: a ritual interval between, let us say, seed-time and harvest is indicated.

The only fact which appears to traverse this induction is that the 28-ft. circle—the presumed wattled walls of the hut—had collapsed inwards under the pressure of the soil barrow in the southern quadrants (p. 134); for, if it was due to decay, it suggests a longer interval than is consistent with the integrity of the 38-ft. circle. But as we have seen, the turf within the hut on the south side was not tightly packed, and the collapse of the wall due to the weight of the soil casing might have occurred long afterwards. Alternatively, the hut may have been intentionally wrecked before envelopment.[1]

---

[1] Mortimer included, in the observations already referred to, evidence that the 'huts' in two of his barrows had been wrecked before envelopment, *op. cit.*, pp. 156 and 183. See also Stuart Piggott, 'Timber Circles, a Re-examination', *Arch. Journ.*, 1939, esp. p. 218. Here he urges that the majority of the Dutch palisade barrows began with a burial made on the floor of a hut, and cites evidence for the collapse of a hut in one barrow. These are described in a famous book: W. Glasbergen, *The Eight Beatitudes*, 1956.

*Summary.* The history of Sheeplays 293′, as determined by fact and inference, may then be summarized as follows:

A well-born youth who probably lived close to a marshy flat fed by the springs now known as 'Six Wells' died about 1000 B.C.; his cremated remains, placed in an overhanging-rim urn, were interred on the adjacent upland. A low earth-dome marked the site; it was carefully built, and at an intermediate and the final stages of its construction tree branches were laid, criss-cross fashion, on it. We are reminded of the vegetation deposit with which the ceremonies associated with the contemporary burial in Pond Cairn ended. Close around the dome, ritual acts were performed, as evidenced by stake-holes and hollows which seem to have played no part in subsequent events.

A circular hut with wattled walls and a roof support of internal posts was built round the interment; the hut was symbolic, not functional—a mortuary house. Two concentric fences were then made, farther out, of close-set stakes (inner) or wands (outer) probably linked by one or more strands of wattling.

While the fences and the hut were still intact, the third phase of the action began. The hut was filled with turves, and it, together with the concentric fencing, was partly buried in a stack of this material. The height of the turf-stack was probably that of the eaves of the hut, and it was approximately circular, with a bulge on the north side which provided a platform presumably for ritual acts; curved ramps led up to this platform on either side of the hut. The platform collapsed, but was repaired.

After an interval so short that no decay had taken place even in the slender outer (48-ft.) fence and while the collapse of the platform was still in progress, a casing of soil was dumped around, and possibly also on top of, the turf-stack.

Thereafter secondary burials also of the Bronze Age were placed in the mound, which probably presented, before modern ploughing reduced it, a flat-topped steep-sided profile.

## SHEEPLAYS 279′, *c.* 900 B.C.

This small barrow was situated 44 yds. (centre to centre) from Sheeplays 293′, lower down a gentle slope, so heavily ploughed down as to be almost invisible. It was dug, necessarily, in wet winter weather, the burial, the

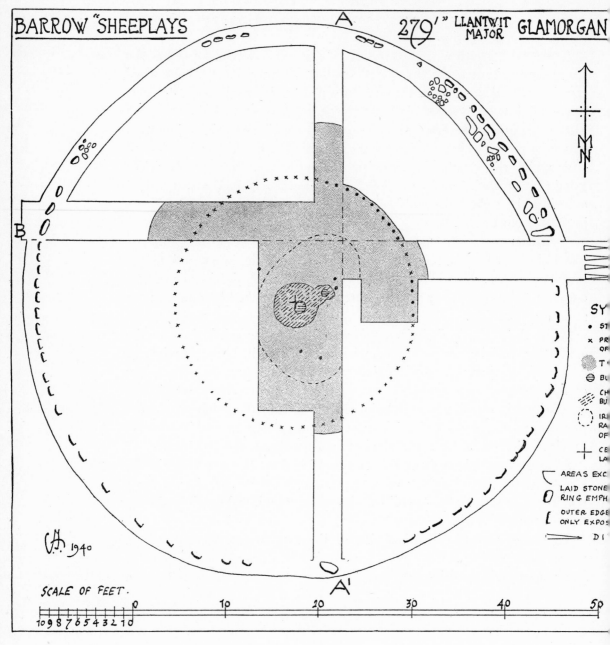

Figure 70

144

stone ring, and the hard-pan floor being recorded. A return to the site, under better conditions, demonstrated the ring of stake-holes. Around two primary cremation burials without grave-goods was a circle of stake-holes, representing the wall of a hut; other stake-holes were found within the circle (roof supports) (Figure 70). The barrow structure was of turf with a casing of soil; it had a marginal stone ring and was possibly ditched. A detailed description follows.

*The Burials.* The position of the two primary deposits is seen in the plan, Figure 70, and their centres are shown by pegs (and a ranging pole) in Plate 42a. The detail is presented in Figure 71. Cremation I was the more

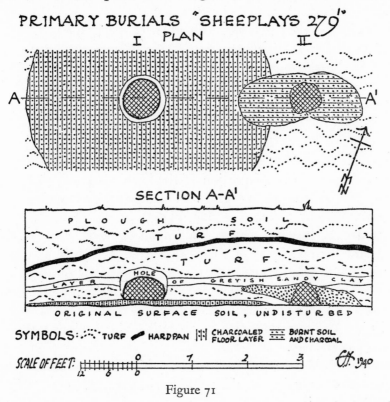

Figure 71

important: it was at ground-level. On a layer 4½ ft. in diameter of greasy dark soil and charcoal—material from the pyre—was a compact mass, 8 in. in diameter, of burnt bones, clean and white, enveloped in a granular reddish-brown substance which had lost all coherence. This substance was

145

about $\frac{1}{10}$ in. thick and was doubtless a leather bag which had collapsed, for there was a hole above the deposit. Orange and black turfy soil of the character familiar in these investigations surrounded the deposit.

Three feet away to the east-north-east was the second cremation. There was a small quantity of burnt bones, loosely distributed, clean like the other. Surrounding this deposit was reddened soil and charcoal which extended on the west side into the layers of turf which surrounded cremation I; *thus it had been deposited after the process of building turves round cremation I had begun, and before it was completed.*

A continuous layer of the usual grey-blue clayey soil covered one deposit, and enveloped the other.

Since both cremations must be regarded as primary, and contemporary, the age and sex of the persons concerned are of special interest. Cremation I is of an adult and a child; cremation II of a child not more than 11 years of age. The contrast between the technique of these two deposits is striking; some day we may hope that the significance of this and kindred phenomena will be understood. Provisionally, the latter may be regarded as sacrificial.

*The Barrow.* The turfy soil which covered the cremations extended outwards to form the central portion of the barrow—a mass approximately circular, probably about 31–32 ft. in diameter; its margins were only determined at four points (see plan, Figure 70 and sections, Figure 74). In or under the turf was a fairly continuous layer of hard-pan. This was domed and hummocky over the central area, being highest above the cremations, and was for the most part at ground-level on the fringe. The existence of the domed portion implies a pause in the construction of the barrow; for trampling, no doubt of a ritual character as at barrow 293′, must be invoked to produce the comparatively impervious layer on which the hard-pan formed.

Over the hard-pan the turfy mass, which showed much grey clay everywhere, extended up to the plough soil; but the barrow at its highest was only 1 ft. 8 in. above the original ground, and there was not much stratified deposit available for study in the cross-sections.

Beyond the edge of the turf there was a casing of loamy soil; on the east side (see section B–B′, Figure 74) this soil was overlaid by the yellow Lias subsoil of the district.

146

*The Stake-holes.* The weather conditions when this barrow was dug did not render the discovery of stake-holes in the quadrant trenches likely: but when these were found in Sheeplays 293' a search was made beyond the trench limits and a series of 15 readily found. When 83° of the arc of the circle had been disclosed (see Plate 42) sufficient had been done to suggest that this barrow had a ritual hut of the same character as, but less well-made than, Sheeplays 293', and the work was discontinued. The circle was evidently set out with the north-west margin of cremation I as a centre; the radius from this centre at one end of the arc was 12 ft. 8 in., at the other end 13 ft.—as close an approximation to a true circle as one could expect to get in prehistoric layouts. The stake-holes were of exactly the same character as those in the second and third circles of Sheeplays 293'; they were *c.* $2\frac{1}{2}$–3 in. in diameter. They ranged from 10 in. to 17 in. apart, and centre to centre, averaged 13·3 in.

A few smaller stake-holes were found in the neighbourhood of the primary interments, which may possibly represent an inner circle. Nothing resembling the irregular holes found near the central cremation in Sheeplays 293' was seen.

*The Stone-ring.* Extension of the four trenches outwards disclosed a ring of stones—Lias boulders and pebbles from the neighbourhood. These were laid flat on the ground and many were 'paper thin'; *the builders had lost interest in the technique* and, spiritually no doubt, in its efficacy. (Compare Talbenny, or Pond Cairn!) The northern half of the ring was completely explored; in the southern half the positions of the rims of the outer stones only were fixed—this in order to determine the exact form of the barrow.

In the northern half there were many gaps, probably due to casual removal of stones long after the construction of the ring. The ring seemed to be in its original condition in the north-east quadrant; here there was a double row of stones, from 1·9 ft. to 2·2 ft. in total breadth (Plate 42b). Two groups of pebbles will be noticed, such as would develop if stones and boulders were collected by all and sundry, including the children, and deposited in heaps on the line of the ring, and if those charged with the business of placing them properly selected those they wanted and left the rest.

The setting-out of the ring is accurate. The margin of cremation I is the centre, as it is for the stake-circle. The diameter of the barrow can thus be determined as 56–57 ft.

147

*Summary.* The barrow is a construction by the same folk who built Sheep-lays 293' adjacent. The domed-up mass over the burial deposit, the stake-circle, representing a mortuary hut?, the turf-stack and the casing, prove this. The secondary cremation is regarded as sacrificial. The structure will be of later date than 293', since the central burials had no grave-goods. The stone-ring, for which 293' offers no parallel, is, as we have seen, met with in other barrows in the district; its character here, degenerate and symbolic rather than structural, also points to a late date. A small surrounding ditch is possible, but unproven. The accuracy of the setting-out of the quadrant of the stake-circle examined, and more particularly and certainly of the stone-ring, is notable: we may surmise that mensuration was part of the ritual, a feature in the training for office, chiefly or priestly.

## 'RITUAL' BARROWS

There are two 'barrows' of the turf-mound type, erected solely or primarily for ritual purposes: Six Wells 267' and 271', both in Llantwit Major parish. As Figure 40 suggests, they are both on the same farmland. 267' was erected for ritual purposes: in 271' the burial is subordinate in the layout to the ritual. It is likely that a 'ritual hut' of some sort was present in each. The former is assigned to the Middle, the latter to the Late, Bronze Ages.

## SIX WELLS 267', *c.* 900 B.C.

This 'barrow' (Plate 43) was situated by the roadside opposite the Elizabethan house known as Six Wells Farm; it was bisected by a hedge-bank and ditch, and measured 49 ft. from north to south, 45 ft. from east to west.

*Argument.* Around a deposit presumably of a ritual character was an irregular 'circle' of stake-holes with an entry on the north-west side: the 'barrow' structure was of turf. A detailed description follows:

*The Ritual* (?) *Deposit.* At a point near the centre of the 'barrow' a small dome was seen with an encircling hollow (rather like a small-scale model of a ditched bell-barrow), the whole being not more than 3 ft. in diameter (Figure 72 and Plate 44A). Excavation revealed a cylindrical hole beneath

(a) 'OHR' urn (primary)    (b) Cordoned urn (secondary)

PLATE 41. SHEEPLAYS 293', LLANTWIT MAJOR, GLAMORGAN

(a) The cremations and stake-holes

(b) Stone ring

PLATE 42. SHEEPLAYS 279', LLANTWIT MAJOR, GLAMORGAN

PLATE 43. SIX WELLS 267', LLANTWIT MAJOR, GLAMORGAN: Site completed; stake-holes pegged

PLATE 44A. SIX WELLS 267', LLANTWIT MAJOR, GLAMORGAN: Dome of the ritual pit

PLATE 44B. SHEEPLAYS 293', LLANTWIT MAJOR, GLAMORGAN: The 28' and 38' circles, north-west quadrant

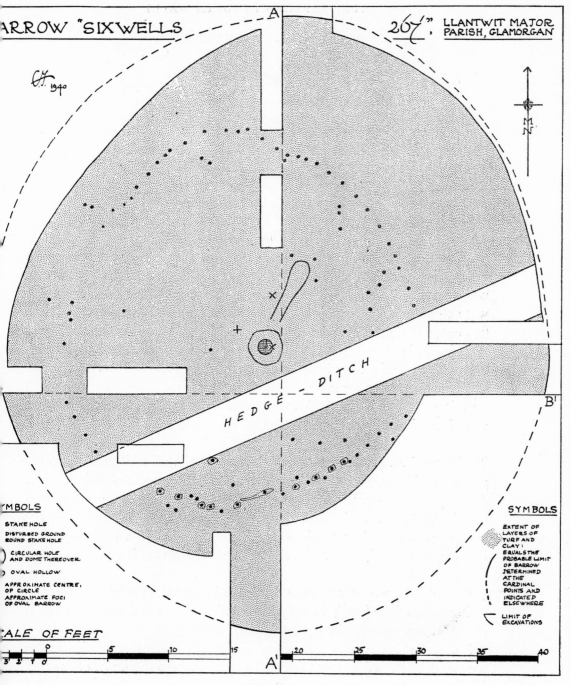

ARROW "SIXWELLS

$26\frac{7}{7}''$ LLANTWIT MAJOR
PARISH, GLAMORGAN

CH. 1940

HEDGE DITCH

A

A'

B'

M
N

SYMBOLS

STAKE HOLE

DISTURBED GROUND
ROUND STAKE HOLE

CIRCULAR HOLE
AND DOME THEREOVER

OVAL HOLLOW

APPROXIMATE CENTRE
OF CIRCLE
APPROXIMATE FOCI
OF OVAL BARROW

SYMBOLS

EXTENT OF
LAYERS OF
TURF AND
CLAY:
EQUALS THE
PROBABLE LIMIT
OF BARROW
DETERMINED
AT THE
CARDINAL
POINTS AND
INDICATED
ELSEWHERE

LIMIT OF
EXCAVATIONS

ALE OF FEET

0   5   10   15   20   25   30   35   40

3 2 1 0

Figure 72

12—L.D.B.A.

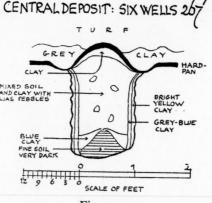

Figure 73

the dome, 1 ft. 2 in. in diameter and 19 in. deep. This was lined with yellow clay to even out the roughnesses of the sides; over the yellow clay was a coating of grey-blue clay about 1 in. thick. At the bottom (which was determined with certainty as 'undisturbed subsoil') was a pile of dark fine earth, not greasy, and containing nothing of tangible size. This was surrounded by fine-grained 'alluvial' clay; over all was mixed stony soil, very compact, of local origin, domed up with clay. There was no trace of charcoal or bone either in or around the hole.

Adjacent to the hole a shallow elongated hollow, 6 ft. in length, attracted attention (plan, Figure 72); it contained no artefacts.

*The 'Barrow' Structure.* The 'barrow' consists of turf and its undersoil—grey clay without stones, similar material to the turf-stacks already studied. A complication—which spoils the sections, Figure 74—is the farm ditch cut diagonally across the structure, destroying every feature in its path.

The present maximum height is 2 ft., but this includes 10 in., more or less, of plough soil, and the surviving barrow structure is thus only 14 in. deep, or less.

'Hard-pan' covers the floor and extends in a smooth unbroken layer to the margins of the 'turf'; the only irregularity being the dome of the ritual pit which was covered by it, as Figure 73 shows.

I suggest that the barrow consisted solely of turf; for an extension of the west trench (12 yd.) and north trench (6 yd.) beyond the limits of the turf disclosed nothing but loamy soil without evidence of stratification and no trace of a ditch. The profile, moreover, suggests a turf-mound rather

150

than a turf-stack. This turf-mound is oval in shape, measuring 48 ft. × 45 ft. No charcoal was found in the structure or on its hard-pan floor, or under the hard-pan.

*The Stake-holes.* Numerous stake-holes were located under the mound, as the plan, Figure 72 and Plate 43, show. The majority form a 28-ft. circle which is fairly true except for a bulge in the north-west quadrant which brings the diameter in one direction up to 30 ft. It is most regular in the north-east quadrant, as the plan indicates; there are occasional stake-holes outside the circle, including three, two on one side and one on the other, of a 6-ft. gap in the ring on the north-west side, flanking the entry.

Distinct differences were noted in the character of the holes in the various parts of the circle. In the south-west and most of the south-east quadrants the holes are large, some squarish, and tending to run together, or close-set in pairs. They resemble the holes under the hard-pan in the central complex of Sheeplays 293'. In the north-east and part of the north-west quadrants the holes are normal orange-rimmed circles, 3–4 in. in diameter; in the rest of the north-west quadrant (working anti-clockwise) the holes became smaller until they were either small black smears or a soft patch of soil. Only those of which one could be reasonably certain are plotted in this segment—gaps will be noticed. Thereafter the orange-rimmed holes pick up again suddenly.

*Inside* the circle are no less than twenty-one stake-holes, none of which can be said to define an inner ring of roof supports. Seventeen of these are concentrated in an area—the south-eastern—less than one-half of the circle, in which the ritual deposit is situated. We may reasonably suppose that they had some relation to the ceremonial. The pattern as a whole suggests that the larger area next to the entry was reserved for privileged spectators.

There was an important difference between the holes in this and in previous barrows; for here none was seen in the hard-pan or in the turf-mound. Had any been present they would certainly have been noticed, for the digging party had gained ample experience. All, then, were found under the hard-pan; showing mostly as circles of yellowish sandy soil with an orange rim in the surrounding natural loam. Sometimes they had a core of dark fine soil. Occasionally the filling of the hole was of grey sandy clay from the turf-mound above.

The inference is clear: every one of the posts or stakes in the area was

151

drawn before the raising of the mound was begun. If, as I suppose, these appearances represent a 'ritual hut' of the usual diameter, 28 ft., the formula had become simplified.

*Commentary.* Six Wells 267′ is a product of the same culture as that manifested in the Sheeplays barrows. The domed central deposit, the stake-circle (ritual hut?), the turf of which the mound is composed, demonstrate this. I believe it to be later in date.

The initial date of the culture must for us, at the moment, be that of Sheeplays 293′, that is *c.* 1000 B.C.; and we can thus approximately place (at *c.* 900? or later) a type of barrow hitherto undated. This type, which I term a *'ritual barrow'*, as being built over a construction which is not a burial, received little or no attention until after this work was first published in 1941; though records of 'empty graves' and 'cists', and cenotaphs—barrows lacking any indication, to the particular observer, of an interment or anything else to account for their existence—are not uncommon in the earlier literature.

In the case of Six Wells 267′ we have an elaborate little structure sufficiently near the centre to justify the view that it is the causative agent of the barrow: a structure in which there is no adequate reason to suspect the former presence of any part of a human body. The absence of charcoal or reddened earth, either in the little pit or anywhere in the central area, and the negative results of the careful examination of the floor for signs of disturbed ground indicative of a burial, buttress this opinion.

Ritual, then, is held to have been carried out in the south-east segment of the floor, the rest of the area being for privileged spectators who entered a broad gap in the stake-circle: the stakes, considered to represent a house, were probably only 2–3 ft. high. The destruction of a broad belt across the barrow by agricultural operations introduces, it is true, an element of doubt; but the plan does not suggest this zone as a likely area for a primary burial deposited by a people of this culture, having regard to the central position of the primary deposits in Sheeplays 293′ and 279′. A barrow of related character awaits consideration, and it is here sufficient to say that a concept and a ritual which involved the labour of erecting such a structure over so materially insignificant a deposit must have represented an important element in the life and culture of the folk concerned.

The stake-circle of Six Wells 267' combines in one structure features found in several circles in Sheeplays 293'. There are numerous holes resulting from the driving-in of stakes, and there are many larger angular holes, similar to some found in the 18-ft. circle. Sheeplays 293' provides also a parallel to the absence of evidence of stake-holes in or over the hard-pan, for many of the enigmatic holes surrounding the central burial in this barrow were only discovered after the hard-pan had been removed.

In discussing Sheeplays 293' it was pointed out that stake-holes found under the hard-pan can only represent stakes removed before the barrow was erected; thus a technique employed at 293' in the case of a comparatively few posts near the central burial was at 267' adopted for the whole of the timber structure. But since some of the holes were filled with material from the turf barrow, the stakes must have been drawn immediately prior to its erection (or they would have been filled, by natural agencies, with soil). Hence stake-structure and barrow form part of the one design.

Professor Stuart Piggott in a paper previously referred to interprets the duplication and erratic distribution of circles of post-holes in many barrows as representing reconstruction and replacement of elements of the original hut; barrow 267' is the only one of mine which offers a possible example of such a practice. The theory would conveniently account for the different ways of placing the posts in the ground and for variations in size. The diameter of the circle, 28 ft., is consistent with the theory. But the inner circle of posts which a hut of such size seems to demand is lacking: moreover, the slenderness of the posts flanking the entrance is surprising. If the structure were a hut it was symbolic like that at Sheeplays 293', not functional, for there was no charcoal or human rubbish of any sort on the floor within the circle.

The two cremation barrows, Sheeplays 293' and 279', and the 'ritual' barrow, Six Wells 267', represent a Middle Bronze Age culture widespread in the South Wales sea-plain and on the opposite coast of the Bristol Channel. Certain features of this culture, stake-circle, turf-stacks, and stone-rings, are already familiar, having been observed in the much earlier barrow at Talbenny in Pembrokeshire (p. 39, above); the huts had not previously been recorded in connection with it.

The view that a barrow may be a structure designed in the course of, and for the performance of, burial ritual, first suggested for Pond Cairn,

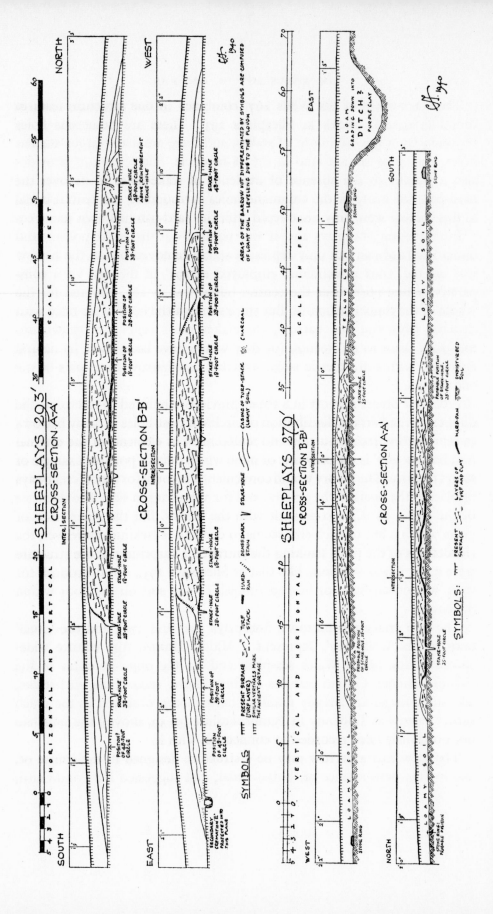

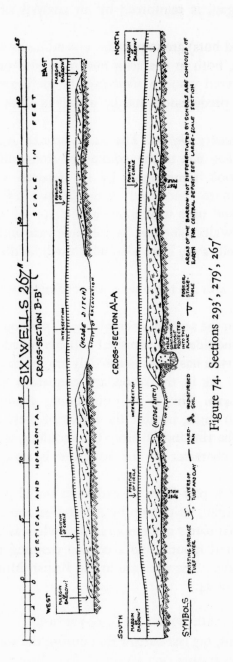

Figure 74. Sections 293', 279', 267'

Bridgend, Glamorgan, is reinforced by an analysis of the turf-stack in Sheeplays 293'.

These circles (and huts) are important, extending as they do our knowledge of the range, both in character and plan, and of the technique of construction, of sacred wooden structures in prehistoric Britain, gained by the work of my predecessors and by myself in West Wales.

*Late Bronze Age Pottery Defined.* The Late Bronze Age which may be dated from about 800 B.C. to the coming of iron-using invaders, *c.* 450 B.C., is in this book represented by (i) debased OHR urns (Plate 49a); (ii) by elaborate 'encrusted' urns (Figure 27) (p. 37); (iii) by straight-sided 'bucket' urns with moulded collars (of which we have no examples in South Wales); and (iv) by a unique vase with flared rim found in a barrow (Six Wells 271', Plate 48b) which will be described in the next section.

The *debased OHR urns* are the only ones needing more precise definition here.

(*a*) *Biconical.* As in the secondary cremation, Ysceifiog, Flints (Figure 5). In this group the shoulder has vanished and the junction of the rim and body of the earlier type has become the only angle the pot presents.

(*b*) *With Cordons.* As in the secondary cremation E, Sheeplays 293', Glamorgan, Plate 41b. This is an outstanding example, with its two cordons rising to an angle, because the *origins* of these elements (*a*) from the lower edge of the rim and (*b*) from the shoulder, is still recognizable, though the visual character of the structure is now something quite different.

Plate 49 provides a pair from an extensive burial group excavated at Colwinston, Glamorgan, written up by Aileen Fox and the writer in 1941. They must be approximately contemporary but whereas 'A' is recognizably OHR, 'B' has a flared mouth, and a cordon defining the upper unit of design, not a rim-edge. The urns are in the British Museum: the plan of the barrow on Figure 84.

### SIX WELLS 271', *c.* 700 B.C.

The account of this, my last barrow dug during the war on Government land hereabouts, illustrating one aspect of Late Bronze Age pot-making

---

[1] *Archaeologia Cambrensis*, 1941, pp. 185–92.

and ritual procedure, will begin—and may also end—with an anecdote.
Six Wells 271', 280 yds. north of Six Wells 267' (Figure 72), was on the
edge of the newly levelled airfield close to a rough hedge with stunted
oaks: being 90 ft. in diameter and over 6 ft. high it was, in this flat landscape,
a dominating, and yet—thanks to the oak trees—a not very noticeable
feature. I had to break off my field work when barrow 267' was finished to
deal with urgent Museum matters; so I begged the Adjutant to have the
mound wired off with an official notice to keep the bulldozers from push-
ing it away. He was a friendly person and readily agreed to do so.

When I came back the mound was wired all right, for the coils lay in
profusion, but it was not the shape I knew! While I was negotiating the
first coil in the long grass a face with an unfamiliar military headgear
appeared at the top and shouted. I was too astonished to retreat, and the
head was quickly replaced by another. This person said in good English
that he was an officer of the Royal Netherlands Army, in charge of the
defence of the aerodrome, and this was one of his machine-gun posts:
'Go away!'

I retreated a few paces, and then said, 'I am an official of a national
museum of my country, and this is a prehistoric burial mound, which my
Government has instructed me to examine before it is destroyed for
security reasons: please come down and talk to me!'

'Ah,' he said cheerfully, leaping down through the barbed wire, 'I
understand! I attended Professor Van Giffen's lectures at Groningen
University, and I know all about it! You shall dig your mound, and I shall
find another place for my guns!' (The Professor is an archaeologist of
international repute, known to me personally.) In a few days my new
friend departed to another point on the perimeter, and I took over: in the
event it was seen that only at four points did his sump-pits pierce the ancient
floor: but some secondary burials (I found none) may have been destroyed.

The barrow (Figure 75) proved to be a turf-mound of the same type as
267', but contained, in addition to 'ritual pit' and stake-circle, a cremation
burial in a cist. The structures disclosed will be described in the probable
order of their making: (1) the 'ritual pit'—and its immediate surroundings;
(2) the stake-circle; (3) the cist; (4) the barrow. It will be appreciated, from
what has just been said, that its condition dictated an investigation on the
simplest lines possible. Two broad trenches were accordingly cut at right
angles to one another across the approximate centre of the barrow; further

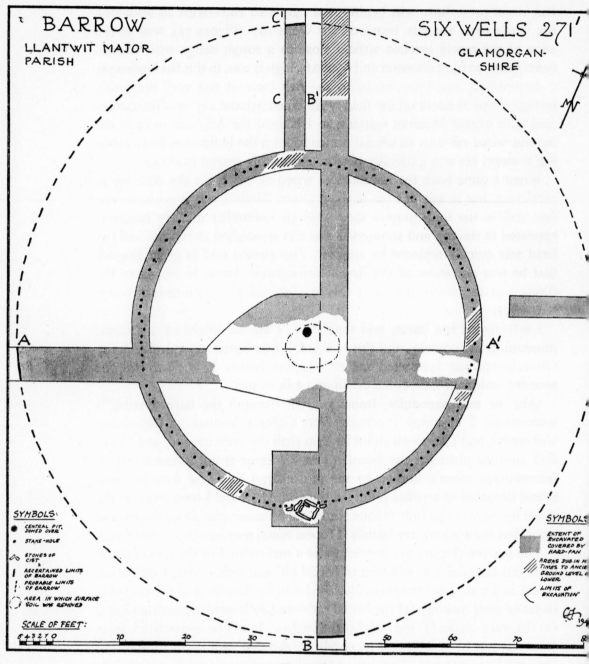

Figure 75

clearances (all down to original ground-level or below it) were limited to the minimum necessary to establish the character and date of the structure. The extent of excavation is indicated on the figure.

*The 'Ritual Pit'.* In the centre of the barrow, at ground level, Plates 45–46, a dome was located, slightly harder than the surrounding barrow material; it was 14 in. high and 16 in. broad at the base, and is seen bisected in Figure 76. It consisted of a shell of mixed soil and clay (Plate 45) enclosing a mass of dark earth with pebbles of the local Lias and chert: and as in the case of barrow 267', there was a circular pit under the dome. This pit (Plate 46a) was 12 in. in diameter, and contained, on one side, similar material to that within the dome; on the other side there was dense grey clay which also appeared to be an artificial deposit.

In order to make sure that the pit did not contain a burial it was opened out to a rock surface (Figure 77), 2 ft. below the base of the dome. The filling here was natural; yellow clay and disintegrating Lias nodules. Figure 76 illustrates the structure in detail; it shows also the character of the barrow around and above it. The layer of 'orange clay', being a colour-change in a natural clay deposit, is probable slightly below the 'floor' hereabouts at the time the dome was constructed. Levels taken at various points suggest that from 6 in. to 9 in. of turf and soil had been removed in the neighbourhood of the 'ritual pit'. This accounts for difficulties of interpretation, and the vagueness of the representation; artificial and natural deposits graded imperceptibly one into another.

Figure 76 shows, in addition to the pit, a dip in the 'orange clay' which can only have been induced by an artificial hollow made immediately above it: the relation of this hollow to the pit is best seen in Plate 46a: it was filled with greyish clay. It will be recalled that an artificial hollow, adjacent to the ritual pit, was demonstrated in barrow 267'.

There was no trace of burning near the pit: no charcoal in it or near it: no evidence of trampling, and no 'dirty' soil around it.

*The 'Untrodden Area'.* Examination of the central portion of the barrow showed that removal of the ancient surface soil extended over a patch of some 30 sq. ft., mostly to the south of the pit. Beyond was an extensive area which, like the central patch, presented a feature rarely seen elsewhere on the barrow floor, namely, absence of hard-pan. This deposit, as we

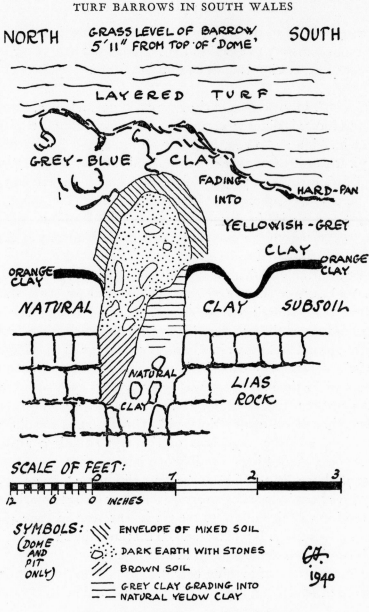

NORTH    GRASS LEVEL OF BARROW,    SOUTH
5' 11" FROM TOP OF 'DOME'

LAYERED   TURF

GREY - BLUE   CLAY

FADING    HARD-PAN
INTO

YELLOWISH - GREY
CLAY

ORANGE              ORANGE
CLAY                  CLAY

NATURAL     CLAY     SUBSOIL

NATURAL
CLAY        LIAS
ROCK

SCALE OF FEET:
0        1        2        3
12    6     0 INCHES

SYMBOLS:    ENVELOPE OF MIXED SOIL
(DOME
AND        DARK EARTH WITH STONES
PIT        BROWN SOIL
ONLY)      GREY CLAY GRADING INTO
NATURAL YELLOW CLAY

CH.
1940

Figure 76. Six Wells 271'. Central dome

have seen,[1] is precipitated on comparatively impervious layers, due almost
certainly to trampling. I conclude then that on the larger area to which I
have referred trespass by the feet of men was avoided; and it is reasonable

[1] Sutton 268', Sheeplays 293', and Pond Cairn.

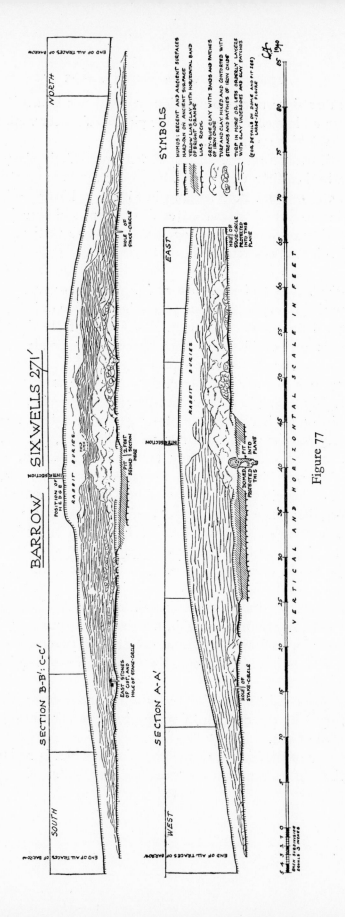

Figure 77

to suggest that since trampling obviously could not be avoided on the patch of ground immediately around the pit, its evidences were destroyed by the removal of the turf layer.

The area is defined on the plan by the absence of stippling, the inner patch by a broken line; under the whole of it the 'orange clay' already referred to was present. Both sections in Figure 77 illustrate the striking difference between the hard-pan-covered (trodden) and bare (untrodden) areas: show the position of the orange band: and indicate the patch where the surface soil has been removed.

*The Stake-circle.* A stake-hole about $2\frac{1}{2}$ in. in diameter and 10 in. deep, defined by a ring of dense black and yellow incrustation of iron oxide, was found in the west trench (Plate 46b). It was 25 ft. from the 'ritual pit'; and a circular trench of this radius being opened up, a complete stake-circle was demonstrated, as shown on the plan, Figure 75.

In the southern part of the circle all the holes were as described above, and were readily found; in the northern part no trace could be seen of the great majority on the hard-pan floor of the barrow; but when the hard-pan was dug away and the natural soil thereunder disclosed, the stake-holes—sometimes unfilled and without any marginal incrustation, sometimes unfilled with a soft black ring, and sometimes filled with earth and so presenting a darker circular stain—were found in the ancient soil and sub-soil. In short, these stakes had been 'drawn' before the barrow was built. This was also the case, it will be recalled, in barrow 267', where the whole of the circle had been so removed (p. 151).

As for the depth, our recording pegs, which were a foot long, some-times dropped into the ancient holes with their tops level with the ground, and it was always possible to press them into a 'yielding' filling for 9 or 10 in. One hole, larger than usual, in the south-east quadrant, was open to a depth of 15 in. As for size, while the great majority seemed to represent stakes from 2 in. to 3 in. in diameter, there were a few of 1–2 in. and still fewer over 3 in.

The number of stake-holes disclosed was 108; there were probably six more, destroyed by the digging of sump pits in recent times (see plan), making a total of 114.

The accuracy of the lay-out of the *ring* of stake-holes is remarkable. A circle struck from the centre of the 'ritual pit' on a radius of exactly 25 ft.

passes through no less than 64 of them, and the maximal error in the case of the other holes within or without the circle thus described is 9 in.: such accuracy is rare in prehistoric lay-outs in this country. Incidentally, of course, it emphasizes the primary importance of the 'ritual pit' in the scheme of the monument.

The distances *between* the stake-holes, on the other hand, was very variable, as a glance at the plan (Figure 75) will show. To the south and south-east of the 'ritual pit', on either side of the cist (p. 164) the spacing of the stakes (24 in number) is most uniform and they were here closest together (± 1 ft); elsewhere only small groups showed any uniformity. Some of the interspaces, especially in the western part of the circle, are so wide (two being as much as 2 ft. 9 in. and 3 ft. 6 in. respectively) as to raise the question of an entrance or entrances. It should be noted that there was a gap in the same part of the circle in barrow 267' (p. 151). The average length of the whole of the interspaces except the two large gaps, 100 in all, is 15·5 in. Both these figures are paralleled in the stake circles of the adjacent barrows. One quadrant of the only circle in Sheeplays 279' was measured; the interspaces averaged 13·3 in. A long series of interspaces of each of three circles in Sheeplays 293' was also studied; they averaged 15·6, 15·3, and 16·0 in. respectively.

It has already been suggested (p. 139) that some standard system (or systems) of wattling or interlacement which provided for a given number of verticals in a given length of hut (or fence) construction would have been employed by the folk living in this district in the Bronze Age: if so, there were two systems hereabouts.

It was expected that evidence of the decayed posts would, on the analogy of the barrow Sheeplays 293', be found in the overlying turf mound; and that since the mound was over 6 ft. high valuable evidence as to the character and height of these fences would be obtained. No such features were present, no stake-hole being found until excavation had been carried close to, or into the ancient surface.

I have said 'close to': for evidence was obtained in the case of three stake-holes widely spaced in the south-eastern quadrant that the stakes were, at the time of the construction of the barrow, some 3 in. high, i.e. above the original ground-level. Plate 46b shows one of the stake-holes, the ground-level being shown by an arrow. The hole ended abruptly and there was no trace of a post in the barrow material above it. Another such hole is described on p. 166. We know that some of the stakes were drawn before the barrow was built; the rest, it would appear, were no more than 3–4 in. high when they were covered up. Two explanations are possible; either the fence formed by the stakes was never any higher than this, being *not a hut, but a hut symbol*, a ritual hut, a 'make-believe' structure: or those stakes which, for some reason unknown, were left in the ground when the barrow was built, were sawn off, a not impossible operation, for bronze saws are known in the Late Bronze Age, and flint saws preceded these. Posts, house-wall high (6–7 ft.), would have got in the way of the barrow-building, as they demonstrably did in barrow 293' at Sheeplays.

Before passing on to the next section, it should be stated that there is no possibility of a second circle having been present within the 50-ft. circle; the floors of the four quadrant trenches, and of the central area, were examined with negative results.

*The Cremation Burial*. The continuity of the stake-circle was broken at one point in a remarkable manner, a cist being encountered on the line of that circle south-south-east of the 'ritual pit' (Plate 47a). It is superficially of a common Bronze Age character and size, consisting fundamentally of four slabby orthostats with a similar stone atop—a stone box, that is, with a cover, the stones being of the local limestone, which dries a dazzling white (Plate 47b). Its minor characteristics are, however, peculiar. It is diamond-shaped, not rectangular; each of the points of the longer axis is extended by a long rectangular stone, and three rounded boulders crown the structure. On the removal of these, and the cover, the orthostatic slabs are seen to be duplicated, in a manner which lessens the area within as well as (on one side) extending it without (Plate 48a).

The cist was constructed in the following manner, illustrated in Figure 78. A broad shallow hole with sloping sides having been made, the stones forming the sides of the cist were wedged up with or bedded in clayey soil. This layer extended round the cist to a height of some 3 in. above the ancient ground-level, and on it the flat stones projecting at either end of the long axis of the structure were laid.

The relation of this cist structure to the stake circle is intimate; its long axis is parallel to the line of stakes, and the placing of the extension is particularly significant. The axis of the cist, be it noted, is definitely outside

PLATE 45. SIX WELLS 271', LLANTWIT MAJOR, GLAMORGAN: The mound (half removed) and central deposit

(a) Dome of the ritual pit—basal portion

(b) Stake-hole in barrow

PLATE 46. SIX WELLS 271′, LLANTWIT MAJOR, GLAMORGAN

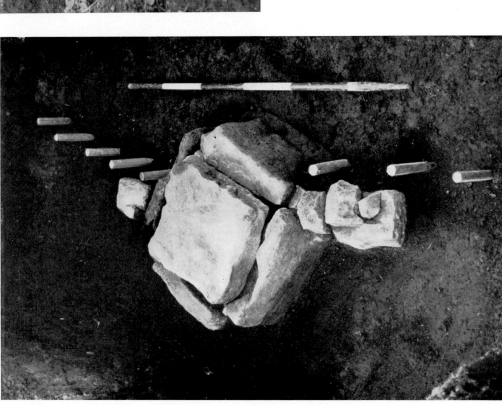

(a) Cist cleared, but undisturbed

(b) Cist in relation to stake circle

PLATE 47. SIX WELLS 271', LLANTWIT MAJOR, GLAMORGAN

(a) SIX WELLS 271', LLANTWIT MAJOR, GLAMORGAN: Cist opened

(b) Urn from cist

(c) ELWORTHY, SOMERSET: Urn

PLATE 48.

PLATE 49. COLWINSTON, GLAMORGAN

(a) Debased 'OHR' urn         (b) Cordoned urn

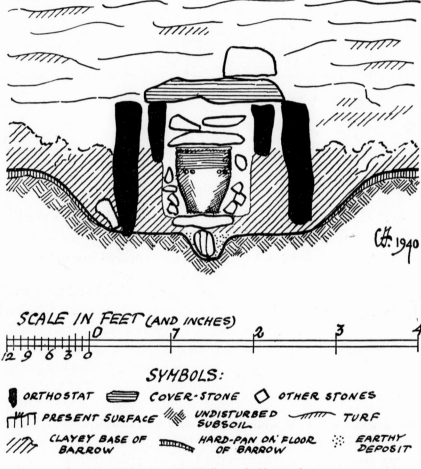

SCALE IN FEET (AND INCHES)

0    1    2    3    4

12 9 6 3 0

SYMBOLS:

ORTHOSTAT    COVER-STONE    OTHER STONES

PRESENT SURFACE    UNDISTURBED SUBSOIL    TURF

CLAYEY BASE OF BARROW    HARD-PAN ON FLOOR OF BARROW    EARTHY DEPOSIT

Figure 78. Six Wells 271'. Cist section

the circle. All these points are illustrated in the photographs and in a plan (Figure 79).

The lay-out, then, conveys an intellectual assurance that cist and stake-circle form one design. We can supplement this by direct proof. We know

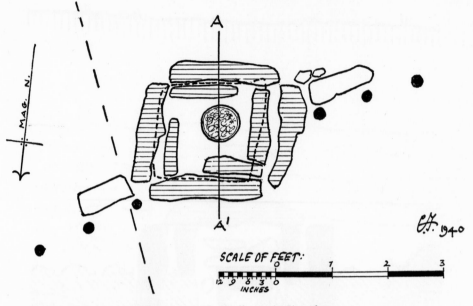

Figure 79. Six Wells 271'. Cist plan

that the cist was present when the turf-barrow was built, for the line of the turves across it was seen to be unbroken (Figure 78); and a further piece of evidence shows that the order of construction was first the circle, then the cist.

Half hidden under a spur-stone beside the upper left-hand corner of the cist in Plate 48a is a small piece of Lias whiter than the rest. The under-surface of this is 3–4 in. above the natural ground-level. On removal it was found to form, as it were, a lid to a stake-hole 2 in. in diameter. It must indeed have originally been resting on—supported by—the flat top of the stake which formerly occupied the hole; for since the upper 3–4 in. of the hole was in 'made' ground, this hole could hardly have remained open unless the stake was in it while this ground was consolidating. The hole, being on the line of the north-south trench, is recorded in section in Figure 77, and it is the third from the left in the plan (Figure 75).

Reference was made on p. 163 to the evidence for short, or shortened, stakes in the circle; here incidentally is the best example of all. From our present point of view the discovery indicates not only that the cist was constructed after the adjacent sector of the stake circle, but also that this stake-circle was then actually present and undecayed. On the other hand, the fact that several stakes were set within the margin of the large shallow basin excavated before the construction of the cist (p. 164) shows that the cist was taken into consideration in the original lay-out: *was in fact part of the original design.*

These things being so, the contents of the cist, in so far as they are datable, will enable us to place ritual barrows of the Six Wells 267' and 271' class more exactly in the cultural sequence of the Bronze Age than was possible when the former was described. These contents will now be considered. Under the cover of the cist, in the centre, a flat stone was seen; this formed the lid to an urn filled with burnt bones which in consequence was shattered (Plate 48a). On clearing the cist the urn was found to have been placed on another flat stone over a small hole in the natural subsoil in which a Lias pebble had been placed (see section, Figure 78), and Lias stones were packed round it.

There was no charcoal in or near the cist; and the most careful search through the burnt bones in the urn (which were quite clean), resulted in the collection of four small pieces only. My colleague, Mr. L. F. Cowley, who has kindly examined the bones, reports that these probably belonged to a male over 20 years of age.

*The Urn.* The urn was rebuilt in the Department of Archaeology of the National Museum of Wales. The fragments were very soft when excavated, and had warped under pressure; the sectional portion of the drawing (Figure 80) more accurately represents its original outline than the photograph (Plate 48b). The urn proves to be just over 9 in. in height, a stocky vessel weakly caliciform, with a flared rim well formed in places, elsewhere irregular. The ill-baked ware, of native Bronze Age character, is gritty but the grits are small. The vessel is on the surface brownish-red to greyish-yellow with ill-defined blackish patches: the core is dead black. The wall is of equal thickness from rim to base. The decoration consists of a series of horizontal smooth-floored grooves firmly drawn with a blunt-point of wood or bone, extending from below the rim to the bulge. Round the bulge are four pairs of dimples spaced at equal intervals. These are carefully modelled and do not show a negative swelling on the inside.

The urn is undoubtedly of a rare type: the change from the cord-ornament, or scratched decoration, of the Middle Bronze Age is as significant as is the complete break with the past, in the form of the rim.

167

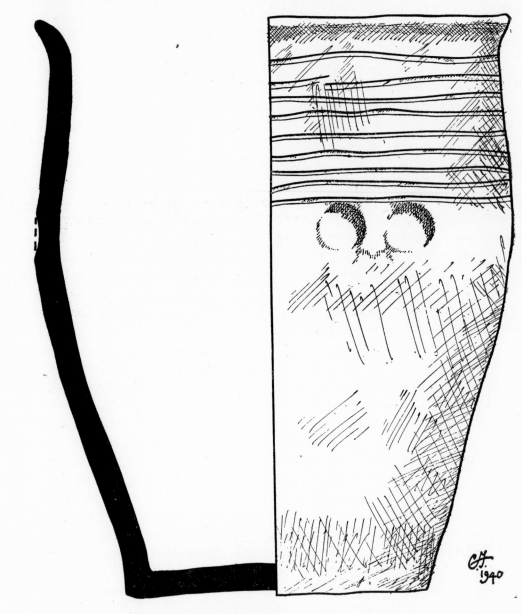

Figure 80. Six Wells 271'. Urn: scale $\frac{2}{3}$

Prolonged search through the literature has disclosed one close parallel only, a cinerary found 'in the winter of 1834–5' in a barrow in the parish of Elworthy, Somerset, on the east slopes of the Brendon Hills, adjoining the coast of the Bristol Channel opposite our group of barrows. This urn is of the same shape and height and has four pairs of dimples; it has similar grooved decoration, somewhat coarser and more varied, with chevron patterns as well as horizontal lines. The record states that 'the burial place contained a circle of upright stones, about six feet in diameter, and three feet high. On one side was a square cavity, about fifteen inches in diameter, enclosed with flat stones, containing this urn, with fragments and ashes of burnt bones. There were also pieces of another urn.'

The Elworthy urn (Plate 48c) has features which reveal its affiliations, if not its origins. The paired dimples show a well-marked intervening ridge; such a ridge, at a slightly earlier stage of evolution from a pierced lug, is seen on a bucket-like urn of Rimbury type of Late Bronze Age date from Crichel Down near Blandford, Dorset.[1] This indication of cultural relationship is rendered certain by another detail of the ornament— the convergence of the horizontal grooves on what we may now call the 'vestigial lugs'. This commonly occurs on globular urns of the Deverel group. Grooved decoration in general and chevron patterns are, moreover, normal to the Deverel–Rimbury wares and their derivatives.

This analysis will suggest that devolution has proceeded further in the case of our Six Wells urn than at Elworthy. This is to be expected: for there is ample evidence that throughout the prehistoric periods cultural trends were from south to north across the Bristol Channel and not in the opposite direction. Since then, the Deverel–Rimbury development can be safely dated from c. 750 B.C. onwards, the Six Wells urn can hardly be earlier than 600 B.C.

The one feature needed to demonstrate the essential identity of this earlier Somerset culture with that at Six Wells is of course the 'ritual pit'. This is supplied in a record of a barrow, also on the Brendon Hills, which was, like our barrows, composed of turf, and which revealed within a 'peristalith' about 10 ft. in diameter (a stone circle) a hole 2 ft. deep and 1½ ft. wide containing no human remains. Our *short-post* circles, then, may be translations into timber of a stone-circle tradition: OR, the stone circle

[1] C. M. and S. Piggott, 'Barrows on Crichel . . . Downs, Dorset', *Archaeologia*, 90, pp. 47 ff.

may be strengthening elements of a turf-walled hut. How little we can learn, in any one generation!

*The Barrow.* The mound is of the turf-barrow class (Plate 45): it was thrown up at one time, and presents no feature needing detailed description. In general, the regularity of the turfy layers with thin bands of clay on their undersides was striking; after rain one could measure the thickness of these layers (3 to 6 or 8 in.) with ease. The barrow was never constructed as a turf-*stack*; nowhere was a vertical face or a steep slope of turf seen. In this respect it resembled the other 'ritual barrow' 267′ and differed from the two Sheeplays burial-mounds 279′ and 293′. Thus the structure tended to fade out at the margins, and determination of its actual limits was difficult. When wet weather had intensified colour-contrasts, and enabled these limits to be fixed, one could not be sure whether they represented the original barrow edge, or a 'spread' subsequent to construction due to a hypothetical instability of the structure. I have assumed the former to be correct (since no means exist of proving the 'spread' or determining its extent), and am probably right in so doing, for the actual limits of the barrow provide a remarkably close approximation to a true circle. The figures are 87·6 ft. in NE–SW diameter, and 90·0 ft. in NW–SE diameter (see plan). The centre of the barrow, as of the stake-circle, is the 'ritual pit'.

Hard-pan was very much in evidence. It covered practically the whole of the floor of the barrow (insofar as it was excavated) except the central area which has already been described; here, descending steeply, it merged into the orange clay (Fig. 76). The level 'pavement' of hard-pan usually met with in turf barrows (p. 131, above) was seldom seen. The floor layer rose in hummocks and then dipped into pits and holes and faded out; thin bands were also seen above and near the ancient surface. Contorted layers of iron oxide, moreover, were found in the body of the mound, in and on the clay masses (Figure 77). Only on the margins of the mound was hard-pan on the floor consistently even. These features are indicated in the sections, in which, however, I cannot hope to convey any adequate idea of the fantastic detail of form, let alone colour, produced after some 2,500 years in (and under) a well-consolidated dump of turf and clay. 'Straight' photography fails to demonstrate the pattern; the wall of the north–south trench with the clay becoming streaky after rain, and with deep rabbit buries above, is seen in Plate 45.

*The Structure and the Ritual.* The importance of Deverel–Rimbury culture—native, not imported—covering south-eastern Britain about 700 B.C. and later, is well recognized, and attention was drawn as long ago as 1933 to features of their ceramic derived from the west. We can, then, reasonably regard the Elworthy–Six Wells urn-type and technique—impressed, not cord-ornament—as one of the western elements of this culture. We are, moreover, fortunately able to prove that domed pit, turf barrow, and stake-circle and ritual-hut traditions were many centuries old on the Llantwit Major plateau when our barrow was constructed. In short, we are dealing with a new Highland, south-western, fashion in pottery, utilized on both sides of the Bristol Channel in structures of traditional forms.

The Six Wells 271' barrow has, it is true, decadent features—the mound is a mere heap and the cist is incompetently built; nevertheless the interesting and important fact stands, that a Middle Bronze Age culture on the sea-plain of Glamorgan existed substantially unaltered, in such of its techniques—pottery apart—as we can study, for not less than 400 and probably as much as 700 years.

Whether the 'ritual' is of the same antiquity here, we cannot say; but since traditional structural forms and techniques were used for it without essential modification, it is hardly likely to have been introduced in 700–600 B.C. Let us now, then, study this 'ritual' at Six Wells 271', first reminding ourselves of the essentials of the problem.

A small hole containing no artefacts, and which therefore is regarded as a 'ritual pit', was domed over with clay and earth. It was surrounded by a small area wherefrom the ancient surface soil was removed, and by a larger area which had not been trodden. This tiny construction was the *exact* centre of a stake-circle 50 ft. in diameter, and was almost certainly also the exact centre of a barrow 90 ft. in diameter. It was therefore the cause of, and reason for, these constructions.

There was a primary burial in the mound, by cremation, in an urn within a cist, of an adult, probably a male. The cist was so designed as to emphasize its structural relation to the stake-circle (with which it was contemporary); it was, however, outside the circle. There are pregnant facts; we receive unexpected and welcome evidence that the stake-circle was in effect the precinct wall of a shrine or sanctuary; burial would pollute an area 'occult, withheld, untrod', and could not be permitted. A votary, marginally interred, might however expect favour from the Power to whom the pit was dedicated, or with whom contact was established by libations, food-offerings, or other ritual centred on the pit. Here we reach the core of the problem presented by our barrow.

It is, in a sense, impossible to penetrate the mind of Bronze Age Man in Britain, and thus, in this particular instance, to know what impelled him to so laborious a creation as barrow 271'; to determine what was the concept behind the ritual; what was the ritual itself which dictated this material form. But there is one European people who were literate, artistic, and introspective, at a time when they still retained a mass of custom and ritual from their Bronze Age past—the Greeks: and it is not difficult to find clues to our problem in their literature and art. 'The chthonic gods,' says Philostratos, 'welcome trenches and ceremonies done in the hollow earth.'[1] Pausanias, giving an account of the ceremonies performed at Titané to soothe the winds, states that the priest does secret ceremonies in four pits. 'Each of the four winds,' commented Miss Jane Harrison, 'dwelt, it is clear, as a chthonic Power in a pit.'[2] The same ideas were shared by the Romans: 'when the *mundus* (the round pit on the Palatine) is open, the gate of the doleful underworld gods is open'.[3]

That the same sort of hole and, like it, domed, was made for a dead man in an adjacent barrow, Sheeplays 293', as for the (presumed) ritual acts in our barrow 271', need not surprise us. Ghosts (spirits of the dead), in the evolution of primitive concepts, become gods or goddesses[4]; the line is hard to draw between them. But that there should be a barrow over a ritual pit, as over a tomb, is harder to understand. It is true that an artificial earth-mound, as representing the home of the earth goddess, commonly occurs in the art of the Greek vase-painter,[5] but I think the explanation of our mound lies elsewhere. We may, at this stage in our enquiry, be content to affirm it as probable that the 'ritual pit' in barrow 271' was a vehicle whereby a chthonic Power was approached, consulted, or appeased. One may further emphasize the classical parallel by stating that we may have here, in pit and stake-circle, a barbarous version of the Greek

[1] This and the following extracts and comments, are derived from J. E. Harrison, *Prolegomena to the Study of Greek Religion*, 2nd ed., 1908. The present reference is to p. 125.
[2] *Op. cit.*, p. 68. Τιτανη was a town in the Peloponnese (in Sicyonia).
[3] Varro: see Harrison, *op. cit.*, p. 47
[4] Harrison, *op. cit.*, p. 240. Cf. J. L. Myres, *Who were the Greeks?* p. 191, para. 3.
[5] Harrison, *op. cit.*, Figs. 68–9, pp. 277–8.

sanctuary with its precinct (τέμενος); but the classical analogies, though relevant, must not be pressed too far. The peculiar feature of our shrine is its ephemeral character. The care taken over the burial of the adult in the cist shows him to have been a person of importance, not a dedicatory sacrifice,[1] and the construction of his tomb was, as we know, contemporary with the construction of the circle. Now it is safe to affirm, on general principles, that definition of a sacred area must either precede or be contemporaneous with the hallowing of the site; were it later, the risk of pollution by involuntary trespass would arise. Contact with the Power in the pit, then, is likely to have been sought and achieved on the death of the individual in question. Furthermore, the holy place necessarily ceased to function when the barrow was built, and this happened, as has been shown, very quickly after the burial. We observe, then, that a month or so might well cover its actual existence.

All this has a bearing on the fact of the mound. It may provisionally be regarded not as the pure expression of a cult of the underworld Power, but as an intrusion of the principle that a barrow was a covering proper to the dead. The barrow was, however, centred on the shrine, not on the burial.

The floor of barrow 271' may then be not a sacred site of a tribe, but a secular plot of ground whereon priests or shamans, on behalf of an important local family with over-estuary connections, who had suffered bereavement, performed ritual acts by virtue of which contact was obtained with an underworld Power, and a place provided for the ashes of the dead in the shadow of Its Presence.[2]

The issue may now be broadened. The striking and dramatic importance of the lay-out in barrow 271' is that we see the Dead Man ousted from the central and dominant position which we have good reason to believe he held in the earlier (Megalithic) religion of the Highland Zone of Britain. Whatever authority the man whose sepulchre we have studied may have wielded during life, in death he was a suppliant. The concept involved in the worship of the dead is here visibly overthrown.

[1] We know what a dedicatory sacrifice among the Middle Bronze Age folk in South Wales was like; burnt bones thrown into a stony pit. See Pond Cairn, p. 109 above.

[2] The classical parallel I have adduced has been applied before, but from a different angle, and not to elaborate structures such as Six Wells 267' and 271'. See, e.g., Thurnam, *Archaeologia*, xlii, p. 181, with reference to holes under long barrows, and Mr. G. M. Young, *Antiquity*, 1934, pp. 459–61, with reference to the circular hollows, miscalled 'Pond Barrows', found adjacent to barrow groups in Wiltshire.

Lastly, there is one correlation, a by-product of our survey, which invites more precise expression. The record of the Elworthy barrow, reinforced (where information is lacking) by that of the Brendon Hills barrow, suggests the presence, on the other side of the Bristol Channel, of a ritual structure similar in plan to that in our barrow, the urn being deposited in a cist 'on one side of' a circle of stones, as our urn was in a cist marginal to a circle of stakes. This apparent identity of function of sacred structures of stone and of wood has familiar parallels, and it increases the interest of a Bronze Age field of inquiry which was expanded by the excavation of Six Wells 271'.

The difficulties in winter of such an investigation as this, and the importance of the presence of the responsible person throughout every hour of the working day, give point to my second 'Six Wells' anecdote, the setting for which is Plate 45. The year is 1940: close to the barrow mass, near a hedge and shed, half a dozen expert craftsmen are repairing, or tuning-up, fighter-aircraft in the open. Kneeling on a folded sack, trying to complete *my* job in threatening weather, I was trowelling the little dome at the mound's centre, below its 'cliff', when a messenger came: 'The Commanding Officer wishes to see you, Sir.' I got up, scraped the mud off my hands with the trowel, and went: the C.O. was by his car with an immaculate top-hatted, frock-coated, patent-leather-booted gentleman, incongruous in such a setting. 'This is Mr. X of the Treasury,'[1] he said, 'who would like to know how your work for the Ministry is getting on.' I made a brief report, and invited Mr. X to come and look at the barrow 'face'. He walked a little nearer, peered, politely declined, and thanked me: I went back to my trowelling on the 'floor'. No sooner was I on my knees again, when a voice from the barrow-top said 'Hoy!' I don't usually reply to such conversational openings, but the 'Hoy' was repeated with such urgency that I looked up, recognizing in the speaker one of the 'plane' craftsmen, who said: "'Ere, was that Sir Cyril Fox with the C.O.?' Grasping the situation, I slowly countered, 'Well, in a way it was, and in a way it wasn't: I'm Sir Cyril Fox.' 'Gor-blimey, Sir, I've bin 'ere a fortnight, and I thought you was the working foreman.'

The stake-circles and the mortuary house seen in this barrow are features deserving of more consideration than they have yet received. Notes on both follow.

[1] This sartorial tradition, for Regional tours, was very near its end, surely, in 1940.

*Stake-circles in Barrows and Cairns, c.* 1550–700 B.C. The circle of stake-holes at South Hill, Talbenny, Pembrokeshire, implying a wattled fence (p. 39) associated with rites which included the deposit of an Early Bronze Age beaker, is now seen to be of considerable cultural interest, since such stake-holes have also been demonstrated in four barrows, of the Middle Bronze Age and later, on the Glamorgan sea-plain.[1] The known chronological range of the technique they represent, associated with mound burial in Wales, is thus not less than 800 years.

It is to be noted that the interspaces between the stake-holes of the fence at South Hill, *averaged* at 24½ in., were wider than in the Glamorgan barrows; the wattling was thus of looser texture. The *average* length of the interspaces in the Glamorgan barrows (measured from centre to centre of the holes) is as follows: Sheeplays 293′, three circles, 15·3 ft. and 16·0 ft., Sheeplays 279′, 13·3 ft., Six Wells 271′, 15·5 ft. The first-named is Middle Bronze Age; the second, averaged on an inadequate range, is also Middle Bronze Age, but was regarded as later than the first; the last is Late Bronze Age. Since South Hill is Early Bronze Age, either a diminution in the course of two centuries in the number of verticals thought necessary by the inheritors of the wattlework tradition for a given length of wattling took place, the number being thereafter stabilized; or two separate traditions are involved. It is to be hoped that future investigators will provide exact measurements of many more such circles—which must be common enough in Wales at all events—and so settle the question.

The facts mentioned above are presented in the form of a graph in Figure 81. I have placed Sheeplays 279′ half-way between 293′ and Six Wells 271′; in my view it lies, culturally, somewhere between the two, but any point chosen must at present be arbitrary.

The obvious explanation of the stake-circle at Talbenny, Pembs., is that the Beaker folk brought this forest- or parkland-technique with them from Lowland Britain, for one cannot suppose it to have been native to the Highland Zone. Indeed the construction of the South Hill barrow seems to illustrate the decline almost to extinction here, of this handicraft

[1] No stake-circle was demonstrated at Sutton 268′, the Beaker barrow in Glamorgan. But I now think, having regard to the relation between the margin of the primary barrow and the wattled fence at South Hill, that such a fence may well have been formerly present at Sutton 268′ *on the site of the rock-cut ditch* that surrounds the primary (Beaker) barrow.

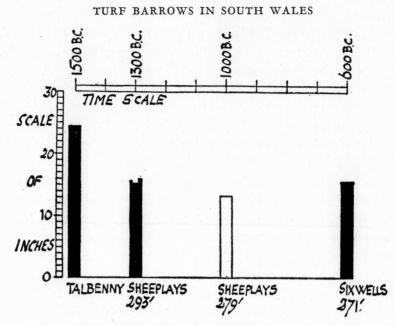

Figure 81. Graph of stake-circle interspaces

as an element of religious observance in connection with burial. The Beaker colonists indeed adapted to their needs the earthfast stone technique of the Megalithic folk who were their neighbours. With these geographical and cultural ideas in mind, one's thoughts naturally turn to Wiltshire, with its Woodhenge and Overton Hill 'A' Circle, as the likely source of wooden construction; but it should be remembered that the driven-stakes-at-short-intervals of Talbenny, and the Glamorgan circles, consistently represent hurdle-makers' technique, while the Wiltshire structures—basically, tree trunks set up in dug holes—represent carpenters' or axe-men's technique. Though post-holes and stake-holes are occasionally found in association,[1] they may well be of different cultural origins, so much do they differ in character; and we cannot yet assume that the circle at South Hill barrow is a primary B[1] cultural element as our 'shorthand' describes it: from Wessex, or acquired by Wessex from Brittany. The hurdle-makers' technique has been found in barrows in Yorkshire and Cambridgeshire, not as yet in Wiltshire; and it may have been taken over by Beaker folk in the Middle Thames region from East Anglians, along with the rim-cordon seen

[1] E.g., at Chippenham, Cambs., Leaf, *Cambridge Antiquarian Society, Proceedings*, 1940, xxxix, p. 36, Fig. 9.

on the Talbenny vessel which appears to have an ultimate source in the Low Countries.[1] Some of the well-known 'palisade' barrows excavated by Dr. Van Giffen may then be related structures.

A hint has been adopted in Figure 38, that the Talbenny Beaker folk arrived by sea, and that Mill Haven was their 'port'. Only cross-channel traffic, it is evident, can explain the settlement of these Beaker folk in Glamorgan on the South Wales littoral; and it is not reasonable to suppose that the slow processes of expansion by land-ways in such difficult country as intervenes between Glamorgan and west Pembrokeshire could bring the culture to South Hill in a similar stage of development as is represented at Sutton 268'. Coastwise sea traffic, then, initiated and may have maintained the settlement; the little implement associated with the South Hill beaker was probably of quarried flint, which points to intermittent contact with the 'homeland'. The deep and safe tidal estuary of the Bristol Avon seems a likely place[2] from which the colonization of South and West Wales, from Glamorgan to Pembrokeshire, started and to which, in the way of trade, the colonists occasionally returned. Returned; for we cannot 'swallow the camel' involved in any rational explanation of the spread, along oceanic shores, of the Megalithic culture, and 'strain at the gnat' of local coastwise trade and traffic on the part of the bearers of the vigorous culture which, in Britain, partially overwhelmed it.

### MORTUARY HOUSES IN TURF BARROWS

This group of barrows, in a limited area of Glamorgan, presents problems of interest to students of Early Man's attitude to Life and Death. We are apparently dealing with a group community with ideas about the after-life as an existence not unrelated in character to the Bronze Age setting which the individuals composing it would be leaving.

Of particular interest to the archaeologist is the incidental indication of the scale of their houses in this world—since no Bronze Age settlement in Wales has as yet been recognized.

The evidence is confined to the two 'Sheeplays', and one 'Six Wells' barrows, in which a ring of close-set small holes for uprights of the wattled wall of a circular hut has within it a number of—often—larger

---

[1] Compare a good example of such a cordon on a B[1] beaker with rusticated ornament from Somersham, Hunts; in *Proceedings of the Prehistoric Society*, 11, 1936, Pl. xii.

[2] Weston Bay, at the western end of the Mendips, is a possible alternative.

holes, presumed to be for the support of the domical roof-framing. The diameter of these structures varies as follows:

|  | Sheeplays 293' | Sutton 279' | Six Wells 267' |
|---|---|---|---|
| Hut diameter | + − 28 ft. | (?) 26 ft. | Oval, 29 ft. and 27 ft. 6 in. |
| Post-ring diameter | + − 18 ft. | (?) 11 ft. | ? |
| Entry |  | ? | 9 ft. (with returns) |

In only one, then, is the entry certain: the 'returns' are bent outwards: it is from the north-west. There is also a gap 3 ft. 9 in. wide on the opposite side of this hut, but it lacks the flanking 'returns'. The gap mentioned in the account of barrow 271' is merely the widest of the variable distances between the circle of holes for the wall-uprights. The post-ring holes vary in character as well as number. Barrow Sheeplays 293' has 30 (and one replacement) sufficiently regular to be called 'the 18-ft. circle'; 267' and 269' have scattered holes within the circular wall; barrow 271' has none.

This last fact is extraordinarily interesting: it is the ritual barrow, the ring-wall of which, being 51 ft. in diameter, could not possibly have been roofed without a central ring of posts. It may have been no more than 3 in. high. Consequently, we may define the structure as hypaethral: 'open to the skies'.

The Power here provided with an earthly resting place, then, must have been conceived as a sky God rather than an Underworld Ruler: Life, not Death, will have been in the minds of those who officiated here.

I should here remind my readers that well-defined and undoubted mortuary houses under Bronze Age barrows are known. They tend to be small, and approximately rectangular; I illustrate an example from the centre of a barrow at Beaulieu, Hampshire, by the kind permission of Mrs. L. M. Piggott (Figures 82 and 83). She concluded that this mortuary house was built over the body, though practically no trace of one was found. Holes in the walls and roof allowed fine silt to collect, and the roof ultimately collapsed, *before the barrow was built*.[1]

This discovery is by no means unique. A barrow at Cassington, Oxford-shire, showed stake-holes of a ritual hut surrounding the grave-pit, and

[1] C. M. Piggott, 'Fifteen Barrows in the New Forest', *Proc. Prehist. Soc.*, 1943, pp. 1–27, esp. p. 6 and Figs. 4 and 5. Also C. A. Ralegh Radford, *Devon Arch. Excavation Society*, 1947, pp. 157, 159, Figs. 1 and 2.

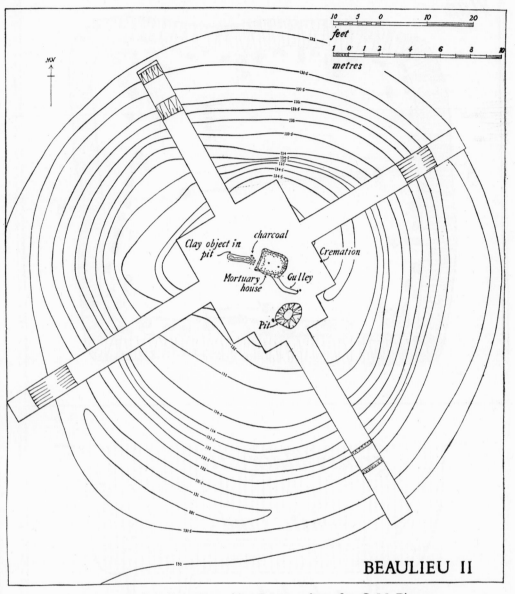

Figure 82. Beaulieu, Hampshire. Barrow plan: after C. M. Piggott

it is likely that the oval platform at Colwinston, Glamorgan, Figure 84, represents a stone-walled hut: the floor area is considerable, 19 ft. × 14 ft.[1]

[1] C. and A. Fox, *Arch. Camb.* 1941, p. 187

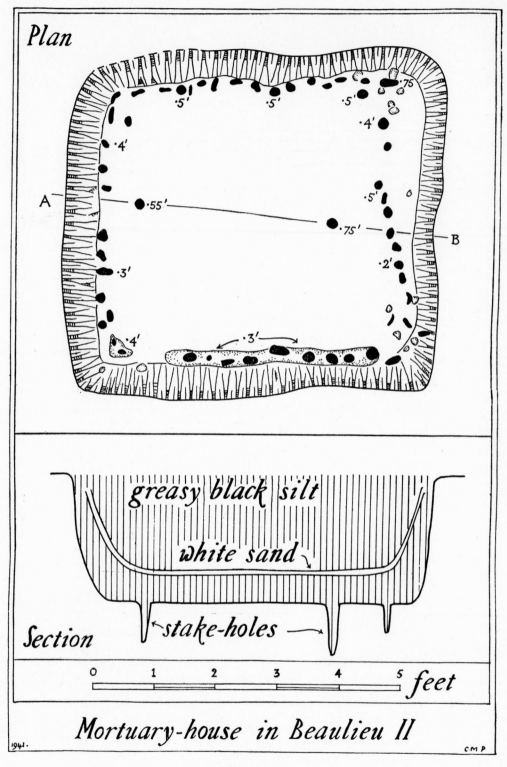

Plan

A — B

·75'
·5'    ·5'    ·5'
·4'
·4'
·55'    ·75'
·5'
·3'    ·2'

·4'    ·3'

Section

greasy black silt

white sand

stake-holes

0    1    2    3    4    5 feet

Mortuary-house in Beaulieu II

1941.                                                                CMP

Figure 83

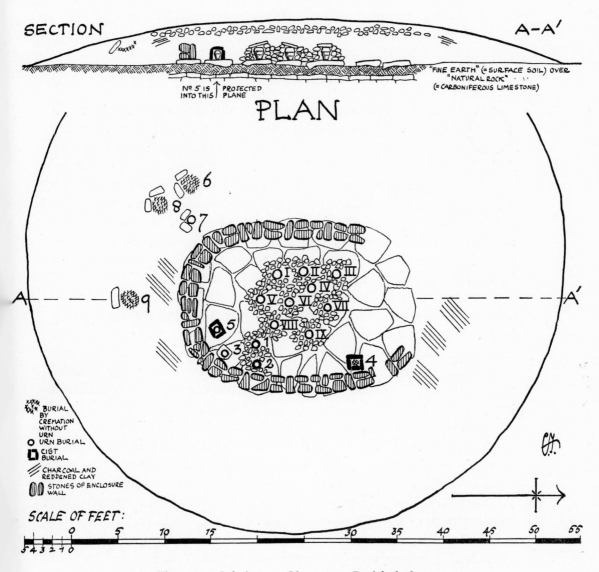

SECTION A-A'

"FINE EARTH" (= SURFACE SOIL) OVER "NATURAL ROCK" (= CARBONIFEROUS LIMESTONE)

N⁰. 5 IS PROJECTED INTO THIS PLANE

PLAN

A — A'

BURIAL BY CREMATION WITHOUT URN

O URN BURIAL

CIST BURIAL

CHARCOAL AND REDDENED CLAY

STONES OF ENCLOSURE WALL

SCALE OF FEET:

Figure 84. Colwinston, Glamorgan. Burial platform

# 7

## COMMENTARY

OUR subject has been Life—and Death—in the Bronze Age: and chance has, to some extent, determined the particular excavation work by which knowledge of both has been gained, chiefly in a limited region, south and south-west Wales. This region, though a long way from the certain and probable centres of culture in Ireland and Britain between, say, 1700 and 600 B.C., may have been one of the traffic routes between them. Between, that is, the Waterford and the Dublin areas, and the Dorset–Wiltshire region. The insular Megalithic cultures of the later Stone Age were thus linked, as the distribution map of such monuments in the *Personality of Britain*[1] suggests: another map, of the distribution of Bronze Age finds in Britain, reveals (*a*) concentrations of finds in—of course—Wessex, and two routes, by the River Avon and the Mendips, by land and water, to the Bristol Channel coast; (*b*) concentrations in coastal Glamorgan and coastal Pembrokeshire south of Milford Haven; and (*c*) a transpeninsular traffic route (to avoid the sea risks of the rocky western headlands) from the estuary of the River Taf at Laugharne to the sheltered bay at Fishguard, crossing Preseli Top (1760 ft.). (The patch of finds in Ireland on the western edge of this map is the site of Dublin.)

We cannot avoid the conclusion that such a pattern is inexplicable except in relation to sea traffic mostly from the southern part of the east coast of Ireland to Britain and vice versa: trade from Dublin Bay and northern Ireland would take the shortest well-recognized route to the Menai Straits: or possibly to the Clwyd estuary.

Whether this southern trade was slight or vigorous, it must have helped the spread of successive cultures into and along the South Wales sea-plain and promontory, and shows how knowledge of the Preseli 'blue-stones', first transported to Salisbury Plain late in the Neolithic Age, could have successively reached the 'Beaker' and the 'Middle Bronze Age' peoples.

[1] National Museum of Wales: 4th. ed., 1943.

The information here set out has come from hurried visits to the sites of chance finds by farmer or workman, or to other people's excavations of burial mounds: one section is a summary of competent work by a skilled investigator, to fill a gap in my 'field' experience: but for the most part it has represented prolonged and detailed study of ancient burial mounds, often helped by my wife, involving an eight-hour day over many months in all, in the field with one or two labourers, with pick and shovel and trowel: the results being written up from the field notebooks, in the winter months.

All the sites investigated have fallen into the known prehistory of the Bronze Age—the coming about 1800 B.C. of the 'Beaker' people (who inhumed their dead), and their spread over Britain: the development in Yorkshire of inhumation burial with food-vessels and the replacement of this rite by cremation about 1450 B.C. in many parts of southern Britain. The new custom persisted down to the end of the Bronze Age. The need of a pot suitable for burnt bones produced the overhanging-rim urn, a shape seen to develop rapidly between *c*. 1450 and 1200—the change involving a deepening of the rim-form which provides its name. While this development was going on, an intrusive, able group of men acquainted with the channels of Continental trade, coming probably from Brittany, brought in the '*Wessex culture*', centred on Salisbury Plain. A notable pottery type, the so-called 'Incense cup', is associated with this culture.

All culture, in early times, is created by the few who through inheritance or conquest control the sources of wealth, but the opportunity does not necessarily result in such development: the forward-minded, dynamic group in power is likely to have been an intermittent phenomenon in prehistoric, as in historic times.

The group we here refer to may have come to Wessex (about 1450 B.C.) as a convenient and safe centre for the exercise of widespread trade control: they seem, from the contents of their graves, to have had agents in Scandinavia (amber), in eastern and southern Europe (faience), and in Ireland (gold). The organization of serf labour here, in Wessex, must be envisaged. The route for the gold trade was probably via the strait of Mona (Anglesey) and Flintshire, rather than Fishguard Bay or Milford Haven—since no gold objects of the Middle Bronze Age are known from South Wales burials or chance finds. But contacts between Ireland and west and south-west Wales, for one reason or another, are certain: encrusted urns found on the coast at Penllwyn and Preseli prove it—for the technique these show was evolved in Ireland, and must have been practised either by Irish potters here resident or, since the products are not *exactly* like the Irish, by potters who had seen and handled their products.

In studying the Beaker culture on the coastal plateau of the Vale of Glamorgan we regarded this area as a likely starting point of its spread along the south coast of Wales, from the Cotswolds or the Somerset coast, into Pembrokeshire. It seems also to have been the focus of development, in South Wales, of a later, more elaborate, burial ritual—or perhaps a concentration here of scientific research in barrow burial, due mainly to the second world war, gives an impression which can only be proved or disproved by further field-work in other south coastal areas.

This later ritual, though it comes, no doubt, largely from Wessex by way of north-west Somerset, as my text suggests, is native, not foreign. The 'Wessex culture' is British, basically. Such foreignness as the exotic content of their graves suggests, did not last. It is held that the influence, in general, of this southern culture might be due primarily to contacts established when the 'blue-stones' were transported from Preseli to Stonehenge—as is here held, by sea along the north shores of the Bristol Channel as far as the Taff estuary and thence up the River Avon to the Plain. The recorded presence of a blue-stone in an earlier structure (Boles Long Barrow near Warminster, Wilts) suggests that the sacredness of Preseli Top to successive prehistoric dwellers on Salisbury Plain began in late Neolithic times, when the Hill may have first become an important transpeninsular traffic route to Ireland, bypassing a storm-swept, rock-infested headland.

A survey such as this involves barrows and cairns which, though their construction can be placed in a highly probable time-sequence, are difficult to deal with rationally because they contain secondaries of various dates. Occasionally, as in the case of Sutton 268′, it was worth while to discuss a barrow in two parts of the book; but to act in this way all through would have caused great confusion.

The survey is also difficult, because the dating of the burial urns by form (and therefore the dating of my record) is in question.

The OHR urn, persisting, it would appear, throughout the greater part of the Bronze Age, has been held to show successive changes in form, 'Phases i to iii', from 'tripartite' to 'bipartite'. It is now, however, very doubtful whether close dating of burials with such urns between, say,

1400 B.C. and 700 B.C., which is the range they seem to cover, is yet possible. Everybody who is interested in the Bronze Age in Britain should be in a position to appreciate the variety of form and the problems presented by these urns. The similarity of the associations of the three Phases suggests that the forms changed rapidly at the outset and were thereafter stagnant. Fortunately, we know what the *beginning* of the sequence is like (p. 87). A list of those with datable associations is appended.

What sort of social order emerges from my studies in burial ritual and practice? These are ceremonials connected with chieftains or members of chiefly families, but the lower orders, surely, on the evidence, join in? A sort of Homeric Age within Britain, a hierarchy of folk comparatively ill-equipped and no doubt barbarously housed, seems to me to take shape.

The similarities in burial technique—and as has long been recognized—in grave furniture, over wide areas suggests, moreover, that men and women of the leading families, having leisure, travelled—on pony-back probably and with attendants—to feast with friends, or indeed strangers, and to take part in or to witness—if need be—such ceremonial observances as cannot but be associated with the structures we study. For it is the acts of living men and women that we archaeologists write up: the choosing of the site, the toil in a circular trench, the access to the centre across this, the digging of the pit: thereafter, the ground well-trodden in the dance,[1] the clouds of charcoal-dust enveloping the performers, who may have been the whole community of full age, the pottery and tools dedicated by the living to the use of the dead, wherever they may be—and so on: Life and Death, with the accent on the former.

[1] A widespread burial custom: see J. G. Frazer, *The Belief in Immortality*, Vol. III, pp. 90-1.

# BIBLIOGRAPHY

If the reader wishes to know more about any one of my sites referred to in this book, it will be found in the named reference to my original papers.

### (A) 1925–1928

(1) 'Beacon Hill Barrow, Barton Mills, Suffolk', in collaboration with the Earl Cawdor, *Cambridge Antiquarian Society Communications*, XXVI, 1925, pp. 19–65.
(2) 'On two Beakers of the Early Bronze Age in South Wales: and the Distribution of Beaker Pottery in England and Wales', *Archaeologia Cambrensis*, 1925, pp. 1–31.
(3) 'Note on Four Sepulchral Vessels of the Bronze Age from N. Wales', *Archaeologia Cambrensis*, 1925, pp. 177–90.
(4) 'A Burial Place of Dwellers in the Upper Taf Valley, near Whitland, Carm.', *Archaeologia Cambrensis*, 1925, pp. 275–88.
(5) 'A Bronze Age Barrow on Kilpaison Burrows, Rhoscrowther, Pemb.', *Archaeologia Cambrensis*, 1926, pp. 1–32.
(6) 'Ysceifiog Circle and Barrow, Flintshire', *Archaeologia Cambrensis*, 1926, pp. 48–85.
(7) 'A Food-vessel from a Barrow on Linney Burrows, Castlemartin, Pembr.', *Archaeologia Cambrensis*, 1926, p. 401–4.
(8) 'Neolithic and Beaker Pottery from Chambered Long Cairn, Capel Garmon', *Archaeologia Cambrensis*, 1927, pp. 39–40.
(9) 'An Encrusted Urn of the Bronze Age from Wales (Aberystwyth, Cards.)', *Antiquaries Journal*, 1927, pp. 115–34.
(10) 'Corston Beacon: An Early Bronze Age Cairn in South Pembrokeshire', in collaboration with W. F. Grimes, *Archaeologia Cambrensis*, 1928, pp. 137–74.

### (B) 1938–1943

(11) 'Two Bronze Age Cairns in South Wales: Simondston and Pond Cairns, Coity Higher Parish, Bridgend (Glamorgan)', *Archaeologia*, 87, 1938, pp. 129–80.
(12) 'Stake-circles in Turf Barrows: a Record of Excavation in Glamorgan, 1939–40', *Antiquaries Journal*, 1941, pp. 99–125.
(13) 'A Dateable Ritual Barrow in Glamorgan', *Antiquity*, 1941, pp. 142–61.
(14) 'The Golden Mile Barrow, Colwinston, Glamorgan' (a re-appraisal), in collaboration with Aileen Fox, *Archaeologia Cambrensis*, 1941, pp. 185–92.
(15) 'A Beaker Barrow at Talbenny, Pembrokeshire', *Archaeological Journal*, 99, 1943, pp. 1–32.
(16) 'A Bronze Age Barrow (Sutton 268') in Llandow Parish, Glamorgan', *Archaeologia*, 89, 1943, pp. 89–126.

# INDEX OF SUBJECTS

INDEX

Burial, secondary, 8, 11, 20, 38, 41, 51, 98, 143
    with 'food vessels', 39, 71 ff.
    *See also* 'Cremation'

Cairn, 3, 43, 59, 64, 74
    character, 68, 113, 115, 124
    lithology, 124
    situation, 31
    structureless, 111
    surfaces, 113
    technique, 123
    thrust-blocks of, 84–5, 87
Cairn-ring, 110, 112, 113, 118, 120
Cawdor, Lord, xiv
Cemeteries, Late Bronze Age, 37
Cereals, in burials, 116, 118, 122, 123, 124
Ceremony, ceremonial, 112, 123, 185
Charcoal:
    floor of, 112
    hawthorn, 111, 119
    hazel, 111, 119
    oak, 108, 111
    ritual use of, xxvi, 62, 76, 111, 112, 123
    also: 51, 52, 54, 71, 100, 101, 106, 108,
        115, 116, 118, 122, 124, 131, 145, 185
Chess (*Bromus*), 116, 119
Child-burial, 20, 122
Childe, Gordon, xix *n.*, xxvi *n.*
Chitty, Miss L. F., xix
Circles:
    concentric, 136–7
    ditched, 10
    earthen, 20
    interspaces of, 163
    'setting-out', 147
    stake-, e.g. 129 ff., 162 ff., 174 ff.
    stone or wood, in barrows, 26, 140, 142,
        145, 174, 176
    'true', 162–3
Cists, construction, 24, 27, 82–4, 164
    *See also* 36, 67, 171
Clay, in barrows, 159, 162, 170
Coal, 86
Collingwood, R. G., xxvii *n.*
Community, Bronze Age, 185
Concept, behind ritual, 172
Construction, order of, 166
Cordons (on beakers), 70
'Corn-king', 123
Copper-trade, 37
Cowley, Mr. L. F., 167
Craftsmanship, decay of, 60

Cremation, 3, 71, 74, 97 ff., 103, 133
    origin, xviii *n.*
    sacrificial, 102, 104
    secondary, 86, 138
    *See also* 'Burial'
Crops, cereal, 116
Cultivation, 121
Culture, cultures, xx, xxii, 90, 152, 171, 176,
        177, 182, 183, 184
Cup, hemi-spherical, marcasite, 82, 89
    pigmy, xviii, 34, 52, 54, 61–2, 96, 98, 102–3
Cup-marks on stone slab, 84

Dagger, bronze, 90, 98; *see also* 'Knife' and
        'Knife-dagger'
Dance: funeral, ritual, xxvi, 39, 98, 185
Death and life, xiii, 173
Dedication, 122 *n.*
Deer, Red, 109
Deverel-Rimbury Culture, 171
Digging, technique of, 1, 2
Disharmonies, cultural, 16
Ditch (of barrow or circle), 10, 49, 50, 54–7,
        67–8
'Dolmens', 24
Dry-walling, 110, 118
Dunning, G. C., 62
Dwellings, 59
Dynasts, xxiv

Earth-goddess, 172
Entrance, ceremonial, 118
Evans, Eyre, 36
Excavation, mechanical, 41
    methods, xiv, 3, 41, 105, 128, 157–8
    range of interest, xiii

Fabricator, flint, 82, 83
Faience, blue, 90, 183
Families, Chiefly, 185
Fences, in barrows, 140, 163, 175
Fertility (symbol), 123
Fires, ritual, xxvi, 116–18
Flint tools, flakes, arrowheads, 8, 44, 47, 54,
        82, 89, 94, 100, 103, 109, 133
Floor of barrow (trodden), 112
Food-grains, 116, 119
Food-vessel culture, period, sources, 32, 74,
        76, 90, 105
'Food-vessels', xiii, xviii, xxii, 32, 35, 39,
        71 ff., 89, 123, 127, 183
Fox, Aileen, xv, 116, 156

188

# INDEX OF PLACES